W. Horace Carter's

CRAPPIE
SECRETS

And Techniques for Catching Other Panfish

Veteran panfishing guide and outdoor writer's handbook of tips that have helped him catch more than 250,000 crappie and bream over the last half-century

Copyright 1991 by
W. Horace Carter

Library of Congress Card Number 91-070622

Printed in the United States of America by
Atlantic Publishing Company
Tabor City, N.C. 28463

Published By:
W. Horace Carter
Atlantic Publishing Company
P.O. Box 67
Tabor City, N.C. 28463

ISBN 0-937866-24-5

Acknowledgements

It is with pleasure that I acknowledge the assistance of Tim Tucker in preparing this book for publication. Tim contributed time, several chapters, photos and assisted with the layout of the front cover. His wife Darlene helped in the typesetting, for which I am grateful. Then there was Judy Walker, who not only set most of the type, she did the proofreading and correcting, a tedious task. Also, the services of Gary Walker in laying out the pages and pictures were invaluable. Likewise, I appreciate the time that dozens of good fishermen spent with me sharing their techniques and experiences that can make astute panfish anglers from even the novices who take the time to read this book.

ABOUT THE AUTHOR

W. Horace Carter is a writer, although he fishes, too. He won a Pulitzer Prize in North Carolina as a newspaper editor and publisher. For the past 20 years, he has been a full-time free lance writer for the outdoor magazines and has sold more than 2,200 stories on fishing and hunting. His articles have appeared in every national and many regional and state magazines. He has written 15 books on the outdoors, two of them with Doug Hannon (The Bass Professor). Both these books rank among the best-selling bass books of all time. *Big Bass Magic* is a first place award winner in the Southeast. His last book, *Lures for Lunker Bass*, with Bud Andrews, artificial lure lunker champion, is among today's most respected bass books. His forthcoming book *Virus of Fear* is a documentary of the day by day crusade he waged against the Ku Klux Klan in the Carolinas from 1949 through 1953, that won him the prestigious Pulitzer Prize for Meritorious Public Service.

A North Carolinian from Stanly County, Carter is now a Floridian and lives at Cross Creek in Alachua County with his wife Brenda. He is a journalism graduate of the University of North Carolina at Chapel Hill.

Carter writes about both fresh and saltwater fishing from Maryland to Texas and is assisted in the photography by his wife. He is a past president of the Florida Outdoor Writers Association, three terms; the Southeastern Outdoor Press Association; and has served six years on the Board of Directors of the Outdoor Writers Association of America. He is a member of the North Carolina Journalism Hall of Fame, and in 1953 was named "One of the Ten Most Outstanding Young Men in America" by the U.S. Junior Chamber of Commerce.

INTRODUCTION

When you make the decision to write a book, you know that there are months and months of painstaking effort putting together the paragraphs and pages that hopefully will appeal to readers. If it is an angling book, as this one is, you are determined to make it attractive to fishermen around the country who occasionally relax in their favorite den chair and read rather than watch another TV show or sporting event.

When I decided to write this book after more than half a century of panfishing all over the country, my focus was to vividly reveal many systems and techniques that would help the ordinary lay angler catch more panfish. I have tried to do that in this book that details a myriad of techniques that have helped me and others put many great seafood dinners on the table.

It is my sincere wish that every reader will learn something in these pages that will assist him in his future panfishing excursions. If it helps the angler catch more panfish and if he will keep only what he needs, releasing some to thrill other fishermen on another day, then I will not have spent my time in vain.

Unless I have failed miserably, you'll be a better panfisherman after you read *Crappie Secrets.*

I would like to hear from you after you read the book. Let me know if it has helped or hindered. My address is: W. Horace Carter, Rt. 3, Box 139A, Hawthorne, FL 32640. Phone: 904-466-3356.

Table of Contents

VIII

The Great Crappie Species

Two different types of crappie are found in the United States—the black crappie (*Pomoxis nigromaculatus*) and the white crappie (*Pomoxis annularis*).

Black crappies are native to the eastern half of the U.S., and they have been stocked extensively in lakes and reservoirs throughout the country. They're scarce in the mountain states from western Texas through western Montana, though anglers still may find black crappie in some waters.

They prefer deep, clear and relatively cool waters, and the best places to fish for black crappie are large ponds, and shallow areas of lakes with sandy or muddy bottoms with large areas of vegetation.

White crappies are also native to the eastern half of the U.S. They have been introduced east of the Appalachian Mountains along the southern U.S. border and the west coast. The species is scarce in the Florida peninsula and in some North, Central and Midwest states.

They prefer shallower waters than the black crappie and are found in warm, weedy bays and ponds, silted streams and rivers, and slow-moving muddy areas of larger rivers.

Both black and white crappie have white flaky meat that is excellent for eating.

World Records

Both the International Game Fish Association and the

Author has a load.

1

National Fresh Water Fishing Hall of Fame keep track of all-tackle and line-class world records for black and white crappies. IGFA All-tackle world records

—**Black Crappie**: 4-pounds, 8-ounces, caught by L. Carl Herring, Jr, on March 1, 1981, from Kerr Lake, Virginia.

IGFA currently recognizes three flyfishing tippet-class records: Max Tongier's 2-pound, 3-ounce black crappie from Lee Hall Reservoir in Virginia in the 2-pound tippet class; Allen Beard's 1-pound, 9-ounce black crappie from Carlisle County in Kentucky in the 4-pound tippet class; and Tongier's 2-pound, 6-ounce black crappie also out of Lee Hall Reservoir in the 8-pound tippet class.

—**White Crappie**: 5-pounds, 3-ounces caught by Fred Bright on July 31, 1957, from Enid Dam on the Mississippi River.

Two white crappies are currently recognized by the IGFA for fly fishing tippet records: Adam Plotkin's 2-pound, 8-ounce white crappie caught in Amelia County, Virginia in the 4-pound tippet class; and Johnny Harper's 1-pound, 9-ounce white crappie for the 12-pound tippet record caught in Smithville, Mississippi.

NFWFHF All-tackle World Records

—**Black Crappie**: 6-pounds, caught by Lettie Robertson on November 28, 1969, from Westwego Canal in Louisiana.

—**White Crappie**: recognizes Fred Bright's IGFA record.

According to both the IGFA and National Fresh Water Fishing Hall of Fame, numerous line-class world records are vacant for both crappie species.

Who Fishes for Crappie

According to the 1985 National Survey of Fishing, Hunting, and Wildlife Associated Recreation, 11,747,000 anglers fish for crappie. This represents 37 percent of all fishermen 16 years and older.

On the average, an angler will spend 20 days a year fishing for crappie, meaning that 229,824,000 fishing days are spent every year by anglers in pursuit of crappies.

• Source: **U.S. Department of the Interior/Fish and Wildlife Service**

Catch Crappie?
Anybody Can Do That!

Anyone can catch crappie. It seems like all a person has to do is throw a line in the water, hook or not, and pull one up. Although it's not quite that easy, millions of anglers, young and old, enjoy fishing for crappies each year.

But catching crappies consistently during the active spring period or the difficult summer months takes knowing where the crappies are, understanding their behavior, and having the correct lure and presentation for the type of water you're fishing. Location, behavior and presentation make up a formula for catching more crappies, consistently, all year long.

The folks at *Field & Stream* magazine and Scientific Anglers/3M understand the importance of this formula and have incorporated it into the newest video in the *Field & Stream* Video Library, "Formula For Success: Crappie." Hosted by Ken Schultz, fishing editor for *Field & Stream*, "Formula For Success: Crappie" teaches the viewer this three-part formula for spring and summer fishing in both lakes and reservoirs.

Formula for Spring Crappies

Location of crappies will vary from spring to summer. Good crappie fishing begins in the spring when the water starts to warm. Different parts of the country will heat up earlier in the year, and some lakes warm up faster than others, so checking with a local tackle shop is usually a good idea to find out how the fish are biting.

During the spring, crappies will move into water less than 10-feet deep, feeding on small fish, insects, worms and crustaceans. Fish can be found in locations protected by the wind, such as shallow channels or canals, because they warm up the fastest. Other hot spots for spring crappies are shallow bays with dark bottoms, which help the water to warm faster, creek inlets, reed beds and flooded timber.

Crappie fishing is usually good during warm, stable

3

A small speck on ultralight.

weather, which pushes them into the shallows. Cold fronts and a drop in temperature will make crappie less active. Crappie are also affected by light levels. Low morning and late afternoon light levels make crappie more active, while high midday light levels slows down their feeding.

Weeds, brush and submerged logs are places where crappies like to hide, and tackle should match the location. A shorter, 5- to 5 1/2-foot rod is best for cover, and a longer rod, 6- to 6 1/2-foot, is better for distance casting. Ten to 14-foot rods can be used to dip the lure in around cover.

Jigs for spring crappie should be pink, white, yellow, blue or black, and weigh between 1/8 and 1/64 of an ounce. Spinners, sinking crankbaits and live bait combined with slow retrieves are also good choices. Crappies will rarely chase after a lure in the spring so a bobber rig helps to match the behavior of the crappies' meal. Bobbers make it easy to detect strikes and keeps the lure at the feeding level of the fish.

Crappies give only a slight tug when they hit, so an instant hook-set is important. Make the set quick and smooth, being careful not to rip the lure out of the crappie's paper-thin mouth. Crappies can simply be pulled straight into the boat, netted, or grabbed by their lower lip. Use safe catch-and-release practices, including keeping the fish in the water as much as possible and using wet hands when handling them. If you do keep some for the dinner table, they'll taste better if you partially clean them and keep them on ice.

Formula For Summer Crappies

Many anglers stop fishing for crappies when the sun begins to make sitting on a lake feel like being a filet in a fry pan. But if the angler uses the proper techniques and follows the three-step formula of location, behavior and presentation, summer crappie fishing can be just as productive and rewarding as spring.

Finding crappies in the summer is the first key to success. When the weather is hot, the crappies move into 10 to 20 feet of water, usually near submerged structure. Summer crappies have frequent feeding periods and, like those caught in the spring, are affected by the weather. You'll have success once the proper feeding level and location are found.

To find crappie in large reservoirs, look on a topographic map and pick out specific locations that look promising. Submerged points near channels, ledges where the bottom drops off or shallow water close to deep water are prime areas. Use a depthfinder to locate these drop-offs, and fish the downstream side of the shallows. Crappies will use the shallows as a shelter from the current.

On natural lakes, crappies can generally be found in three locations: in weeds, suspended just outside the weedline, and suspended over deep rock piles where the bottom drops off, known as the breakline. To locate the crappies, cruise in a pattern or troll slowly just outside the weedline. When fish are found, anglers should continue to scout for new spots, looking for similarities among locations and adding to their list of spots to try when the fishing slows.

Crappies will school in the open water during the summer, making them difficult to find without a depthfinder. Once a school is spotted, a simple minnow rig jigged up and down is an excellent method. Or a countdown method—counting ten seconds while the lure drops, retrieving it, counting 15 seconds, etc.—keeping track of lure depth. By counting down, lures can be returned to the feeding level after each strike.

If open water is unproductive, anglers should try casting small spinners between weed beds. Or, drifting just outside the weedline and casting to its edge is also a good summer technique, allowing the angler to cover large areas of water with minimal effort. Anglers should work slowly through all areas before moving on.

As the sun goes down, crappies move close to shore feeding on insects just beneath the surface. This makes crappies easy prey to even the most novice fly fisherman. Late-afternoon fly fishing for crappies is an excellent way for anglers to increase their proficiency with a fly rod, or to work on new techniques.

More than anything else, fishing for crappies is fun. By using the three-step formula of location, behavior and presentation, anglers can catch crappies consistently, any time of the year. This formula for success will make a smarter, more successful angler, for any species of fish.

- - -

Along with the new "Formula For Success: Crappie" video, Scientific Anglers/3M has introduced Fly Fishing Systems that take the guesswork out of choosing the right fly tackle for bass, panfish and trout. To pursue crappie with a fly fishing outfit, Scientific Anglers' System for panfish includes Concept brand fly line (weight forward, 5 weight floating version), a 7-1/2 foot 5X (4-lb. test) System tapered leader, and 100-yards of 12-lb. System backing.

For more information on the Scientific Anglers/3M Fly Fishing Systems, contact John Mazurkiewicz with the Walker Agency at 800/248-9687.

Crappie and Bream—Humble Species for the Unsophisticated

A cane or fiberglass pole is sufficient.

Extensive surveys indicate that more people go fishing to put meat on the table than for any other reason and that translates to the fact that crappie and bream are sought by masses of unsophisticated anglers who wouldn't trade their panfish food and fun for the pressure of stalking bass with all the gadgetry patented by modern scientists.

Bass rarely make it to the dinner table as restoration and conservation demand that this member of the sunfish family be caught and released. Not so with the humble crappie and bream that are so prolific that their populations remain near constant in waters everywhere with suitable habitat despite the growing number of freshwater seafood dinners that they provide.

While there are some avid crappie anglers who would not stoop to fishing for bream, in truth the species are equal in catchability, gourmet taste, reproduction and challenge. Yet, there are as many contrasts between these species as there are similarities. Bream fight and pull harder and crappies have the thinner tissue mouth that aids escape.

When Can You Catch 'Em?

Crappie generally are caught the fastest and therefore in the largest numbers when they are spawning. This may occur as early as late fall in Florida and right on through February and March. In other areas of the South, crappie spawn from early April through May and June. All other states experience the crappie spawning a few weeks after the first warmth of spring until summer and beyond.

But crappie can be caught in deep water in any month of the year if you can find them, as many trollers and drift fishermen have discovered. And they may spawn in ten feet of water or ten inches of water. They simply spew out their eggs and go on their merry way, but hundreds may choose the same room-size area in which to deposit their eggs. That's why you catch a limit in the same spot when you find them spawning. Crappie do not guard nests from predators. Bream do.

Bream, and that is a broad term used in the South to denote bluegills, shellcrackers, warmouth perch, pumpkinseed, redbreasts, stumpknockers and a few insignificant flat species of panfish, start nesting as early as March and often continue bedding through September in several Southern States. In virtually all states, they will bed as long as the water stays warm, from about 72 to 90 degrees.

Bream do guard their eggs and fry on the nest and both male and female often take part in this protective instinct that makes it possible to catch them in the same small area day after successful day. They may stay there a week or more.

How Do You Find Bedding Fish?

Both crappie and bream like to bed in cover, that is grass, weeds, lily pads, brush piles, around logs and stumps, rocky shorelines and on gravel or sand bottoms. Neither can always find the ideal terrain and a crappie, when impatient in locating the ideal spot, may elect to push out her roe in fringe areas near cover. It's difficult to find such a nesting area, but you may see or hear these fish breaking on the surface, feeding or frolicking as males and females may be plentiful over an area as large as the foundation of your home. Bedding crappie are always hungry. When the crappie are bedding in aquatic cover or even brushpiles, they often give their locations away by bumping and shaking the weeds and limbs. Even on a windy day you can see this tell-tale bump that looks like someone took hold of the base of the object and shook it on purpose. That's a dead giveaway of their whereabouts.

While these observations often locate crappie, they help find bream beds, too. But there are several other documented ways to find and catch bream on the beds. In the warmer weather, bream on the beds produce a distinct odor that can be smelled over a wide area by fishermen with sensitive noses. Describing this smell differs with every astute bream angler you question. Some say it smells like an open watermelon. Others say it smells like fish. I think it smells like a musty, damp cellar. On a calm day, you often are right on the bed when you smell it. If there is a breeze, you may have to follow your nose into the wind for a few yards to pinpoint its origin.

Bream often nest in just a few inches of water and you can see their beds as white spots on the bottom where they have rooted out saucer-shaped indentations. They may spook and swim away but they will return in a few moments.

One of the most sure-fire observations that locates bedding bream is the rooty fibers that they dislodge from the bottom when they are bedding in grass, weeds or spatterdock lilies. These roots are snow white the first day that they reach the surface and where you find an accumulation of these roots, you will find the mother lode. The bedding bream will be right there on the bottom and they will bite anything flaunted in their faces. If the roots have turned brown, they have been uprooted several days and discolored from the sun. The fish may still be there, but often they have left or been caught. What you look for are the white, hair-like fibers, not big roots. The fibers cluster on the surface, often by the handfuls.

Differences in Tackle and Expertise

Crappie fishermen a generation ago almost all fished with cane poles, minnows impaled on big hooks under a cork and a lead shot or two on the line, in or near cover. Some fished from boats but the bulk of the crappie anglers sat on the hill and propped poles up with stones and stumps. They waited for the fish to come along to ease off with the bait and the cork. You snatched him out of the water and put him on a stringer that you tied to a bush while the fish stayed alive in the water along the shore.

Fishing in that manner years ago, my father looked out across the half mile expanse of water in the Great Pee Dee River in North Carolina and observed: "How on earth are we going to catch fish here when they have all that water out there to live in? There's no reason for them swimming here to bite our hooks." While we caught fish even then, there has been a revolution in crappie fishing, even though it is still humble when compared to bass angling today.

Most of today's crappie anglers have boats, some homemade but many with moderately expensive craft like Ranger's 622-The Fisherman, a sturdy and safe boat that will carry three and four anglers. Skeeter, Glastron, Bass Tracker, and many others have good boats suitable for the crappie fisherman. Many fishermen mount pole holders on the gunnels and troll or drift a dozen or more lines at a time in the open water. This productive style has become a favorite crappie-catching technique for many in this decade.

Hack Curran gets a crappie.

While the old-fashioned minnow on a hook is still widely preferred by crappie fishermen, many veterans have gone to Betts and Super Jigs, Hal-Flies, and others. Fished in combination with minnows or jigged expertly in the holes of the cover, the artificials now often produce heavier stringers of fish than the natural bait. At times, a Beetle Spin will catch crappies when all else fails if retrieved slowly near cover.

Cane poles are not the vogue that they once were. Fiberglass telescopics by B 'n' M and others have replaced many of the bamboo traditionals. Crappie rods and reels by Silstar, Cabelas, Zebco and others are increasingly popular for the lay crappie angler as well as the tournament oriented fisherman. These modern innovations are not sophisticated but they are a far cry from a popash limb cut from a shoreline tree used often between World War I and World War II.

In some ways, the new rods and reels for crappie add to the thrill of tussling with a nice fish on the line. You play him longer and he may jump more.

The wind of change has not been as apparent with the devout bream fisherman. Hundreds of thousands of bream are caught every year in the warmer states from bridges, banks and railroad trestles by cane pole anglers with a wriggling worm on a hook, the original Izaak Walton natural bait.

Yet, years of experimentation, trial and error, have changed bream fishing for millions. Stalking bream on the beds in boats is the modern way. While this can be done in open water with flyrods, light and ultralight spinning tackle, and even some bait casting equipment, most bream are caught by fishermen with cane or fiberglass poles in cover and with natural baits.

A gray cricket floated to the bottom on a 6- or 8- pound test line, No. 4 or 6 hook, small shot, and a tiny bobber threaded on the line so the bait hangs just off the bottom is a bream catcher. Eagle Claw and TruTurn, among others, make long-shank bream hooks that are easy to remove from the fish's mouths. Short shanks are more difficult to retrieve and you may lose a dozen in the fish bellies on a busy morning. It takes a much smaller hook for bream than crappies.

Other natural baits catch bream. Sapheads from the bark of rotting pine trees, mealy worms, wasp nest larvae, catalpa worms turned wrong side out and even the traditional Georgia wiggler earthworm help put bream on the table. But there is no natural bait as productive as the freshwater grass shrimp that inhabits virtually all the Southern lakes and streams.

It is best fished with a short cane pole no more than eight or nine feet long, often discarded as being useless by other anglers, with a six pound test line only as long as the water is deep, and a No. 4 hook tied securely on the end. Impale the tiny translucent shrimp from the chin to the tail, and find the honey hole in the cover where the roots and smell testify to the presence of bream. With that tackle that I call a "Nothin' Pole," let the shrimp filter slowly to the bottom. Twitch it a time or two. If there

11

is a bream in the neighborhood he will strike it and you can wrestle him out of the cover with that short line and pole. Pound for pound there is no fish that pulls and fights harder on this humble tackle. It never ceases to thrill every angler.

Many bream anglers use too much weight on a line and a cork on the surface that turn bream off. As a native Florida bream expert said years ago, "Corks are made to be put in bottles and lead is for plumbers. It is not made for catching bream." He was so right. The nothing pole and live grass shrimp is the greatest of bream catchers, whether you are talking of bluegills, shellcrackers or warmouth perch, among others. It looks natural and they jump on it.

Bream at times in the summer seasons can be caught with popping bugs on the surface near shoreline cover with flyrods or just long cane or fiberglass poles with light line. They will also sometimes hit a Super Jig flipped in tiny holes of the cover where they are nesting. Mepps spinners will attract them when they are in the open water and feeding, as will Rooster Tails. It's these and other artificials that many of the purists prefer, some vowing that they wouldn't eat a bream that was caught with live bait.

One man's trash is another man's treasure and that is part of what makes fishing for panfish the recreation it is for throngs of outdoorsmen today. You are never quite sure of what you have on the line until you put it in the boat.

Whether you are exclusively a crappie catcher or an avid bream buster, there are thrills a'plenty on the waters of America even when you are without sophisticated boats and equipment. But the similarity of these species makes it possible for you to enjoy almost year 'round excitement catching panfish that delight the old and young, men and women, veterans and novices, North and South, when you fish for both of them with educated know-how.

The two species go together like pork 'n' beans, ham and eggs, French fries and hamburgers.

You'll never be sorry you know how to catch both these species and you'll get a lot of compliments from your picnic guests or family and friends at the dinner table after success in your favorite honey hole.

Tips To Catch More Crappie

America's Favorite Panfish

Whether you call him speck, white perch, papermouth, calico bass, sac-a-lait or crappy, the crappie is considered by many as the finest eating of the panfish.

Ranging throughout the United States, the two species of crappie share a similar appearance that sometimes makes it difficult to tell them apart at a glance. The black crappie usually has a darker, mottled color, while the white crappie has vertical bars on its sides. The easiest way to tell them apart is the way the scientists do, counting the number of spines on the dorsal (back) fin. The black crappie has seven or eight spines, as compared to six spines for the white crappie.

Although many anglers feel one species prefers one type of water or angling technique over the other, I have never seen any major differences between the two. Their behavior patterns appear to be the same. As long as habitat ingredients are suitable, either can be found frequenting most any kind of water, from gin-clear to turbid spring runoff. The same angling techniques seem to work equally well for both.

Long Poling

While many types of tackle and techniques will catch crappie, one of my favorites is long poling, vertical fishing with an extra-long 10- to 12-foot rod. Tight-lining or with a cork, the technique offers year-round advantages. You can fish cover where casting and retrieving isn't practical, dropping a jig or bait straight down into pockets or branches. You can lift a fish straight out of cover, with less chance of his tangling your line. The extra rod length lets you get your jig or bait out to cover a wider area around the boat and to prevent spooking fish in shallow water.

When fish are suspended and/or inactive, vertical fishing lets you hold a bait in one spot longer, with better depth control.

Linda England and the author land specks.

It also lets you cover a wider depth range faster, to locate the most productive depth zone.

When it comes to serious long poling, my favorite outfit is Daiwa's Crappie Pole with a matching Underspin reel. Unlike the old cane pole, the Crappie Pole telescopes down to a length that's a lot easier to tote around and can be easily stored in your boat's rod locker. Collapsed, it looks like a club, but you'll be amazed how light it actually is. The soft, parabolic bend of many crappie rods makes swinging a fish into the boat like trying to lift a bowling ball with a noodle. But the Crappie Pole is stiffer in the butt, bending more in the last 30% near the tip. The soft tip action reduces tearing hooks from a crappie's soft mouth. Its backbone lets you lift them straight out of cover and swing them in. The Underspin reel not only makes controlling depth a whole lot easier, it lets you make a cast when you want to.

Of course the right technique and tackle will help you catch more crappie, but only if you're fishing the right spot, at the right depth. That brings us to the most important key to catching more crappie year round, gaining a better understanding of their behavior. Once you do, you've got a lot better chance of locating them, and that's one of the most important steps in filling a stringer. So let's talk a little more about crappie behavior.

Breakline Crappie

Crappie are definitely a fish for all seasons. However, many anglers believe the summer and fall months to be the most difficult. They can be, but by adapting their techniques to match the fish's behavior, experts bring in fine stringers in even the toughest months.

Crappie like company, and where you find one, you'll find a school. Understanding that these large concentrations of crappie are structure oriented and spend the majority of their lives relating to breaklines, is a key factor in learning their behavior patterns.

A breakline is that area on the floor of a lake where there's a rapid or sudden change in depth. For example, the edges of channels, points or secondary banks, submerged ridges or even high spots. It's anywhere the water depth changes suddenly. Along the breakline are areas known as breaks: weeds, rocks, stumps, brush or other objects that provide fish cover. When these breaks have the depth, temperature, oxygen, pH and food availability to the crappie's liking, that's where you'll find them holding, especially in the warmer months from June through about October.

About the only time crappie are not tied to the deep water breaks is during the spring spawning season and in bodies of water that remain extremely muddy most of the time. Crappie in muddy water are usually found shallow, maybe two to six feet deep, and are extremely object-oriented. In clear water they'll hold just below the level of greatest sunlight penetration, from maybe 10 to 30 feet deep. In stained water they may be from 10 to 20 feet deep.

The major first step in locating crappie is determining the depth pattern they are using. Information from other anglers or local bait and tackle dealers can be helpful; otherwise, it takes trial and error. If you find crappie are using a 10-foot pattern,

15

fishing that hot spot you found last trip in 20 feet of water is probably a waste of time. Your efforts should be concentrated along the 10 foot breaks.

Crappie in Standing Timber

Standing timber can be one of the greatest structures for holding crappie, especially that which still holds most of its limbs. Not to be confused with willows or oxbows that infest some lakes, standing timber is the flooded timber that is still standing on many of the man-made lakes.

I'm often asked, "When confronted with acres of visible standing timber, how do you decide where to fish?" Well, it can be like looking for a needle in a haystack. They could be in there anywhere, but there are ways to narrow the search.

As I mentioned earlier, finding the depth pattern fish are using is a key starting point. From there a Corps of Engineers or U.S. Geological Survey map can narrow the search for areas with the right depth. If a good map isn't available, you must rely heavily on your depth finder or graph.

Remembering crappie are structure oriented, what you're looking for is anything irregular, anything that is different in that standing timber. It could be a slough, ridge, creek channel, old road bed with cover, slope, pocket, terrain change, hump, depression or even an old field. Don't forget, it has to be at the right depth.

When I find a likely spot, I drop my jig and prepare to stay or move on, depending upon the results. Now just because you don't catch fish at that good looking spot doesn't mean you couldn't at some other time of day. Schools of crappie are often on the move and could temporarily hold in any number of places. When you do find them, fishing may be productive for only a short time before they move on. So keep track of those likely-looking spots and try them at different times of the day.

Spawning Crappie

The spring crappie run is an excellent time of the year when everyone from beginner to pro shares in the catch. As soon as springtime water temperatures reach about 54 degrees, crappie start moving into the shallows to spawn. Almost any good sized cove or pocket is a potential spawning site, but the action usually starts first on the north or northwest side of a lake. There, coves warm quicker because they receive more radiant energy from the sun and south winds blow in warm surface water. That doesn't mean all the fish run to the north side of the lake. They don't, but the fish that live in that warmer area will start their spawning activity first.

Males move in first, setting up spawning sites to attract females. Sites can be on just about any kind of bottom, from mud, clay, rock or sand to even gravel and concrete. Spawning depth depends upon water clarity. The clearer the water, the deeper they'll spawn. Murky water moves them closer to shore.

It's easy to determine the depth at which a large percentage of fish will spawn with a simple tool you can make yourself. Cut an eight inch circle from sheet metal, paint it white, and attach an eyebolt and nylon cord to its center. Without sunglasses, lower the disc on the shady side of the boat until it just disappears from sight. That depth, or up to two feet below it, is where crappie will spawn when the temperature there is at least 54 degrees.

Suspended Crappie

During the summer and fall months, crappie are particularly prone to suspend. Their swim bladder lets them stratify at a level providing the preferred light, temperature, pH and oxygen levels. If there's cover around at that depth, that's where you'll find them. Otherwise, they'll suspend in open water. In colder weather, they pack tightly in a school and move closer to the bottom. The clearer the water, normally the deeper they go.

If you have fished objects along the shoreline and structures in deeper water without success, you can pretty well believe crappie are suspended out in open water. Locating them can be a difficult proposition. Often as not, they're located by accident, but a good graph or depth finder can help immensely.

Trollers are a good clue to suspended crappie. When you see a large number of boats trolling, you can pretty well guess that a high percentage of fish are suspended and that's why trollers are having success catching them.

Good places to look for suspended crappie are at the mouths of creeks and coves along deep drop-offs. Crappie also love to suspend in standing timber, especially timber that still holds most of its limbs.

17

In clear water, they tend to suspend deeper, in larger schools than in murky or muddy water. In some lakes, it's not uncommon to catch them at 30 to 40 foot depths in clear water conditions. At times like these, vertical fishing lets you drop a jig right on top of them and hold it at a constant depth, especially important when fish are inactive. It's a lot more productive than trying to cast and count down.

Inactive Crappie

Although we would like them to, crappie just don't remain active and in a feeding mood all day long. The barometric pressure changes that come with changing weather highly affect a fish's equilibrium. Fish in shallow water are affected even more. They move into tight cover and become very inactive. Cold water also lessens their activity.

It's during these inactive periods that vertical fishing is one of the most effective techniques. You can get right down into cover and hold a bait in a highly productive strike zone for a longer period of time than by trying to cast and retrieve. A non-aggressive fish just is not going to chase a bait very far. Putting that bait right down on top of him and holding it there can make all the difference in the world.

When fishing a jig this way, the size of the jig can be very critical and it's wise to experiment. I've seen times when changing from a 1/8 oz. to a 1/16 oz. or even a 1/32 oz. jig made a tremendous difference in the number of fish caught.

A Learning Experience

As I mentioned before, acquiring information from others as to current conditions can save you a lot of time looking. Otherwise you'll have to depend upon your own trial and error to find crappie. But even here there's a distinct advantage one shouldn't lose sight of. Every time you fish a particular structure you learn a little bit more. You should never look upon a fishing trip as a wasted day, even when you fail to catch fish. The more you fish, the more you learn. It's smart to be observant, make notes and above all, think positively. What you learn today will pay off down the road.

The best of fishing to you.
Bill Dance

Crappies-By Hook or Crook

     Generations of sportsmen have hauled in creel limits of crappies from cover and in open water with finger-length minnows impaled on a hook and dangled in the vicinity of these plentiful panfish. A hook and a morsel of food is the traditional crappie catcher, but today there are many of these gourmet perch mistaking a bit of plastic, feather or hair for something of food value and falling to a con game being played by purist anglers—they make mistakes and find the attractive, twitching minnow-mimicking lure is a counterfeit. Yet, all is fair in war and fishermen for a hundred years have been outsmarting fresh and saltwater fish with phony morsels that pit the ingenuity of man against the instincts and cunning of crappie and other finny creatures. This man-against-the-fish battle has taken on great sophistication in panfishing in the last decade. It is no longer just the real meat bait that entices the black and white crappies to strike an angler's hooks as a society of artificial lure fishermen get their kicks by conning the species and putting big panfish in the skillet. Fried, broiled or baked, few freshwater fish make a gourmet meal comparable to a mature slab caught in a clean lake or stream anywhere in the country.

Crappie by Hook

Half a century ago when few fishermen other than doctors and lawyers had any kind of fishing boat, Southern sports fishermen sat on the banks of lakes and rivers, baited a hook, tied a cotton line on a cane pole with a bobber, and watched it fiddle around near stumps, brush, grass or other cover until a school of crappies came along. A twitching, struggling three-inch minnow hooked under the dorsal fin enticed any crappie that eyeballed the natural bait. They hit it and ran. Fishermen fed a lot of families for a generation with shoreline success.

As my dad once said when we sat with our backs against a tree and he was impatient for lack of any action, he looked out across the Great Pee Dee River from the Stanly County, North Carolina side and said, "How on earth do you expect to catch any fish right here at this little spot when the fish could be anywhere out there in that half-mile wide river?" He was right! It did cut down the odds of success when the fish had to do all the traveling.

Then came the fishing revolution. Homemade bateaux at first were about the only boats on the streams. Made from either cypress lumber or some other hardwood, later from marine plywood, it put the meat-hunting angler in a position to look for the schooling fish when they didn't come to the bank where he had his poles extended, waiting patiently for a cork to go down.

Boats changed the pattern, a word never heard of outside of the mother's sewing room, and fishermen after these abundant crappies began dropping lively minnows in brushpiles, around stumps, aquatic growth, and deep near submerged ledges in creek mouths and swamp runs. The fish succumbed to the hook with a meal on it for years, and they still do. Today a minnow, small crawfish, maybe even a cricket, grass shrimp or wad of worms dangled in the territory where crappies are nesting or feeding, will put fish in the livewell. It's a foolproof enticer that

20

doesn't con the speckled perch, as they are known in Florida, to swallow something with no real food value. It's truly an "honest" way to put crappies in the boat.

Crappie by Crook

Since the days of Lauri Rapala and long before, man has tricked fish into biting an inanimate object. In so doing, fishermen have proudly broken their suspenders with a puffed-out chest, inflated because they learned to outwit, outsmart and catch fish that are prone to make mistakes when confronted with hundreds of inventive gimmicks of man's superior intelligence.

Today, crappies are caught in virtually every state with a wide assortment of artificial lures that directly or indirectly resemble a stomach-filling meal for a predator fish that mistakes it for a bit of live nutrient. Except for largemouth and smallmouth bass, there are perhaps no other species caught in such abundance on man-made lures as the humble crappie, not a great fighter, but a cooperative panfish hauled in by men, women and children virtually the year around in the warmer South. And in the North, they are still caught through holes in the ice in the dead of winter. Despite the heavy harvest year after year and a minimum of attention by fish and game agencies, the crappie species continues to thrive and thrill sportsmen everywhere. Not even prominent professional bass men and women can hide their pleasure at catching a big stringer of slab-size crappies when they are not competing for dollars or big boat prizes on the tournament trails. And the pros, along with many others, get kicks from catching this flatfish on artificials—they want to con the species like they do the larger, heavier lunker bass. Part of the pleasure is proving you are smarter than the fish. That's one reason so many people who make their own lures are especially happy when they catch a fish on their own creation.

One of the first artificial lures to attract speckled perch in Florida was the tiny red and white No-Alibi. Cast on ultralight or light spinning tackle along grass and weed lines, in nooks and holes of the lily pads, or under overhanging limbs of the shoreline, then slowly retrieved, this bit of metal and paint has put millions of fish in the boat at Okeechobee and throughout much of Florida. It takes a little know-how to catch fish with that lure on a line. If you retrieve it too fast, the fish spook and disappear. The lure had to come up off the bottom slowly, and with a few twitches, that made it appear to the fish like a wounded minnow. It then often brought strikes. It was also jigged vertically from the bank or a boat in a relatively deep hole with the same results.

Hundreds of other artificials have successfully enticed crappies that are mistake-prone to bite anything dead or alive in the last two decades. They are easier to con than most bass

The popular Hal-Flies, a Georgia-made jig that combines a hook with various colors of plastic and some tail-feather trailers of hair, has enough weight in the head to take it down, but not too rapidly. The orange, yellow and clear Hal-Flies remain among the best of artificial crappie catchers on the market. It can be jigged, cast or trolled, and generally is the most successful when flicked near cover on light tackle, then twitched all the way back to the boat.

Bob Garland, of Arizona originally, and now in Utah, marketed dozens of colors of Mini-Jigs that fooled a lot of crappies. He is turning out a similar jig now in his new location. It had a lot of action. It was nothing more than a half-inch tube of plastic with tentacles cut for a tail. Wriggled in the water, it closely resembled something alive. An identical product is now on the market by Midsouth Tackle, of Jonesboro, Arkansas, and is called a Super Jig. Made in natural colors and fluorescent, the white, yellow, orange and chartreuse will catch crappies when handled gently on a light rod in any territory where crappie are congregated. But pink has been the most productive in Florida since 1985.

Mepps has tiny spinners, preferably the gold-colored leaves, with small treble hooks that are good crappie attractors trolled or cast. Many natives in swamp rivers of coastal areas of the South still catch good stringers of crappies with a spinner that they tie on a light monofilament line and cast or slingshot under cover. When you have a bluebird day with a lot of light and bright sun, this spinner will attract specks better than on cloudy, overcast days. The glint of the sun's rays gives it added life, and helps you con the crappie. It often works when jigs fail on bright, sunny calm days.

Another excellent crappie bait is the Rooster Tail spinner. It's a fine lure when you have a lake or stream with a lot of aquatic growth, but with enough holes and coves free of obstruction that you can cast and retrieve. It works better retrieved slowly than fast. It needs to move with enough speed to keep the spinner spinning. That's all! It is too life-like for crappies to resist.

For the fly fisherman, the popping bug on the surface with its big eye painted on a peanut-size piece of cork with rubber legs, is the best of the crappie catchers. Flipped inches from cover and allowed to float calmly, it often draws crappies out of hiding. Perhaps they think a bee or beetle has fallen in the drink. A few moments of stillness and then a flick or two, often does the trick. Almost every fly fisherman I have ever talked with about catching crappies on a bug prefers the white or chartreuse color. A few like yellow and many clip off about half the length of the rubber legs so it can be swallowed easier.

Sometimes you can doctor your con game lure and make it even more productive. A Mepps or Blue Fox whisper spinner with a couple of pieces of Uncle Josh red and white pork rind often makes a lot of difference. The pork rind should be narrow and no more than an inch long. One red and one white together is a better lure than a single color. Prior to the Uncle Josh fish lure additives, many anglers cut strips of white and red balloon, and fastened them on the spinner hooks, or they made these color appendages from bathing caps.

In recent years, a galaxy of small crankbaits have gone on the market. Storm, Rat-L-Trap, Norman, Rebel, and Bagley among others have many that are not too big for crappies to strike. Rebel has several colors of lures designed like small crawfish crank baits. These are less than two inches long and crank so that the crawfish moves backwards, his natural movement. These are particularly productive around rocky shorelines or ditches where the crawfish is plentiful. There are many more types of "dishonest" lures that catch crappies than "honest" ones with real food value. The species succumbs to the con game.

Crappies By Hook AND Crook

While the age-old live baits are proven crappie catchers, and the newer, more sophisticated artificials get their share of the panfish too, there are many followers of Izaak Walton who prefer the best of two worlds—they combine the live and the dead, the real and the imposter. They catch crappies by hook and crook.

Trolling is the most practical way to combine artificial lures with a dab of meat. Super-Jigs, Hal-Flies, Beetle Spin grubs, Cotee grubs, Stanley jigs, Mepps Spinners, and a dozen other small lures, will get more strikes and help the angler put crappie in the boat if you impale a minnow on the hook along with the man-made attractor. Hooking a small, two-inch or smaller minnow through the lips or the eyes and letting him move through the water on a cane pole, Lew Childres and Sons Breambuster, a B 'n' M telescopic pole, or on a six-foot lightweight rod, will bring crappies in a hurry. This combination crappie catcher should be used in open water, and trolled baits should run a foot or two off the bottom. Small and lunker-size slabs will hit the combination providing you do not use a minnow that is too large, and move at the proper speed. Small ones catch big and little fish. Big minnows are often tackled unsuccessfully by the small fish and even the huge ones prefer the smaller offering. After all, the man-made lure and minnow together make a rather big bite for panfish.

Those crappie anglers who dislike trolling can catch a skillet full in the holes of hydrilla, lilies and grass beds, as well as brushpiles and rooty shorelines, with a 1/8 or 1/16 ounce jig and minnow combination. It is most successful when flicked in the cover with a small bobber a couple of feet up the line. A single small shot six inches from the hook takes it down quicker, and seems to prompt more strikes. Minnows fished with jigs and spinners and moved should be hooked through the lips or eyes. Those that are flipped into cover and allowed to maneuver on the line for awhile, are more apt to attract strikes if hooked through or under the dorsal fin. The minnow will run and show more life.

One man's trash is another man's treasure. There are crappie fishermen who wonder why anyone would use jigs, spoons and spinners when going after a meal of this species when a real live minnow is hard to beat. Yet, there are just as many others who say, "I wouldn't eat a fish that I had to catch on a live bait. I want my fish to hit a lure." Still others have their best "luck" going after panfish with a lure and a live critter.

Crappies are not hard to catch. As long as they are a delight on the dinner table, there will be thousands of man hours spent with minnows on the hook. The crappie gets caught when he is after a real morsel. Other crappie catchers will get their kicks from outfoxing the species, and they will still enjoy the protein on the table. They win the confidence game. By hook or crook, crappies are sought by 20 million Americans and even the pros admit it's a lot of fun when the bass have lockjaw or even when there's no cast-for-cash event and plain recreation is the objective. Crappies are food and fun.

Crappie: By Any Name Spells Food and Fun

A crappie is a crappie whether he is black or white, and even if fishermen are confused about the species when they hear it referred to as sac-a-lait, speckled perch, goggle-eye, calico perch, papermouth, bachelor or even strawberry bass. By any name, it spells angling thrills and gourmet eating all over the country, and that is really the name of the outdoor game. In Florida it's a speckled perch, and they are plentiful.

Black crappie have long been in abundance in most of the states and its prolific power to reproduce has kept the population generally healthy even while most game commissions have virtually kept a hands-off policy. The species has seldom received much attention or much assistance from governmental authorities, yet it is among the very best fish for old and young, men and women, amateurs and the skilled. It has the fun-for-all garland around it, and the added attribute of being easily dressed and a tasty main course dinner.

Opinions about the best way to catch this species, and where, are about as varied as the many monikers it has in sectional nomenclature. There are veterans with long track records for success who swear by specific lures, large and small, white and black, fished deep and shallow. They are just as sure of its hiding places in dark shadows, buried in the brush, or open water places where the bottom is clear. Avid advocates of crappie fishing say it spawns in shallow water, and just as many know that it often lays its eggs in ten feet of water. Some say it has a small mouth, and just as many others think its mouth is large. Crappie enthusiasts often catch their limits at night and would fish no other time, while others find there's plenty of action in the daytime.

There's just about as much difference in the thinking of the fraternity of crappie fishermen about the rules for success as there is in day and night. Succinctly, the rule is that there really is no rule. Crappies make their own, and the fishermen who are confident with their own system usually are successful regard-

25

Fishing was slow...Angler takes a nap.

less. . .yes, regardless. But they have to adapt a bit from time to time.

My system of crappie fishing at Cross Creek is novel, and I stumbled upon it accidentally five years ago. With a documented catch record of many thousands a year ever since, the confidence I have is unshakable. Furthermore, a dozen or so close fishing friends, who have adopted the principles of my crappie fishing have been equally adroit at filling their stringers and live boxes. I know it often works when everything else fails.

The technique that I use has the added advantage that you do not have to wait for the fish to spawn to catch them. It doesn't have to be early in the morning or late in the afternoon, fair or cloudy. You catch both large and small the year around. Several years ago, my wife, a West German tourist and I caught 142 specks, as they are known at Cross Creek and throughout Florida, on the 16th day of June in Lake Lochloosa. We ran out of minnows three times. The catch was about equally divided between two hours early in the morning, two hours in the middle of the day, and two hours just prior to sundown. They had no roe. They were in open water from eight to 12 feet deep. Mind you, it was a hot summer day when most anglers have given up fishing for speckled perch in the Sunshine State, and wait patiently for January, February and March when they spawn in the lily pads.

Then they must surely have been little fellows? That's the common query from fishermen who have become conditioned to catching this species in the shallows in the spring when they are spawning. No! Some were small, in the 6- to 8- ounce range. But many weighed more than a pound and two topped 2-pounds. And while some may frown on the smaller specks, I'll pick them off the platter every time when I have a choice at the picnic table. I do not believe in filleting specks, regardless of size. I consider it gross waste of the resource. I prefer to eat the smaller specks cooked whole after de-heading and gutting. It's no trouble for me to remove the bones by pulling the dorsal and anal fins out after frying and then simply folding the white meat off the backbone with my fingers. The meat easily slips away and is much tastier than a deboned, skinned fillet. You can fillet with your fingers after cooking as easily as you can with a knife before cooking. After cooking there's no waste.

Exception! If I am expecting small children or senior citizens who have difficulty removing bones, I fillet the bones out of **one side** of the larger specks, leaving the skin on. Then I fry the whole remaining carcass. The kids and oldsters get the boneless portion, others eat the balance and nothing is wasted.

But back to my simple system that I accidentally discovered.

I was fishing alone in the middle of the morning in the middle of Lochloosa in March. I was sitting on a couple of cane poles with Missouri minnows on the lines, snap-on bobbers, a shot or two of lead and letting the wind push me along slowly. It was peaceful, but I wasn't putting any meat on the table. And a nationwide survey reveals that meat on the table is the number one reason fishermen give for angling.

Rummaging through my tacklebox menu, I ran across a couple of small hooks with a bit of purple plastic on the shank, followed by a few squirrel hairs. I tied it on my worst cane pole and dropped it over the side. I drifted only a few yards before the pole bent, the bobber was gone, and I pulled in a flouncing speck. I tried it again, but got no immediate response. I pulled it in and impaled my smallest minnow through the eye sockets on the hook with the purple plastic. When it hit the water and straightened out, it didn't even stop. Bingo! Another speck. Time after time that day I got almost instant replay every time I put that combination of minnow and lure in the water. Then a mudfish or gar or something took hook, line and sinker, and I was out of luck.

In the following weeks, I found some more of these little lures and successfully caught my limits on them. I don't even remember the name of the product. But it dawned on me that I could use a homemade version of that rig, and perhaps do as well. It was then that I began cutting up plastic worms, like bass fishermen use, into half-inch pieces, threading them on the hook, pushing them up to the eye where the line is tied, then stringing my minnows on a No. 2 gold hook. It worked beautifully, and I have caught thousands with that makeshift speck attractor.

I have regularly refined the system until today I am reasonably confident that I'll catch some speckled perch every time I take to the lakes when there is no more than a ten-mile-per-hour wind blowing.

I later began using my electric variable speed trolling motor instead of relying upon the wind to move me. I found I could control my speed and direction, something you can't do just drifting. Then I found that I could always do better with the stern of my boat to the wind, not broadside like I had been fishing.

Sitting on two or three cane poles is one way of holding

them in the boat, but if you are moving along, get a couple of strikes at the same time, or shift your weight, you often have a messy system. I installed heavy pole holders, the steel unbending kind made in Taiwan, on both sides of the bow of my bass boat, and also two pairs of the same holders just forward of the front seat in the bow. I am usually fishing with someone. I adjust these holders so they will hold my 14-foot cane poles parallel to the surface of the water and perpendicular, or slightly pointed forward, to the boat. I do much better with them in this position than I do with them hanging out the back or sticking up in the air.

I use a 12-pound Stren monofilament or Trilene line and a No. 2 gold hook because it is thin in diameter and does not kill my minnows quickly. I put three No. 4 Water Gremlin, clothes-pin type sinkers on my line scattered six to eight inches apart from the hook. If it is windy, I may have to put five or even six such sinkers on the line to keep the hook down to within a foot or two of the bottom of the lake. I always fish the open water in the deepest part of the lake.

The bobber that you use is all-important. I prefer a two-inch styrofoam, elongated bobber no more than half an inch in diameter. It will not support your shot, hook and impaled minnow when the boat is still. But when you troll along at the proper speed, the bobber will rise to the surface. The line will trail downward at an angle of about 60 degrees. It is imperative that the bobber not be big and awkward. The crappie will turn the hook loose many times when it offers resistance to his tugging of the bait. And when you get a strike, you'll know it. Often the first warning you have is the jiggling of the pole in the holder. Other times you just see a bouncing pole half-submerged in the water.

You give the specks no line and no time when you see a strike. Any slack is an invitation to let the fish escape. You simply pull him in with no jerk and no deliberate setting of the hook. The fish will surge sufficiently to drive the hook through his paper-thin mouth. If you are afraid he will fall off the hook before you get him into the boat, then maybe you better take along a landing net. I use no net, but simply lift the fish out of the water and over the boat quickly. Often he falls off about the time he clears the gunwales, and saves you the trouble of unhooking when he lands on the deck. I lose a few that shake the hook before they are boated, but not many. Using a net for crappies when they are biting well is slow and messy. The hook, line, bobber and sinkers get entangled in the net and it takes time to get back to fishing again. Then, too, I think the sporting thing is to give the fish that additional chance to escape. If he's really a wall mount above 2-pounds, you can always lead him up to the boat and lift him over the side with your fingers in his mouth.

Being the notorious gregarious schooling species that he is, you'll do well to mark the open water spots where you get more than one strike trolling. There will always be more than one fish there. I throw out a plastic milk jug with a piece of brick for an anchor, and circle it several times. Sometimes I leave the marker in place for days. Specks have a habit of frequenting the same area for long periods of time, and can be caught in numbers when they are thick enough to fight over the bait.

One thing about this plastic speck attractor and the trailing minnow: almost any color plastic will help, but red is the proven leader of the homemade lure. The Missouri minnow that you hook behind the plastic should be small, preferably about two inches long. Larger ones will curtail your catch. And if you are a bed fisherman in the brush, grass or cow lilies, don't use the plastic attractor. It only helps when you are trolling the open water using the system outlined here. But it will work every day of the year where water is shallow enough that you can reach the fish with a line on a cane pole.

Every system calls for change and adaptation as fishermen are constantly looking for a better mousetrap. And while my homemade tackle has done the job well for me for years, I ran into a slow period one winter. Suddenly, instead of catching 20 or 30 specks in the morning and an equal number in the afternoon, I was lucky to get ten or so. Trying hard, I could not get back to my long established success with this species. The first impulse is to think that the fish are not there any more. But biologists refute such thinking.

I took off some of my crude plastic attractors and tied on various colors and sizes of Super Jigs, pretty little lures with lead heads, gold hooks and plastic skirts that virtually obscure the hooks. The 1/16 ounce jigs have gold hooks almost as large as the No. 2/0 I had been using. I knew it was large enough to hold even the slabs.

Those jigs revolutionized my speckled perch fishing.

Fishing with Del Thompson, an Illinois friend and long a proficient speck fishing believer in my plastic attractors, we landed 27 nice fish on a February morning despite a strong 15-

mph northeast wind. We caught nine of those specks on a purple jig, four on green, three on white, four on black, one on yellow, and six on my original homemade tackle.

Again in February, we ran the same test. This time we trolled for two hours in calm waters on Lake Lochloosa and landed 22 fish.

Eight of them were on green jigs, four on yellow, two on purple, three on black, two on white, two on clear, and unbelievably, we did not catch a fish on the old reliable cut plastic I had invented.

Since then we have experimented time after time with all colors of jigs and the formerly used attractors cut from the bass bait plastic worms. Specks have some preference for colors—apparently pink and purple are best—and they definitely will strike them in Lochloosa now better than my original, although we are back to catching good numbers with the old bait. While the jigs come in weights from 1/32 of an ounce to 1/8th of an ounce, I like 1/8th ounce. I simply impale my same little minnow through the eyes on the hook of the jig, just as I did on the clumsier lure I made myself. Specks will hit.

And not only will you catch crappies with this pretty little lure, you'll likely hang on to several other species. I have landed chain pickerel regularly, up to 4-pounds, while trolling that open water. Recently I landed two yearling bass, one weighing 2-pounds, 13-ounces, on the green jig.

The schooling crappies don't have to be flushed out of cover and places difficult to reach. You can put them in the boat without staying hung on the cover. You can catch your fish without costly rods and reels, just plain old country fishing poles or B 'n' M fiberglass poles. But the dyed-in-the-wool basser who wants to catch all his fish on spinning tackle, can have success with the jigs too. After all, casting and retrieving this lure into the havens that hold the fish creates a situation virtually identical to trolling over the honey hole. And you can troll the stern with rods.

So if you have been waiting for another spring when the water reaches about 60-65 degrees and the crappies start spawning in the shallows, thinking you can't catch them until then, shrug off that attitude. You can catch them in the summer and winter. There's no need to catch this species just a few weeks out of the year when it is such a table delight in all seasons and readily catchable today. Fashion yourself one of my funny-looking plastic attractors with a trailing minnow or get yourself some jigs and minnows. Then troll that bait alongside your boat in the areas where you believe the crappies are lurking. You'll catch 'em. They can't resist it.

(This technique for year 'round crappie success in open water will be repeated in part in other chapters of the book. Each circumstance may be slightly different, but the general system remains the same whether you are fishing a slough off the Great Pee Dee River, Santee-Cooper, Kentucky Lake or the shallow, natural waters of Florida. You simply adapt the idea to the depth of the water, wind currents, etc., and it works everywhere.)

Crappie Team Secrets

Increased knowledge on crappies' habits, preferences and reaction to environment has resulted in new techniques and equipment that help catch more fish. Two techniques that have been used increasingly by Crappiethon Winners are "tight lining" and "vertical fishing" with small tube jigs. Martin Reel has developed equipment that has been specifically designed to be used for this type of fishing. It allows you to feel the strike better, land crappie faster and quickly get back to the strike depth.

Crappie Characteristics

A crappie leads a rather regimented life, and knowing why and when it reacts to its surroundings will get you to the right spot to catch them. In the spring as the water warms up to the mid-50's, crappies leave their deep water home of winter and approach the shallows, which warm up quicker, in preparation for spawning. They generally hold suspended over cover until the water temperature rises to the mid- and upper 60's. Then the males go into the shallows, select territories and hollow out nests on the bottom. The females then come in, lay their eggs in the nest and retreat to deeper water. The males remain behind, fanning the nests to provide oxygen and protecting the eggs and hatchlings from predators. After the fry leave the nest, the males join the females and form schools that suspend over cover and drop-offs. As summer comes on and the water continues to warm up, the crappies form tighter schools and head for deeper water near cover, generally in the 12 to 22 foot range. Crappie continue a little deeper and stay near the bottom as fall and winter come in and remain there until the water starts to warm up in the spring.

Zooplankton is the major food of most young crappies. As they grow, aquatic insects become important and as they become adults, small fish make up most of their diet. Seasonally, a typical pattern for adult crappies features plankton and insects during spring and early summer, with minnows and young-of-the-year fish the mainstay for summer and fall. Since they tend to suspend near their natural food, you must get your bait down to their level. Their non-aggressive nature keeps them from moving very far to strike a bait.

Locating Crappies

After spawning, crappies migrate towards deeper water. Depending on how far along the season has progressed, you should look for fish to be in increasingly deeper water. They suspend near drop-offs and underwater growth. Some spots can be located using topographical charts of the water to be fished. Look for submerged creekbeds running back into bays, concentrations of deeper water, stumps and brush, deep water rockpiles and tapering rock drop-offs. Depth/fish finders are great for locating structure, and often can spot schools of suspended crappie.

Tight-lining Technique

Since most of the year crappies spend most of their time in deeper water, professional crappie fishermen have developed a technique of fishing that methodically locates crappie schools, gets hooked fish quickly into the boat and gets the bait back into the water to the strike depth while the fish are in an active feeding mood.

Tight-lining, as the name implies, uses a rig with artificial or natural baits, anchored at the bottom by a bell sinker. After you've positioned the boat where you want to fish, you get your bait to the proper depth by stripping line off the reel in increments. Initially, with a nine foot rod, you'll already have about 8 feet of line out (from the tip of the rod to the hook hole in the trigger of the CM-1 Reel).

Step 1. If your depth finder shows crappie at 18 feet, for example, you'll need to strip off 10 more feet of line. Grasping the line at the reel and with a sweep motion of your arm (towards the tip of the rod) you'll pull off about 2 feet of line each time. Stripping this way 5 times will get your bait down to 18 feet. The rod should be held so the tip is just 4 to 6 inches over the water.

Step 2. Work the retrieve trigger on the reel with your rod hand, "jigging' up the bait a few inches at a time. This degree of control will come to you after a little practice. Since you can do this with one hand, your other hand is free to "feel" the line for that very soft strike as the crappie takes the bait.

Step 3. Set the hook when a strike occurs. Immediately raise the rod tip high while depressing the reel trigger to keep tension on the line.

Step 4. "Strip in" the line with your non-rod hand, keeping the trigger depressed to keep tension on the line. When the crappie breaks water, stop retrieving the line. Just swing the crappie into the boat, unhook, check bait and re-bait if necessary. You'll still have the 8 feet out, so all you'll have to do is again strip off 10 feet of line, and you're back in action at the same depth you started at the time before. If the strike came at 16 feet, adjust accordingly.

Fishing two rods at once

Once you get accustomed to tight-lining as described above, you can fish with a rod in each hand because you don't need an extra hand to "crank in." The CRAPPIEMATIC Reel does the cranking for you . . . and it is fast.

Martin CRAPPIEMATIC
Rod/Reel Sets

The Reel, Model CM-1 has been specifically designed for this type of fishing. The spool has an enlarged hub that provides the correct line capacity of 40-50 yards of 20 lb. monofilament and can handle the monofilament pressure. Heavy duty gears are used that can take the constant jigging action and frequent retrieves. A special insert rides between the spool and the frame to prevent line from getting behind the spool. And the long proven Martin ratchet and pawl brake system stops the retrieve instantly, controlling jig action.

The Rods have been developed from fly rod blanks especially adapted for vertical jigging and tight-lining. They are long (9 and 10 feet), two-piece graphite composite rods which have sensitive tips to detect the slightest nibble, yet have the backbone to swing a slab into the boat as soon as it breaks water. The guides are ceramic to stand up under mono wear. The "R" rods have a 4 1/4" butt section to be used with rod holders, while the others have a shorter, more traditional fly rod handle with removable fighting butt. The heavy duty construction of the tip is designed to allow for dislodging hang-ups.

Tight-lining Bait Rigs

Live Bait Rig—There are many variations of this, but here's one rig that has proven very effective for L.D. Davis of East Prairie, Missouri, and his fishing partner, "Shorty" Akers, two of the best fishermen on Kentucky Lake, fishing live shiner minnows 3 to 3 1/2" long.

Bouncing the bottom with the sinker of this double hook

rig gives you a "feel" for underwater obstructions and cover. And while two fish may be taken at the same time, the real purpose of this rig is to present the bait at two different depths. Whether the fish are hiding in cover or suspended above it, you'll be able to reach them.

Steve McCadams of Kentucky Lake, a well known guide, writer and crappie fisherman, uses a similar rig with hollow bodied tube skirt jigs tied 18 inches apart. Another variation is tying on a jig in one position and a minnow in the other.

Equipped for Jigs

At times jigs will prove more productive than live bait. Dr. William Kobler of Cairo, Illinois, and his son, Bubba, won the 1986 Crappiethon on Kentucky Lake using Martin automatics, ten-pound test monofilament line and tube jigs tied directly to the line. This allows you to "twist" the jig to a horizontal position which can't be done using swivels. Small tube jigs of 1/32 to 1/16 oz. are used. The Koblers also took 4th place in the 1988 Crappiethon Classic.

Burel Goodin and Bill Voegele Jr. of Keyesport, Illinois, wholeheartedly agree, saying the "horizontal" tie is the only right way—and they won the 1987 Crappiethon on Carlyle Lake, Illinois.

Goodin & Voegele Variation—Burel and Bill use lead head jigs 1/32 to 1/4 oz. (depending on depth) with the 1/16 to 1/8 oz. jigs producing the best on Carlyle Lake. With murky water they find they can use 6- to 10-lb. mono on the "jig rig" since the fish aren't suspended as deep as they would be in clear water. One of them will use a 2 foot shorter rod so they can fish the same structure at the same time and cover different depths. Using a 2 to 3 inch "up and down motion," they consistently take crappie from 1 to 10 feet down. They use a slower retrieve when the water is cold.

We hope these tips will help you in being successful in locating and catching crappie, and you will be pleased with your new Martin CRAPPIEMATIC equipment. If you discover any additional techniques or fishing tips that you'd like to share with other crappie fishermen, you're welcome to submit them to:

CRAPPIEMATIC
MARTIN REEL COMPANY
30 Main Street, Mohawk, NY 13407

There's a Revolution in Crappie Tackle; It's Not Always A Cane Pole and Minnow Anymore

Mepps spinners catch crappies.

Another generation or two of panfish anglers may put crappie on the dinner table with the traditional cane pole, cork, lead shot and gold hook with an impaled minnow. Eased in to a brush pile, weed bed or near a submerged ledge, crappie fishermen have been feeding families and showing off trophy size fish since the time of Izaak Walton. That old humble system still produces, but with the advent of Crappiethon competition and tagged panfish that bring the lucky anglers big bucks, tackle manufacturers have gone to the drawing board and a revolution in rod, reels and poles has emerged.

Johnson Reels is now lauding its Cast A Country Mile closed-faced spinning reel that is designed to cast 6- pound test line further than ever before. Tangle free, the reel will not allow the line to twist, has an anti-static rotor and is specifically designed for panfish, although it is adaptable to bass fishing with 10- and 15-pound test line. Long a crappie fishing proponent, Johnson Reels is engineering more and more products for crappie enthusiasts.

B 'n' M Pole Company, of West Point, Mississippi, has already introduced its top of the line, 10-foot, two-piece graphite

37

jig pole that works with a West Point Crappie reel FR-2. Operating like a miniature fly rod and reel, it is a semi-sophisticated tackle for the panfisherman looking for something better than a cane pole. Already the professionals on the Crappiethon circuit are swearing by the revolutionary innovation. Pulling crappie out of tight holes in brush cover is being made easier than ever before.

B 'n' M's new glass fiber Crappie Duster-Jig Pole that telescopes for ease in transporting and handling, makes the cane poles of yesteryear obsolete. It's a strong yet lightweight fishing pole that comes in a variety of lengths, the 12 footer the most popular. These sleek crappie poles can be fitted with additional guides if anglers wish to modify them, and reels are made to fit if fishermen want to reel in their fish.

Broken sections of the B 'n' M pole can be repaired and replaced by the company at a minimum charge. Already in use by many of the pros, the Crappie Duster became increasingly popular in '89 in tournaments as well as by lay panfishers around the country.

Zebco, a name synonymous with crappie fishing for decades, has long marketed low-cost, simple crappie rods and reels that are almost trouble-free. Now engineers have concentrated on designing more sophisticated crappie equipment at Zebco and the world's leading seller of rods and reels is launching new products expected to attract panfish enthusiasts on the professional circuit as well as the family weekend fisherman.

Zebco's tradition has advanced with the CR60 Crappie Classic reel with a depth locator that enables crappie anglers to drop a lure in deep water to the exact depth at which he previously caught fish.

When fishing deep impoundments or holes in the lake and river bottoms, this new twist in reels gives the fisherman a distinct advantage. His suspended quarry will have the bait in its face repeatedly by plan and not by accident.

Because of the success of the CR60, Zebco introduced a full line of products designed to meet the needs of crappie fishermen. Among these are the six-rod Crappie Stick series, the CR6 Crappie Mate reel and combination, the CR10 spinning reel (the first spinning reel with controlled depth adjustment), and a special nine-foot doodlesockin' rod and matching reel. The new concepts are revolutionary improvements in fishing tackle that transform crappie equipment from the humble to the sophisticated, yet highly functional.

"Crappie are not always easy to catch, especially when they hide in heavy cover or in flooded timber. That's why Zebco has developed the Crappie Classic 2140 combination—an outfit that includes the sensitive ultralight CR40 reel and a nine foot telescopic rod that is ideal for fishing hard-to-reach areas," says Denny Jackson, Zebco's spincast product manager.

"The key is the nine foot rod. It's light, compact and portable. It allows the angler to reach a long way to catch a crappie in an area where he cannot simply cast," Jackson says. The light action doodlesockin' rod is the CR40 ultralight reel. The reel offers the convenience of spin-cast with the balance of the under-the-rod, closed-face spinning design. The CR 40 has a cut brass pinion gear and Zebco's Magnum Drag for smooth retrieves and smooth drag performance. It weighs less than five ounces, but comes spooled with 8-pound test line for pulling big crappies out of the brush.

The reel also has interchangeable handles for right or left handed retrieves.

Zebco's Crappie Sticks are no less impressive. These are rugged rods designed to meet almost any situation from pulling slabs from 20 feet of water to doodlesockin' in heavy cover in less than two feet of water. These attractive white rods with red accents and guide wraps range in length from five foot light action to an 11 1/2 foot telescoping dipping rod.

"Crappie anglers are serious about their sport and they deserve rods to meet their needs," says Steve Vogts, Zebco's rod products manager.

Zebco's new CR6 spin-cast will give crappie anglers a lower priced companion for the popular CR 60 Crappie Classic reel. The CR6, ergonomically-shaped to fit naturally into an angler's hand, comes with the convenient, wider angle dial, adjustable drag and positive pickup system. This allows for the pickup of the line every time on the first turn of the handle—important on a reel with 6-pound test line.

Equipment manufacturers have made this the era of the crappie fishing revolution. While there will always be those who prefer the good old days of cane poles, corks and minnows, there's going to be continuous testing of new fangled equipment that may make it easier to catch slabs in deep or shallow water, in cover or in the open. It will be interesting to see what professionals and lay anglers do with real sophistication in crappie tackle.

Even youngsters use modern tackle.

Crankbaits Catch Crappie Near Cover
In Spring and Summer

Hydrilla islands polka-dotted the surface of the 8,000 watery acres of Lake Lochloosa in Central Florida. Some of these aquatic meadows were the size of your living room, others smaller, but all were so thick with stalks attached to the mucky bottom in 14 feet of water that you couldn't possibly retrieve a lure through it. There were few holes in the exotic growth patches where you could even vertically fish a jig. A live-minnow crappie angler couldn't get his bait through the weeds to the bottom.

So, it was one spring when Mark Emory and a friend stopped casting along the shoreline for uncooperative large-mouths. They turned their attention to speckled perch or specks, as crappie are known in the Sunshine State. They had observed a lot of fish action around these hydrilla islands all morning, and no bass had bothered to strike. The feeding fish there logically must be specks, a species found in abundance in virtually every Florida lake and stream. When specks strike on the surface, the noise of their tail flailing the water is a sharp clap, and is discernible from a bass break noise. It also differs from the bream-feeding noise that is a sucking noise.

"Let's tie on some of our smaller crankbaits, and cast around these islands. This hydrilla attracts a lot of forage fish, and it is a natural speck hideout almost year around. It is even better than the man-made, submerged tree reefs that the game commission planted around Lochloosa in its deepest water. We can't cast into the stuff, but the outskirts may be holding specks that maraud here stalking the careless gambusia," Emory conjectured. "Anyhow, we are not doing anything with the bass."

A couple of hours later, Emory and his fishing friend tied their boat up at the Cross Creek Fish Camp pier. They began unloading their livewell into a 32-quart cooler. Their speck catch nearly filled it. They had 56 slab-size crappie that averaged over a pound. A few reached 2-pounds, and one even topped that.

It was an example of how really big specks like the looks of slow retrieves and small crankbaits. When these lures are intermingled with the real live forage fish, crappie do not decide to analyze the situation. They don't gulp down just those with real nutritional value, they jump at the chance to hit artificials. Specks make one mistake after another until the fisherman tires of the sport or simply catches all of these tasty giants that he can use. Emory had more than he could use. He was leaving for his salmon-guiding job in Alaska in a few days, and didn't need to take any fillets along. He generously doled them out to some unsuccessful anglers at the dock who were enviously admiring the crankbait catch.

Strangely enough, there are times when these artificials around clumps of hydrilla and other dense cover will attract strikes and catch fish when live minnows fail. The angler can give a crankbait a lot of action, perhaps more than the wriggly, squirming movement of the hooked natural bait. That could account for the super success of the lure.

There is also the chance that the behavior of small fish is the reason for lure advantage over minnows. Every size crappie in the neighborhood will gulp a minnow. There are none too young or too small to attack a two inch gambusia flitting in his face. He will go after it. But generally only the giants of the species attack a crankbait, even a small one. In that the little specks often rush for the minnow, it cuts down the angler's chances of reeling in another slab. There is competition for the food. The artificials usually catch just the big fish, sometimes real trophy size.

Discovery that crappie are anxious to strike lures is often a bass fisherman's find. He may get strike after futile strike on a worm or big crankbait, spinner or buzzbait, but hook nothing, or he may bring in a speckled perch or two. If no largemouths are caught, the angler is convinced that it is the specks that have been after his lures. If he is one of those bassers who wouldn't be caught dead fishing for panfish, he may ignore the hits, and stay after the lunker largemouths. But if he wants to put something in the boat that will later make it to the dinner table, he may shift to smaller crankbaits, and put this gourmet species in the box.

Crappie often hit plastic worms, particularly the short three or four inch ones. It is a common discovery of crappie fishermen to find pieces of plastic worms in the stomachs of specks at the dressing table. Unfortunately, these plastic worms will not digest. They may clog up the crappie's intestines, and eventually kill the fish. Small pieces pass through the fish, and are excreted, but larger chunks may stay in the fish's stomach for days, even weeks. The worm's color fades to a dirty brown, and

Big enough for the net.

they are usually that color when you find one in the speck's insides.

While crappies will hit worms, spinners, jigs and buzzbaits, the small crankbaits are hard to beat around aquatic islands where dense growth of hydrilla, milfoil or other weeds attract abundant food. A crappie may not have the intelligence of man, but he certainly knows that crankbaits look more like the normal stuff he feeds on than do the other artificials. He makes mistakes, and goes after the fake food, but when it looks and moves much like his everyday meal, he is more likely to strike, swallow and get hooked.

Nothing is forever true, but most crankbait crappie fishermen find their best success in medium-deep water. Where hydrilla grows to the surface in eight to ten feet of water, crappie may hang out month after month. They will hit the year 'round. In water considerably deeper, they may suspend at about that depth or deeper in the hottest weather, and they can be caught. The hydrilla has been known to grow to the surface in 45 feet of water, but few fish are ever caught at such depths with crankbaits or anything else. In shallow water where aquatic growth is found, usually it is not a good place for crappie on crankbaits. Hooks stay fouled, and it is a nuisance that tests the patience of the fisherman.

Some crankbait crappie anglers have color preferences. Others have little reason to believe the fish can tell the difference. Those with the blue-grey-white colors of the natural forage species are logically the most desirable. There is no doubt about their productivity. But you cannot discount the bright chrome, silver and gold colors. When there is good light on a bluebird day, these reflective hues sometimes bring the crappie running.

How about twitching the lure or rigging them so they will dive and dodge on the retrieve? There may be rare situations when twitching the rod tip or making the lure change directions will help. There are fishermen with a kind of magic touch, a special feel, who catch crappie with lure maneuvering. But most often, the fish strike with a simple, slow retrieve around the cover. You will lose the fish if you are too fast. Very slow retrieves catch the most fish around hydrilla islands, and similar speck hideouts. There are a few astute crappie anglers who can vertically jig a crankbait in holes in the cover and get strikes. It takes a special talent and experience.

The weight of the lure is important. The best crappie

crankbaits are no heavier than 1/4-ounce. Many of those in that weight made by Bill Lewis in his Rat-L-Trap series are deadly. They look natural on 6- or 8-pound test line and retrieved on light or ultralight tackle. It's light enough, and small enough to allow even medium-size specks to mouth it quickly. It has good hooks that hold. You may want to sharpen them a bit, but even without that, the hooks generally penetrate the soft tissue of a crappie mouth easily. There is no need for a gusto hook setting. Specks hit and are hooked, and you'll land most of those that strike by steadily and gently reeling the fish to boatside. Some fishermen net all their fish. It may save a few that would drop off, but the time lost getting the fish and hooks loose from the net may cost you a chance at an additional bite.

Rebel has a bevy of fine, tiny crankbaits. They will catch fish. Some are so light that it takes the best ultralight tackle to handle efficiently. They look natural, and crappie can't resist their slow retrieve in their feeding range. The brownish-orange crawfish is about as natural a look as any man-made bait can be. Crappie love crawfish near shorelines in four or five feet of water or even shallower. It's the one crankbait that may be more successful when twitched. Crawfish in the wild move in spurts backwards. That's how they flee from predators. When it is twitched a few times near feeding fish, it has the real-thing look. It may attract specks when some minnow-like lures are rejected.

There are other great crankbaits, like those made by Storm and Norman, that are small enough to be successful for crappie fishermen. Every fisherman makes his own selection, and fishes those in which he has the most confidence. Once he learns the feel, catches a few crappies on crankbaits, locates the feeding fish, and is acquainted with the light, hook-setting technique and retrieve, he will put fish in the boat. He may never be able to use it in the lily pads and sawgrass where the crappies may spawn, but when they sneak around the islands in the open water, a crankbait in the face of the really big ones is irresistible. Browned good in the skillet, it is irresistible to most seafood lovers, too, when eaten on the river bank or even at a more sophisticated meal in your dining room.

Crank a few crankbaits for crappies. It just might save a fishing day for you on one of those warm days when bass have decided it is Lent season and are fasting.

Minnesota crappie caught in walleye tournament
in Rainy Lake.

What, When, Where and How to Catch Open Water Crappies

Darlene Tucker lifts in a speck.

Nine plump laughing gulls nestled on the calm surface of Orange Lake a half mile from the nearest cover on the shoreline. It was high noon in mid-October, and there was a slight chill in the Florida air. What were these water-oriented, meat-eating birds doing here? They betray feeding striped bass in both fresh and salt water, and the dubious distinction of being "Judas birds" is an accolade that they rightfully wear. Anglers for big predator species follow the gulls, especially the diving birds, and their antics often lead to the demise of giant stripers to the delight of the astute anglers. The gulls go wild over bits and pieces of forage fish mutilated by the predators, and they gorge themselves with the residue. That feeding frenzy is the dead giveaway that observant striper fishermen look for. They rush to the spot and generally catch the fish that have ravaged the bait species, disrupting the banquet meal enjoyed by the circling, squawking sea gulls. But do these waterfowls pecking on the surface have a message for crappie anglers?

Indeed they do. I eased my boat near the gulls with my trolling motor, and carefully looked into the water, my polaroid glasses making it possible to peer below the surface in semi-clear water. Millions of tiny minnows flitted and frolicked, creating a bonanza for hungry fish. I trolled my combination jig-minnow bait through the melee. It was bingo time. Every line stretched, bobbers went down, my B 'n' M poles bent, and there were several minutes of havoc in the boat with flouncing slabs everywhere. It was the moment speckled perch fishermen live for. That observation, along with many others, is how veteran crappie anglers unlock the secrets of what, where, when and how to catch open-water speckled perch in lakes and impoundments not choked with hydrilla or other dense cover. Experience leads to expertise that nearly guarantees successful panfishing where the species population is abundant and the elements are reasonably cooperative. The "when" to fish for crappie in the open water is argumentative. In the waters of most Southern states, experts can catch limits of crappies every month of the year with the best results usually enjoyed from September through April. But I have seen limit catches in Florida lakes in May, June and July too.

On June 10th a few years ago, blind mosquitoes covered acres of open water in Lake Lochloosa, Alachua County, Florida. Specks literally were working alive in this enticing food-spread where a heavy fog dampened the insects so that they tumbled into the lake and could not recover. They were easy pickings for hungry specks. We caught 142 slabs before the honey hole played out around noon. I saw a similar heyday in Lake Waccamaw in Eastern North Carolina once when mayflies struggled on the surface, inviting both crappie and largemouth bass to fill their stomachs.

The species can be caught the year 'round. Yet, the best months in the open water are generally the same months that shoreline anglers catch the fish in the shallows where the spatterdock lilies, grass and weeds abound. When the specks are bedding in the shallows in the winter and spring in Florida, they are also active in the open water.

A crappie is just as likely to spawn in ten feet of water as ten inches of water. If they are on the beds in the grass, they will most certainly strike tied-out food in the open if it is convenient. So the "when" is answerable as "anytime of the year." There is one time when success in the open is difficult. If there is a gale-force wind 15-miles- per- hour or more, that would be a good day to fish a cove or slough. Or maybe stay at home. Keeping the bait in the face of the fish in such a wind is almost impossible in the open water.

What about the "where" in the lake or impoundment? If you have the good fortune to find the feeding gulls, patches of insects on the surface, or otherwise discover a school of fish flipping and feeding, that's the bonanza location. You need not look anywhere else. These obvious honey hole revelations are not always available. In their absence, in shallow-water lakes like those in Florida where generally the natural waters are from eight to 15-feet deep, start your search for specks in the deepest water. If there is a creek run through a portion of the lake, that may be the deepest water by a couple of feet. Fish there!

The fish like the dropoffs and the bottom structure. They will feed and often spawn in such spots. If there are underwater springs that feed the lake, give that a try. Crappie like the 72-degree water flowing from the bowels of the earth, and they will hang out in the spring runs all months of the year. If there is bottom structure, rocks, logs, stumps or dropoffs, specks will school and spawn in those areas whether it is a natural lake or an impoundment. They look for bottom change. There are few impoundments in Florida where there is very deep water. Where there is deep, open water, (more than 20- 25 feet) you'll probably do better to hunt coves where the depth is less than that. You may catch them in water that is deep by anchoring and dangling a bait near the bottom, but that is not the technique I prefer. Most Southern impoundments have some open backwater that is fishable where there are congregated crappie schools.

The "what" in catching open-water crappie focuses on what bait is the most productive. Using my system of crappie angling, you will catch some fish with a plain minnow hooked through the lips, eyes or dorsal fin on a No.2/0 gold hook (I prefer TruTurn) with two or three medium-size lead shot eight inches apart above the bait. A small oblong cork on the surface that will sink easily, but keep the bait off the bottom, helps. A 6- or 8-pound test line will get more strikes than a heavier one. I fish this rigging on 12-foot cane poles or the popular B 'n' M telescopic fiberglass rods that are easy to transport if you move from one lake to another. They will fit in your car trunk. This same general tackle will catch some fish if you use a small jig on the line instead of a live minnow. The tentacles will quiver, enticing some slabs to mistake it for a nutritious meal, and they may gulp it down.

One of the largest specks I ever caught was on Lake Woodruff on the St. Johns River with a plain jig on the line. These minnow baits and jig lures do produce. But when you combine them, giving the crappie a little something extra, you may double your catch. After years of trial and error, experimentation and documentation, there is an inescapable conclusion: A Super Jig with a No.4 gold hook (made in Jonesboro, Ark.) on the line with a two-inch minnow hooked through the eyes or lips, will put more specks on the stringer, and bigger ones too. Larger minnows reduce your strikes. Don't use them.

SuperJigs are made in dozens of different colors. I have experimented with these in Florida, South Carolina, Georgia and North Carolina. The solid pink color catches more fish than any other regardless of the season. The white and yellow will catch some fish, as will the brown with natural colored tentacles. I usually fish with six poles. I give the crappie some choice with three pinks, one brown, one white and one yellow.

There is a tip here worth considering. If you have dragged a minnow so long that it is stiff and white, re-bait with a lively one. Dead minnows will catch some crappies, but your chances are enhanced if you have one on the jig that looks alive. Also, if the action is not up to par, in addition to your minnow impaled through the eyes, hook another smaller one under the dorsal fin. By fishing the two minnows on the jig hook simultaneously, it often attracts reluctant specks that ignore the single bait. They are real meat eaters. That's the "what" of my open water crappie fishing.

The "how-to" catch speckled perch my way includes all the above when, where and what information. But the details of how-to may make the difference in going home with a mess of fish or the proverbial hungry gut and wet posterior. Sturdy pole holders mounted on the gunnels of your boat help. You may catch a few fish by sitting on the poles or propping them under minnow bucket handles, gas cans, seats, etc., but the baits and corks will ride better, and look more alive if the pole is fastened to the boat with adjustable pole holders that allow you to fish straight out from boatside or directly in front or in back of the boat. I like to have six poles in front of the boat and the same number for a partner in the stern. Two of the front poles are at right angles to the boat on each side. The other two are directly in front. In the stern, two are off each side and two behind the boat. A trolling motor with variable speed is a must for best results. I use a 12-volt Motor Guide with ten speeds. Your speed must be such that the angle of the lines from the end of the pole to the water surface is about 60-degrees. If it is less than that, you are going too fast or do not have enough weight on the line. If it is more than 60-degrees, you either have too much lead or you are trolling too slowly.

If the wind is blowing, head directly away from the breeze. The wind on the stern will let you reduce the trolling motor speed. I never troll into the wind, and I cannot catch fish when the boat is broadside to the wind. There are some good fishermen who drift in the open water with poles sticking out from the gunnels into the wind. The corks, lines and bait jump up and down with every wave. I contend that this makes the crappie work too hard to catch a minnow. I can do better by letting my jig-minnow combination move smoothly through the water. I know it looks more natural than an acrobatic jumping bait.

Often the wind is just right to keep you moving along at a pace that keeps your baits down without help from the trolling motor. You may have to touch it from time to time to keep the boat straight, but it floats along at a desirable speed. It is good to remember that if your outboard is down, make sure it is straight. If it is turned even a few degrees, the wind will push the boat around. You'll have to constantly use the trolling motor to keep the wind directly on the stern. Generally, when I reach the lake, I head into the wind and run for a considerable distance. I want to keep fishing for several hours without having to wind in the lines, crank up and move back to the windward end of the lake.

On lakes that are several miles long, you can often fish your half day without veering from your course. And you may keep catching fish from one end of the lake to the other. If you troll over an area where several poles bend at the same time, and you haul in some nice slabs, it may be advisable to drop out a marker, (a gallon Clorox jug with a piece of brick tied on a string for an anchor is as good as anything). You can then make figure eights around the marker, and you may load the boat if a big school has staked out the area for spawning or feeding. This is the easiest to do successfully when there is calm water. Troubled waters make it difficult to circle. While I use a plastic jug on a string anchored to a weight on the bottom, the late Preacher Travis Clark of Gainesville, Florida, always carried a long pole in his boat with a jug tied to the top. When he found a honey hole, he stuck the pole in the muck, and you could see the marker for a mile or more.

51

One morning when the lake was dotted with dozens of boats, he located a good spot and put out his pole and jug. He began catching specks. A tourist angler unfamiliar with Orange Lake fishing tactics, observed the success. Envious, he asked Clark if it was alright for him to fish around the marker. No one had ever asked for such permission before, but jokingly Clark said it was OK. "But as a matter of ethics, when we fish some other angler's spot, customarily we put a quarter in the jug," Clark said, as he suppressed a smile. Some time later when the honey hole was no longer producing, Clark moved several hundred yards away from the marker, searching for another good spot. When he returned to pull up his stake, he was startled to find three quarters in his jug. The tourist anglers were appreciative. So was Preacher Clark.

Speckled perch have tender mouths, and in many places are referred to as "papermouths." For that reason, many good fishermen believe in large hooks and a landing net for saving the strikes. Normally, neither is really necessary. No hook is better than a No. 4 or a 2/0. Anything larger may turn the crappie off when he tastes the steel. Those hooks will hold almost any speckled perch if you keep the line tight, horse the fish to the surface and quickly lift him over the gunnels. The fish has the most power when he is in the water. Horse him out without a hook-setting yank. Come in steadily, no jerking. You will lose very few unless you get trigger happy and pull on the fish before he has a chance to gulp down the bait.

When caught while trolling in the open water, most fish have the hook swallowed, and the end of the pole flutters in the water before you can grab it and pull. The crappie hangs himself if he is given a moment. Many speck anglers drag every fish into a landing net when the crappie reaches the surface. I net no specks unless I think I have a real trophy fish on the line. Most of the hooked fish will come in without a net that often complicates fishing as hooks, leads, bobber and fins tangle in the netting. It takes too long to get the bait back in the water. If you must use a net, you'll do well to buy one of the large-mesh nets with plastic-coated cords. Fish can be retrieved from these without the hassle of hang-ups. This is my what, when, where and how to catch crappies in the open water. I know it works. Over a lifetime of crappie fishing I have put more than 250,000 in the boat. You can, too, with a little experience and expertise.

Many Crappie Anglers Now Catch Open Water Slabs Every Month of the Year

Veteran crappie fishermen, guides and outdoor writers have their own best way to catch this gourmet species, and many readers have absorbed enough media advice to practically talk the fish into the boat. In truth, there is no one best way to catch crappies. There are many proven successful techniques that apply to almost any state where the species abounds. You do have to adapt a particular system to this fish based on the season, the cover, the available bait, your equipment, and your own ability to discover

A 2-pounder is a big crappie.

the tell-tale signs that pinpoint the location of schools. Then, when the fish are located in sufficient numbers, you may carry home enough fish for your dinner table or enjoy a festive neighborhood cookout. Above all, you must have the expertise to catch crappies in the open water if you want to enjoy success almost every month of the year.

Disdained by some bass fishermen, and accepted for its true value as a fine edible species by others, crappies (also known as specks, sac-a-lait, calico perch, bachelors and myriad of other monikers) are fun to catch and delightful to the palate. That doesn't mean they will fight from first strike to the gunnels every inch of the way like a bluegill or a shellcracker. It doesn't mean that they will jump a foot above the surface when hooked, and tail dance with gills flaring like a largemouth bass. The crappie won't do any of those things. But a 2-pounder on a cane pole or a 12-foot telescopic Lew Childres Breambuster, will run, pull and challenge you from a half dozen feet under the water, and make you wonder if you'll ever get the bend out of that pole once you put the fish in the boat or lead it into your landing net. You get the same challenge on ultralight spinning tackle if you prefer the more sophisticated equipment when angling for panfish.

First, let's talk about natural baits for crappies. The age-old enticer is a Missouri minnow, called more correctly today an Arkansas minnow, in that the bulk of them are raised at Lonoke. It is still the number one natural bait, but variations and additions to this little fish will make it more attractive and productive. Crappies can also be caught with live freshwater shrimp that are plentiful in most lakes of the South, and usually two or three of the little creatures impaled on the hook at the same time will attract strikes.

There are various ways to impale this minnow that make it more acceptable to crappies. In cover and water usually two to six feet deep, a No. 2/0 gold hook is desirable, and the minnow should be stuck just below the dorsal fin, and fished under a cork with one small shot eight inches above the hook or no lead at all. That's when you are going to still fish in cover. You may want to set out more than one line, and watch the corks carefully as the minnow flits and flips. If there's a crappie in the neighborhood, he will eventually take the bait.

If you are the kind that likes to hold the fishing pole, dropping a hook in one hole after another in the cover, and that's a fine way to catch crappie in the spring when the water warms up and these slabs start researching the territory for food and nesting space, impale that minnow through the eyes. A socket is there that lets the hook through easily. The minnow will live for hours. It won't slip off the hook easily when you hang up. You can let it flutter down near the bottom then jiggle it every few seconds up and down, and drive any crappie within sight into a frenzy. They'll hit it.

Minnows fished with the hook impaled under the dorsal fin should be about 2 1/2 to 3 inches long, no bigger. Even smaller ones work better when hooked through the eyes and twitched. A 2/0 gold TruTurn hook is ideal for this fishing, and a 10-pound test line is heavy enough.

These are old, familiar systems of crappie fishing that are

54

Even kids catch crappies.

still productive, particularly when fished during the warm months of spring when the fish are either spawning or feeding in relatively shallow waters. The system works in every state as the water reaches temperatures near 70° F.

If you catch your crappie before the water warms up, perhaps in 15-feet of open water, as many astute anglers do in impoundments, you use those natural baits differently. You still hook the bait through the dorsal fin, but you may have to use a larger lead shot to get the minnow down quicker. You may "stump jump" fish by dropping it around submerged stumps, logs, ledges, and let it fall near the bottom. When it gets a strike, and it will if crappies are there, often it moves the cork only inches or makes it just wriggle a bit. You waste no time. You tighten the line and come up pronto.

Second, there are other ways to catch crappies that are workable a greater part of the year. Fishing the minnow on a line in the cover is successful at best a couple of months of the year in most places, perhaps three or four months in some warmer states. If you have the time and go to the trouble, you can make fish hides in the deeper open water, and the crappies will gather there to forage for food much of the year. This technique catches barrels of big crappies with rod and reel, heavy leads, two hooks, and minnows dropped in the man-made fish hides or around natural cover.

Third, if you live in an area where most of the water is shallow lakes, eight to 15-feet deep, and not too much hydrilla or other aquatic growth, you have an advantage over most other crappie anglers. You can catch fish the year around. They need not be spawning. You'll carry your enticer to the fish, and you don't have to find him in the shallows or even in cover. You look for the open water where most anglers wouldn't even think about fishing.

For the best success, you must have the right equipment. That means a boat with a variable speed trolling motor that you can adjust to your system. You need good pole holders that will allow you to set several poles in the bow, and an equal number in the stern. The 12- or 14-foot poles are desirable with an oblong styrofoam bobber about three inches long, a 12-pound test monofilament line or lighter, and three or four medium-size shot spaced eight inches apart up the line from the hook. The hook should be No. 4 on a Hal-Fly jig, preferably orange or yellow, or a SuperJig made by Phillips in Jonesboro, Arkansas. On that jig hook, you impale a 2-inch minnow through the eyes or the lips. You are ready to fish.

Set the poles perpendicular to the boat, and parallel to the water. One should be almost straight out from the bow, the others at right angles to the sides of the boat. It isn't very productive to fish out the stern directly behind the boat unless you use a rod and reel with a bobber 50-feet behind the wake. Put the wind on the stern, never broadside, and move with the waves, never against them.

Start your trolling motor and move through the open water of your lake, trying to pull your bait across the deepest spots. Move at a speed that will force your cork to the surface when you have it set so the hook will drag along a foot or two off the bottom. That usually means the line will slant down from the end of your pole at a 60-degree angle. The bobber will sink immediately from your three or four shot if you stop or if you move too slowly. But it will ride the surface if you troll at the proper speed. That's what you want. The cork lets you know when you are moving at the proper speed.

When you get a strike, you'll know it. The end of the pole will slap the water. You grab the pole and yank it from the holder. Lift upward gently, always holding the end of the pole, not "choosing up" the pole like you would a baseball bat. You need not set the hook. The tender mouth often will not stand a jerk. Don't play the fish. Put him in the boat by lifting him out of the water.

There is absolutely no best season for that kind of troll fishing for crappies. The system works well in any lake where you can get the jig and meat near the bottom. In deeper water, suspended crappies will often strike when trolled baits are eight to ten feet below the surface.

Fourth, I have no explanation, but there are days in the summer when crappie will strike small jigs cast on light spinning tackle into deep holes in the open water, and allowed to sink slowly, much better than they will any natural bait. There are things you must know in this type of fishing to bring home the protein. The jig should be tied on the line in a manner that will make it stand out at 90 degrees, not dropped downward on the end of the line. You must have very light monofilament, 4- to 6-pound test is best.

It's important to know how to fish a jig, and perhaps the best advice is DON'T JIG THE JIG. All you do is swim the jig back to the boat slowly after you have allowed it to settle. It needs to be retrieved steadily with no action, no fancy twitches. Slow and steady are the right words. Your retrieve depth will vary with the length of time you allow the jig to sink, the weight of the jig head and the diameter of your line. But the retrieve speed at whatever depth must be slow and steady.

You can also have some productive crappie jig fishing days by letting the fluorescent glowing Super Jig simply suspend near the bottom. The tiny tentacles on the jig skirt will flutter and quiver even when there is little current. Without any twitch or jerk, it is realistic enough to fool hungry crappies, and they will often gulp it down when they congregate in deep, open water holes.

Fifth, night fishing is not always comfortable, but there are times and places when crappie will get on the hook at night when they refuse the most delectable dinners in the daylight. Coleman gas lanterns bounce light off the water around the corks a dozen feet from the hill. Other fishermen are anchored out in the middle of the river, in the lake itself or under the bridge with similar lights either from lanterns or the more sophisticated DC current electric bulbs that allow you to use your boat's battery. Some of these lights will burn underwater. Insects and minnows flock to the light, and the specks are never far behind. Minnows and jigs catch great stringers of crappies in state after state where avid anglers defy the darkness to outfox the fish with lockjaw in the daylight.

Sixth, how do you know where to fish for crappie in your favorite fishing spot whether it's in The Great Pee Dee River or Lake Jordan? Experience here is the great teacher. But here are things to look for that will bring success.

If you use your sight, hearing and smelling senses, you learn to put the bait where the fish are. Watch for shakes or bumps in the aquatic growth or brush piles when you are around cover. Crappies rushing for a morsel make mistakes, and hit objects that are dead giveaways. Listen for splashes and strikes on the surface in the open water. Crappies go after minnows and insects floating on or near the top, and they will strike your bait if it is dropped in front of their eyes where they are feeding. During spawning season when you are fishing waters with lilies and weeds, scan the surface for floating, white hair-like roots. Fish frequently dislodge these roots from the bottom when nesting, even though crappies are not good family-oriented spawners.

Remember, crappies will spawn in ten feet or ten inches of water. They tend to spew out their eggs, and go their merry way. But in the laying and fertilization, they do loosen many tiny roots, and these are real Judas tell-tale signs.

Your nose is important too. You can smell schools of crappies, particularly in summer, on lakes when the wind is calm. The smell is different from that musty smell released by bluegills on beds. The crappie smell is a fresh fish odor, like a fish market.

Look for maidencane, bulrushes, stumps, weeds, lilies and grass in relatively shallow water. Even if you hear, see or smell nothing, crappies inhabit this kind of cover. In the Currituck-Back Bay section of North Carolina and Virginia, they have a rule of thumb for fishermen—put your bait down every place where there is wood in the water. There is a lot of open water wood in that area where many duck blinds have been built. Duck blind pilings, bridges, sunken boats and other man-made obstructions attract crappies.

Look for crappies in open water trolling, that has been discussed here. If you have a depth finder, let it point out to you where the deepest channels are. Crappies that are not bedding will often school in these old creek runs or sink holes. When those jig and minnow combinations pass over the schools, you'll know it. It is a good idea to have some kind of marker in the boat. It makes it possible for you to keep a fix on the school. Nothing works better than an old gallon milk jug or Clorox bottle with a line tied to the handle, and a piece of brick or metal on the other end.

The crappie species is not very smart. They reproduce in such numbers that few lakes are ever fished out. They provide meal after protein meal for families all over America. They are caught in many states, and the year around with the best stringers in most waters dragged in during spawning months, this period varying from winter in Florida to summer and fall in the most northern lakes of the United States. In the Carolinas and Georgia, it is from March through June. While the world record fish weighed 6-pounds, generally the crappie you catch will not quite reach 1-pound. But even the midgets are tasty.

You have both fun and food when crappies flounce on the deck. It's an all-American species that thrills men and women, even children, and should forever have a place on a pedestal for anglers with a love for even the commonplace events as long as they happen outdoors.

Author and Darlene Tucker fish the open water.

Three Ways for Crappie

Springtime means crappie to the majority of the anglers in America and one of the best tactics for taking home a limit of crappie is jigging. Actually, jigging covers a wide variety of tactics, each of which can be effective in different circumstances. The most common is probably vertical jigging. This is a good tactic early in the spring when crappie are in fairly deep water, and is nothing more than sitting over a known crappie bed and dropping the jig straight down into the bed. Usually the lure is allowed to fall all the way to the bottom and is then brought up very slowly, stopping frequently to twitch the lure in place or "jig" it up and down slightly. Usually the fish will hit as the lure falls downward. Once a crappie is caught at a particular depth, lower the jig to the same depth for continued success.

Another type of vertical jigging is "dabbling" or dropping a crappie jig down into pockets and holes in brush and other cover used by crappie to spawn in the shallows. In the past a short section of line was tied to the end of a cane pole and used to reach into these tight spots. These days any number of modern graphite "crappie" rods make the job much easier. Merely move from one spot to the next, dropping the jig in place, "jigging" it a bit, then pulling it up and moving to the next hole.

Casting jigs and bringing them back in a slow "swimming" retrieve is a deadly tactic for locating crappie during pre-spawn and post spawn when they're not concentrated in the shallows. Cast the jig up on the shoreline and bring it back in a slow swimming motion. Vary the depth by speeding up or slowing down the retrieve until you start catching crappie, then use the same depth to continue your success.

The **ROAD RUNNER**® jig from Blakemore Sales Corporation is a great crappie producer. It features a tiny spinning blade on a "horsehead" design jig. Tail or dressing is available in the old standard marabou, tinsel skirt, living rubber, curly tail, and Turbo Tail which features a solid plastic body welded to a serrated tube tail. **ROAD RUNNERS**® are available in sizes ranging from 1/4 down to 1/32 ounce, the latter the top choice for vertical jigging and 1/8 often the best for casting and retrieving.

Make sure you take along a wide assortment of colors as crappie are known for their color finickiness.

Bass Fishing Techniques Can Aid Crappie Anglers

Tommy Biffle is best known as a bass fisherman, but he's more than capable at catching crappie when he's not following the bass tournament circuits.

Biffle's reputation as a bass angler is well deserved. He has won dozens of tournaments in Oklahoma in the past decade. In fact, there are few fishermen in the nation who have won as many bass events as Biffle, who has averaged more than ten tournament victories a year for the past five years.

But while he spends perhaps half of the year fishing for bass, he spends as many days as possible guiding and fishing for crappie. In 1989, he and his clients caught 150 to 180 crappie a day on better days, and 50 to 60 on "slow" days.

One of the secrets of Biffle's success at crappie fishing is his bass fishing experiences. That is, he knows the bottom structures of many lakes in intimate detail, and has the locations of dozens of brush piles committed to memory.

In one lake, for example, Biffle has 38 brush piles from which he catches crappie when the fish are not in shallow water. A few he built himself, but most were built by others or left by nature.

Some are as shallow as four feet. Some are down 40 or 50 feet. No matter at what depth the fish are holding, Biffle has brush piles in the appropriate range. Some are on deep ledges and creek channel edges. Others are on shallow, otherwise barren mud flats.

"When crappie are in a biting mood, you can catch dozens of fish from a single pile," Biffle says. "But on days when they are not biting, it is more like bass fishing—two or three fish from any single pile. On those days, knowing the locations of many brush piles gives a crappie fisherman a real advantage. By taking one

63

Tom Biffle shows off a speck.

or two fish from nearly every spot, you can wind up with quite a few at day's end."

The key to successful brush pile fishing, Biffle said, is placing one's bait at the correct depth. On any given day, most of the active fish will be suspended at a certain depth. If that depth happens to be near the lake bottom at the place one is fishing, it is easy to put the bait in the right spot. One merely lowers the bait to the bottom, then raises it a few inches and waits for the bite. But more often, the fish are suspended somewhere in the middle, making the process more difficult.

"Finding the correct depth at the beginning of the day is a trial-and-error process," Biffle says. "Generally, I start fishing near the bottom, or at a depth where the bulk of the crappie are seen on a sonar screen, and work up from that spot until the best depth is determined.

"There is a fisheries biologist in Missouri who spent three years observing crappie behavior while scuba diving in reservoirs. He found that crappie may rise as much as two or three feet to take a bait, but seldom will swim downward to do so. That's why it's important to fish exactly at the depth where the crappie are suspended or slightly above it—never below it.

"If you follow this technique, you will find that crappie often hit a jig or minnow as it is jigged upward—not on the fall. That's against common belief, but it's true."

Biffle says that depth control is just as crucial with jigs as it is in minnow fishing, especially in slightly stained water that limits the visibility of the lure. In general, he relies on 1/16-ounce tube jigs fished on 4- to 6-pound test Magna Thin small-diameter line. The colors he finds most productive are black-and-white or black-and-chartreuse in stained water or pearl in clear water.

In the past, some crappie anglers have resorted to marking line with felt-tip markers or tape, or tying small portions of rubber bands on a spinning reel spool so that they can return a bait to the same depth quickly after each catch.

"Those methods work, but there is no need to go to all that trouble," Biffle says. "Zebco's Depth Locator reels have solved that problem."

The Zebco CR60 spin-cast reel and the CR10 spinning reel both have depth-setting devices that enable the angler to return a bait to exactly the same depth, time after time.

Once an angler hooks a fish, all he has to do is push the

Depth Locator button forward and reel in that fish. Then he can immediately drop the bait back to the same depth.

"Once I find the right depth, I keep the boat moving until I find a spot where the crappie are concentrated," Biffle says. "I use my MotorGuide to troll slowly around and jig around brush piles until I get a bite.

"Crappie fishing is like any other kind. To catch fish, you have to keep your bait in the water."

A crappie angler studies the shoreline cover.

New Techniques for Catching More Crappie

Lightnin' Strikes come on spinning tackle.

To catch more crappie this year, learn the tactics of the crappie fishing pros like Alan Padgett from Kathleen, Georgia, and Bobby Martin of Warner Robins, Georgia. In the past four years, these two anglers have earned more than $70,000 while tournament crappie fishing.

"To catch big crappie, you must find spots to fish where the average crappie fisherman is not fishing," Padgett says. "Most of the obvious treetops and brush piles will be picked clean of slab crappie by local anglers. To locate very large crappie, look for underwater cover and secret places where most crappie anglers don't or won't fish."

One secret hideout that these two anglers always search for is underwater brush located on river and creek channels or at the mouths of creeks.

"These sites are hard to find and can be hard to fish—particularly if the wind is blowing," Martin explains. "But often these are the places where bigger crappie stay."

Padgett and Martin also have learned through days spent hunting crappie that the color of the jig is the key to catching more crappie. On any given day on any lake, the big crappie usually prefer one color more than another.

"If we can locate a school of crappie on our depth finder, we can catch them," Padgett mentions. "By changing the colors of the jigs we fish, the crappie will tell us which color they like best. Then we fish the color that produces the most crappie on that day on that lake."

A productive tactic Padgett and Martin use year round is trolling. Often they'll have from 12 to 24 lines out as they move slowly along creek channels, river ledges and/or stump rows.

"We know at all times how deep our baits are trolling," Martin reports. "If our baits are moving through the water at ten feet and we see a school of crappie at 13 feet, we slow the speed of our trolling motor down. This action allows our jigs to fall deeper in the water and pass through the school of crappie. If we spot a school at eight feet, we speed up our trolling motor, causing the jigs to rise and allowing them to pass through the school. The ability to control the depth that our jigs are swimming at is one of the critical keys to our catching more crappie."

During the winter months, Padgett uses a dead cork tactic when he's fishing a jig.

"A crappie's body metabolism slows down in the winter," Padgett explains. "Crappie don't want to expend very much energy to chase baits. Therefore I'll often cast a jig with a cork above it out in six to eight feet of water. I'll let the cork sit on the water and give it no action. Often crappie still will bite. When a crappie sees that jig holding steady with only the marabou tail moving with the current, the fish thinks it's found an easy meal that it can take with no effort. So it'll attack."

The newest strategies in crappie fishing are being developed on tournament crappie circuits like Zebco's U.S. Crappie, which offers three one-day fall tournaments and 16 spring tournaments with three categories of competition: husband and wife teams; adult only teams; and adult and child teams. This circuit pays back 100 percent of all entry fees and has an annual Classic tournament which pays out $27,000 in cash and prizes.

To become a member of Zebco's U.S. Crappie and to learn how to enter these lucrative crappie fishing tournaments, call or write the U.S. Crappie Association at (205) 244-7860, 6224 Wynfrey Place, Montgomery, AL 36117.

Lethal Lures for Crappies

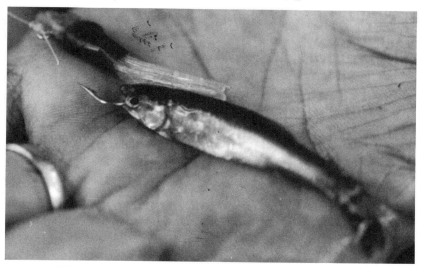

There is no better crappie catcher than a Super-Jig/minnow combination trolled in open water.

Crappies are one of America's most beloved gamefish, and by far the most common bait for these panfish is the small live minnow. Yet, there is a legion of crappie anglers who have discovered that lures catch fish on a consistent basis and will often out-produce live bait, including minnows.

There are four basic types of lures that catch crappies and which offer good fishing without the mess and bother of handling live bait. These are plastic body jigs, marabou-body jigs, tiny spinnerbaits, and small crankbaits. They are often lethal for crappies.

Plastic-Body Jigs

"The most common artificial crappie bait used in all geographic locations has to be the jig," says Steve McCadams, a guide on crappie-rich Kentucky Lake in Kentucky and Tennessee and a recognized crappie-fishing expert. "Small fish, such as shad, are their main food source, and jigs simulate small baitfish with their movement and often their color, although matching the color is not extremely important."

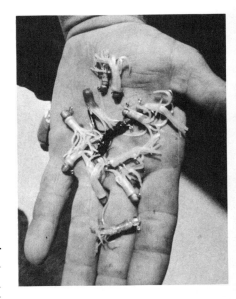

McCadams says that jigs have really gained in popularity over the last five to ten years for crappie fishing, and that the issue of which is best—minnows or jigs—is hotly contested in some areas of the country where crappies are prized gamefish.

There are basically two types of soft plastic-body jigs: the tube-skirted, hollow-bodied version and the solid one-piece version with straight or curled tail. Both are fashioned to a small leadhead hook and range in size from 1/80 ounce to 1/8 ounce, the larger sizes geared to big crappies.

"I prefer the hollow-bodied tube-skirt jigs when I am able to jig straight down over structure in fairly deep water and don't have to cast to it," says McCadams. "The skirt on these lures breathes, and it expands when it sinks. You put that in front of a crappie and it almost can't resist the lure's motion."

He says the action of straight or curl-tailed soft plastics is better suited for casting and a slow retrieve. "I use those types of jigs for casting with ultralight gear," he explains. "If I'm fishing in clear water and find an underwater brushpile that I know is holding crappies, the fish will be spooky because of the clear water. I'll then back off and cast to that brushpile. That's a good application for that type of jig. On the other hand, they don't have the right action for fishing a deepwater brushpile vertically. They have to be retrieved to have any action."

Selecting jig size can be crucial and perplexing since such a wide range of sizes is available.

"You have to gauge lure size by the average grade of

crappies you're catching," McCadams advises. "In the Southeast, where there are plenty of big crappies, they'll hit a good-sized lure because they're feeding on good-sized shad. I've caught crappies that had 5- or 6-inch shad in their stomachs. Big crappies will take a big bait. But where the crappies are a little smaller you have to use a smaller jig. Instead of fishing an 1/8-ounce jig head, you might need to go a 1/16- or 1/32-ounce head. You have to match your tackle to the fish."

Selecting the jig colors that crappies are most attracted to is anything but an exact science. Veteran crappie fishermen say color preference seems to be dictated by several factors, including the region of the country, water clarity, and the whim of the fisherman.

"The standard colors that I use are all-chartreuse and chartreuse combined with other colors—pearl, pink, black, and white," McCadams says. "I think water color and clarity are probably the most important factors in selecting color. For example, on a sunny day when I fish water of average clarity, I like to use jigs with metal flake, which really reflects the sunlight. In very dingy water, I think the darker colors like black are more effective. In clear water, I have good success on a red body with a hot-pink skirt."

However, according to McCadams, depth regulation is more critical than lure color in crappie fishing. "Crappies are basically a lazy fish," he says. "By lazy, I mean they're not going to go a whole lot out of their way to strike a bait. They're not going to do like a bass that might run 6 feet to hit a buzzbait. You're going to have to put that bait right in front of crappies on their level to catch them most of the time."

There are a couple of ways to do that. The most common is the use of a plastic bobber, although many crappie aficionados avoid using a float, believing the slight resistance it offers can be felt by the panfish. But it remains the easiest way to regulate the depth you are fishing. A good way to determine that depth is to troll several lines at various depths. The rod that gets the most action usually indicates the depth at which crappies are holding and feeding.

"I prefer to fish a tight line instead of using a bobber," McCadams says. "Sometimes the strike is so slight, you have to feel it to detect it. I use a bobber in the spring and fall when we're fishing depths of ten feet or less.

"In deep water, though, you have to either tight-line it or

71

use a special rig that's been very effective for me. I tie a bell-shaped (dipsey) sinker to the end of my line and tie one jig 18 inches above the sinker and another jig 18 inches above the lower jig.

"The rig is deadly for fishing 15- to 20-foot depths around cover, such as an underwater stump line where stumps are scattered throughout the area. The sinker regulates the depth of the jigs and also works as a depthfinder. You can pinpoint the underwater structure by feeling it with that lead weight and you can then work around that structure more thoroughly. You can keep those two suspended jigs in the effective zone much longer."

In weedy lakes, fishing a jig is extremely difficult since the vast majority of the jigs on the market have the tiny hook exposed. Weedless jigs that are rigged similar to a Texas-style plastic worm, with the hook embedded into the plastic body of the lure, slide through aquatic vegetation easily.

Marabou-Body Jigs

Marabou-body jigs offer a different action from their plastic counterparts. Their soft, feathery body makes them flutter as they fall, so they're naturals for vertically fishing an underwater brushpile or working the pilings of a bridge.

"Marabou skirts have that same good breathing action as hollow-bodied tube-skirt jigs," McCadams says. "But you can also retrieve them slowly and get a pretty effective action." Many crappie enthusiasts find that a marabou jig teamed with a live minnow is a deadly combination.

Marabou crappie jigs tend to be brighter and flashier than most panfish lures. In Florida, many crappie fishermen swear by colors such as hot pink, red, and orange. But Ricky Green, a tournament bass fisherman who admits to being a "crappie nut" during the spring of the year, prefers a jig that combines marabou and plastic.

"The most effective lure I've ever fished includes both a plastic tail with a little bit of marabou around the head," Green says. "I think a small amount of marabou gives that bait better action than just the straight plastic tail does." During the spring spawn, Green says white is the most effective color.

Spinnerbaits

One of the most effective ways to cover a large area and locate crappies, particularly in deep water, is to cast and retrieve one of the many tiny spinnerbaits on the market.

These miniature spinnerbaits are equipped with one or two small blades which flash and reflect light when retrieved. The baits also have a soft-plastic body, usually in the form of a straight tail.

"These lures are easy to use and catch a lot of crappies throughout the year, particularly when the fish are really aggressive, like at spawning time," McCadams says. "I really like to use these baits when I'm fishing fairly clear water and I back off of a brushpile or a man-made structure of old tires, cast past the structure and bring the lure past the fish.

"You need to pay attention to the speed of your retrieve, though. You want to move it fast enough so that the action of the lure is right, but you don't want to buzz it so fast that the fish won't hit it."

For fishing deep water, crappie experts will often add a split shot or even a light worm weight to the line to help these spinnerbaits run deeper.

Crankbaits

Bass fishermen using small crankbaits are often surprised to find panfish at the end of their line. But experienced crappie fishermen know that these fast-moving diving plugs are extremely effective under certain circumstances.

Tiny crankbaits will generally get deeper quicker than a jig or spinnerbait and will cover more water, which are important factors when you're searching for crappies. Preferred baits are in the 2-inch-long range, with an active swimming motion.

"These miniature crankbaits are especially effective in the early spring and through the spawn," McCadams says. Crappies are very protective of structure where they are going to spawn, and they'll hit a crankbait for that reason.

"There are other times of the year when crappies will hit a small crankbait out of pure hunger. But the biggest problem is that the hooks get hung up a lot."

Small crankbaits are good weapons for catching spooky crappies in both shallow and deep clear water. With the added weight of the lure, you can make longer casts with ultralight tackle.

No lure will ever evoke the affection many crappie fishermen feel for the sight and feel of having a lively minnow dangling beneath a bobber. People like to see that float go under. But lures are a viable alternative to the mess and hassle of stalking crappies with live bait. At times, some of them might even be considered lethal.

Author jigs in yearling crappie.

Crappie After the Spawn

Spring is the season when every angler becomes a bona fide crappie expert. In April, as the water warms up into the mid-60s, a massive influx of spawning crappie move shallow to make beds and lay their eggs. They create a standing-room-only situation along shallow, visible shoreline cover like willow trees, brush, logs, and vegetation.

During this time, the world abounds with crappie experts because almost any fisherman can catch these tasty panfish when they are spawning. Although the crappie is primarily a deep-water, offshore species, the annual spring spawning migration makes them especially vulnerable by stationing them in obvious, common-sense places where the neophyte angler can find them. And the protective nature of the fish—like most freshwater game fish— makes it easier to catch while it is guarding the eggs or fry.

All the world is a carnival during the spring spawn, but immediately after the spawn, it is as if Freddie Kruger comes to town. Nightmare on Your Crappie Lake. Crappie fishing becomes the toughest it will be all season, even for the knowledgeable, experienced anglers who are able to follow the crappie migration throughout the year.

Post-spawn crappie are the most difficult version to catch.

"That's a common problem in most lakes," says Steve McCadams, perhaps the country's most renowned crappie guide, biologist, and author of *Crappie Wisdom*, a highly successful book on crappie-fishing strategies. "And that's one reason why some people actually believe that crappie only bite in the spring.

"Of course, that is a common fallacy that was even written about for years. You can understand their way of thinking because they'll really catch them during the spawn, but when that post-spawn period comes in, the fishing begins to get tougher each week on the same shoreline bushes where they had slain them a few days earlier. Every weekend they find less fish there, and by late May they can hardly catch enough to take home

75

and stink up a skillet. They say, 'Well, the season is over,' and put away their poles."

Even crappie experts like McCadams, who guides on the famed slab-crappie mecca, Kentucky Lake, admits that post spawn crappie often baffle him.

There is a three-to four-week period that usually occurs in late May and early June in most of the country during which crappie go into a recuperative period to rejuvenate from the rigors of the spawning process. To understand why they are difficult to catch and, hopefully, use that knowledge to improve your post-spawn success, a little biology lesson is in order.

Immediately after spawning, biologists tell us that female crappie leave the nest and move off onto nearby brush or vegetation. After a short stay in shallow water, the females then move to the nearest mid-depth drop-off or vegetation. The males are left to guard the eggs and eventually the fry, until the tiny fish disperse and do what scientists have never been able to actually document. After leaving the fry, the males and females will re-group during the later stages of the post-spawn period before finally moving to their summer positioning in the deeper water areas.

You can begin to comprehend the reasons why post-spawn crappie are so difficult to catch. It begins with the challenge of finding them. That can be tricky because of the lack of concentrated females immediately after the spawn. It becomes more difficult as the wide-ranging tendencies of the species move into less-conspicuous places—even suspending in open water. This in-between stage for crappie separates the true experts from the instant springtime experts.

And once you locate post-spawn crappie, it can be an even greater challenge to get them to bite.

"Post-spawn crappie are tough to catch for the same reasons that post-spawn bass are difficult to catch," explains Oklahoma's Ken Cook, best known as one of America's elite tournament bass pros, but a crappie enthusiast who studied the species extensively during his days as a state fisheries biologist. "The reasons begin with the fact that they are hard to find, but they certainly don't end there.

"First of all, Mother Nature provides a fail-safe mechanism in sunfishes, of which species crappie are a member. That is, they don't eat while they're on the bed. So during a portion of the post-spawn period, the fish still have that ingrained in them. And they're tired and lethargic from the stress they go through during the spawning process."

Cook's first approach to catching post-spawn crappie is to avoid fishing for them. Instead, he moves around the lake and concentrates on spawners for as long as possible before turning his attention to the post-spawn fish. It is the same process that many bass anglers use to avoid being confronted with the sluggish post-spawn members of that species. You can accomplish this by simply following the natural heating cycle of a lake and reservoir. Start on the northern banks, bays, and protected coves where the water warms up the earliest in the spring and take temperature readings to find spawning water (about 64 to 70 degrees Fahrenheit) throughout the lake.

"Eventually, we all have to face up to post-spawn crappie," Cook laments. Locating post-spawn crappie is the first test of skill and patience.

Post-spawn crappie move off into deeper water, but not the depths in which they will ride out the summer temperatures. Cook looks for them along any drop-off adjacent to the shallow spawning area that has some type of wood or weedy cover.

There are three areas where post-spawn crappie are especially abundant, according to the experts:

• The mouths of bays. When crappie leave the shallow back of the spawning bays, they usually move out to the entrance of the bay where it meets the main lake. Look for them to hold around sunken vegetation, brush, or wooden structure on drop-offs bordering the open lake.

• Creek mouths. Crappie that have spawned along the shorelines of a creek will move to the mouth of the creek and hold along brush or weedy cover that is positioned along a change in depth. A key to locating these fish is remembering that these stressed crappie will avoid the current from the creek. They will usually be positioned off the side of the creek mouth where the water is calmer.

• Steep shorelines. In shorelines that have varying degrees of depth, like a long point, crappie will use structure on the shallowest portion to spawn and then will move onto brush or vegetation located in deeper water for the post-spawn recuperation period.

If adequate cover isn't available nearby, many post-spawn crappie simply suspend in open water—the panfish specialist's nightmare.

McCadams has utilized knowledge gleaned from a study of post-spawn crappie by Missouri state biologists to catch more of the non-aggressive fish. In that study, divers documented the movement of crappie from pre- through post-spawn periods in the clear waters of several Missouri reservoirs. To McCadams, the most telling discovery that the biologists made was a tendency of post-spawn crappie to deviate from their normal structure-oriented pattern, scattering and moving off into open-water flats where they simply suspend.

Although most post-spawn crappie are found in depths of 10 to 20 feet, legendary angler Bill Dance, one of the country's true crappie-fishing authorities, emphasizes that the clearer the water, the deeper post-spawn fish will suspend.

"Crappie suspend a little differently from bass," Cook explains. "They pick out a level and suspend uniformly at that level throughout that portion of the lake. Crappie suspend like a blanket—side by side at the same depth—while largemouths, white bass, and almost any other game fish tend to be grouped at all levels of depth. Depending on what that level is, they will suspend above structure like a brushpile, instead of relating directly to it. That is why a lot of people miss suspended crappie. They fish under them."

The depth at which post-spawn crappie suspend is directly attributable to two natural factors in the makeup of the water column—the thermocline and pH breakline. The thermocline is the water temperature level that is most comfortable to fish (meaning it has adequate oxygen as well), while the pH breakline is the point at which the level of alkalinity or acidity in the water is acceptable.

By measuring those two factors, you can determine the likely depth of the fish. To determine the depth of the thermocline, lower a temperature gauge probe down until you reach a point of significant change. Note that depth and check for a pH breakline, which will pinpoint the depth of the fish even further. A thermocline can have a variation in depth of 5 to 10 feet, but the pH breakline (which will be located in the upper part of the thermocline) will be somewhere in a 2- to 3-foot zone.

"They will stay at that depth until some factor changes," Cook adds. "The sunlight level can change, which causes the photosynthesis to change, which will alter the composition of the water column, either the oxygen, pH, or temperature. One of those factors will change and the fish will move up or down a foot to ten feet to again find the level that best meets their needs."

The next step is to locate structure at the depth indicated by those readings—although suspended crappie don't always relate to underwater objects or changes in the bottom contour. If you don't have a temperature probe or pH gauge, a quality depthfinder can show a thermocline.

The suspending nature of post-spawn crappie is the major reason why most fishermen get frustrated in their late spring/early summer efforts. Crappie anglers are structure-oriented and tend to move from brushpile to brushpile without fishing the open water in between. Ironically, this open-water no-man's land may be where the post-spawners are holding.

That is the reason why guide Steve McCadams spends more time making random casts with a jig—instead of vertically fishing specific spots—during the post-spawn period.

Trolling may be the most productive method of locating suspended post-spawn crappie, Dance says. "Trollers cover enough water to find post-spawners," he emphasizes. "When you see a large number of boats trolling, you can pretty well guess that a high percentage of the fish are suspended and that's why the trollers are having success catching them."

In many parts of the country, crappie fishermen use a technique commonly referred to as the "spider rig" to run baits at several different levels while drifting or using trolling-motor power to cover open water. Four to eight poles are positioned all around the boat with minnows or jigs swimming at variable depths from 6 to 20 feet. After a couple of strikes at the same depth, the trollers then adjust all of their lines to fish that depth. Trolling is the easiest way to pick up scattered, individual fish—typical post-spawn crappie.

Rather than confront the challenge of locating and catching these inactive crappie, many fishermen choose to simply sit out the post-spawn period and wait for the fish to move to their structure-oriented summer lairs. Generally, once you can no longer find beds, the post-spawn stage is over and it is safe for less-determined crappie fishermen to return to the water.

"The best crappie fisherman is one who can change when the fish change," McCadams says. "Crappie don't just disappear when the spawn ends. The best crappie fisherman works hard enough to follow post-spawn fish through the transition period from shallow to deep, and that determination pays off."

B 'n' M Fiberglass poles and rods are
great crappie catchers.

How to Catch Crappie the Old Fashioned Way

Before the era of automatic transmissions, sliced bread and monofilament line, panfishermen put a lot of crappie and bream on the dinner table caught with humble gear from the banks, bridges and cumbersome homemade bateaux. Today's modern gadgetry would have been helpful, but angling was not a big business, and industry didn't envision opportunity in manufacturing and marketing until the middle of the century.

A few rods and reels have been available for nearly a century, and the first freshwater tackle that made much of an impression on fishermen was the Pfleuger Supreme reel and hollow steel rod. It beat anything that most lay anglers had seen prior to its introduction. But by today's standards it was a joke.

There were few bait and tackle shops early in the 20th century. Hooks and lines were generally sold over hardware counters in the back of the store. Some areas had shops where you could purchase cane poles from 10 to 16 feet long, but most panfishermen cut their own from dense growths of reeds found in some river bottom jungles. They were free. The store-bought poles cost a quarter, something that few people had to spend on recreation.

Families bought vinegar in gallon jugs. The cork stoppers were the common big bobbers used by panfishermen. Anglers looking for a smaller bobber used the half-inch diameter corks from castor oil bottles and SyrupPepsin, the two most commonly used laxatives of that period. If you ran out of these choice corks, you could always fashion a makeshift bobber from a piece of pine bark or even a splinter of white pine. (Castor oil was such a famous cure-all for everything that those small corks were almost always available.)

Split lead shot for sinkers was introduced much later. The store-bought sinkers were inch long wrap-around lead. Most country fishermen of the era tore open T- and A-Model Ford batteries, and stripped out the sheets of lead. You could cut it with a pair of scissors, and flatten it out enough so it would wrap around a line above your hook a few inches. It made a satisfactory sinker, and you could suit yourself as to how heavy you wanted it.

Fishing line was the most difficult, cantankerous product that early panfishermen had to use. There were times when the only line available was black No. 8 thread from a spool on your mother's foot-treadle sewing machine. This was cotton and perhaps compared to 2-pound test line. It would tangle on everything it touched and, of course, break when a sizeable fish thrashed around and ran. There were other cotton lines made for fishing, and some linen, too. These were used by the anglers who could afford them, and were the only things available for rod and reel fishermen, generally the doctors and lawyers of the community. A backlash with these flimsy cotton or linen lines often took hours to unravel. It was not easy even on a cane pole.

Monofilament was not discovered until 1937 when DuPont introduced it for women's stockings, and it created fights as ladies crowded stores everywhere to purchase these almost transparent hose. Prior to that, the most glamorous ladies wore silk or cotton hose that were quickly destroyed by even slight picks that caused long runs. Nylon, a form of monofilament, glamorized ladies' legs, and two years later it began the revolution in fishing line when it was first put on a reel and tried by Doctor Carouthers in Brandywine Creek in Delaware.

Hooks generally were bought, and most panfishermen chose a No. 4 all-purpose size. Whether for bream or crappie, the No. 4 steel hook did the job. A dozen hooks sold for about a dime. A few desperate fishermen forged hooks from tempered hay-baling or barbed wire, and many children bent straight pins for hooks used in the creeks for little bluegills and punkinseed, called "sun perch" over much of the South.

The few boats that were used for crappie fishing were made from 1 x 6 cypress boards, cured for months in the sun, and then bent to the desired contour of a clumsy, blunt-end boat, bateaux to the outdoorsmen of that period. This humble craft was a luxury. The masses fished from the shorelines of the rivers and lakes. Homemade plywood boats came later.

Wild creek minnows, some known as "stone-toters," were scooped from the branches and creeks with crude seines made from coarse-fiber, 200-pound size, fertilizer sacks. Fastened to a couple of popash limbs cut from the creek bank, it was sufficient for the bait-catching maneuver. Normally a few dips in a knee-

Many crappies are caught from the bank.

deep, unpolluted stream trapped dozens of lively, two-inch minnows, enough for a day's adventure in quest of a stringer of crappie throughout the South.

There were no aerators. You kept the minnows alive by regularly changing the water. Once you reached the river bank, you tied a bucket to a bush after punching it full of holes. It sat in the shallows with the water passing through it. The minnows would endure almost forever in this humble prison.

Easter Monday was the gala opening of the freshwater fishing season. Indeed, up until about the middle of the century, many states had closed seasons on gamefish until about this time in the spring. In North Carolina you could catch only catfish and German carp until Easter. The reprieve was in force to keep the fish from being "caught out." Easter Monday opened the fishing because almost no one fished on Sunday. That was a no-no in much of the Bible Belt.

After you had your "tackle" and bait and headed for the river, you faced the decision as to where you would fish. You had to pick a shoreline where the crappie were likely to be feeding or perhaps nosing around in search of a choice spawning spot. You didn't have the luxury of a boat and motor so that you could ease along miles of shoreline until you found the mother lode. There were no trolling motors until after World War II. You had to choose a place where you could get a car close enough to the water that you could carry your poles, bait bucket, drinking water and a little food. A few old sawmill roads helped fishermen reach the banks where they believed crappie were holding. Often other fishermen had picked the same spot, and you moved a few yards up or downstream to what appeared to be another likely site.

What made one small stretch of shoreline better than all the others on large rivers like the Great Pee Dee in the Carolinas; Savannah, in Georgia; the St. Johns in Florida; among others in every Southern state? What did the early bank fishermen look for?

With it being difficult to fish more than the length of a football field on any one excursion, the crappie hunter had to use his knowledge of the species to pick and choose the most likely stretch to put out his poles. Regulations in many states prohibited anglers from fishing more than two poles at a time. Again, biologists considered this a conservation decision. The two-pole limit was in force until recently.

Shoreline natural grasses blessed the banks of many rivers. When you found a spot with a couple of yards of grass along the bank, and open water five or six feet deep on the fringe of the aquatic growth, this was indeed a good spot to crappie fish. Honey holes are made from such habitat.

Other ideal bank-fishing hot spots were around fallen, half-submerged trees with enough depth that crappie could spawn, and where you could get a flitting minnow between the limbs and down near the bottom without staying constantly hung up.

Several stumps near the bank with perhaps a log or limb or two on the bottom was always a desirable location. In rocky rivers, an accumulation of boulders a fishing-pole length from the bank would hold crappie. Then there was always a spot or two where sharp drop-offs only a few steps from the shoreline would have crappie moving along the ledge stalking forage food or just exploring for spawning grounds. Fishermen of the era learned where these holding areas were, and they fished them year after successful year.

Those few fishermen with tiny boats in coastal areas often found crappie schooling around cypress knees and standing trees along shorelines where the water was a couple of feet deep. They squeezed in around the trees and flipped minnows in the shadows. Some waded into these wilderness waters and caught fish on long cane poles and later on rods and reels.

Most anglers of that generation inherited patience—an attribute that then and now often makes the difference in going home with a stringer of crappie or just going home. They kept bait on the hooks and slack in the line as they fished diligently for any hungry critter in the territory. The astute anglers knew that when the cork went under you gave line to the striker for three or four seconds, and then set the hook with not too much gusto. The tender-mouthed crappie needed a little time to swallow the hooked minnow, and you had only to wait a moment, then gently drag your slab along over the surface to high ground and the stringer. You caught the fish that bit.

Those humble fishermen without sophisticated equipment also knew that crappie like a moving bait. Generally, they hooked lively minnows under the dorsal fin so that they would swim and struggle much more than one impaled through the lips or eyes. When the minnow died, they quickly put on a fresh, healthy bait. They also learned that when your minnow became lethargic, you could dip him up and down in the holes in the cover and often bring a crappie a-runnin'. You could tight-line a minnow and make him look alive.

Fish were obviously more plentiful in those early days before pressure and pollution reduced their population. Often you could catch two dozen slab crappies from a single tree top without moving from your stump seat on the bank. The same was often true of a dishpan-size hole in the grass or spatterdock lilies. There were no hydrilla or water hyacinths.

Much of the expertise that those early anglers learned about panfishing from the bank, is just as appropriate today. They acquired knowledge from their experience and observations. They learned patience, the need for gentleness in landing the papermouths, what the species sought for feeding and spawning grounds, and how to make a bait more attractive to the fish. Those lessons are pretty well set in concrete. That knowledge is adaptable to today's panfishing and has changed little with time and sophistication.

Modern panfishermen with excellent tackle, electronics

that can pinpoint a single stump in an offshore hole, trolling motors that allow you to slowly fish miles of inviting shoreline, outboards that can put you anywhere quickly, and tasty-looking morsels of life-like replicas of everything a crappie ever ate, have a myriad of advantages over the pioneers. Combining that modern technology with the expertise garnered from generations of observations, gives today's panfishermen unsurpassed opportunity to put fillets on the dinner table.

Time has marched on and fishermen have profited from the storehouse of knowledge multiplied by the scientific discoveries of innovative manufacturers. Like everything in America, fishing has witnessed a renaissance—transition continues even as the 21st century approaches. It makes fishing much easier but not necessarily more fun. Or has it?

Curt Layser fishes the grass.

Fears Shares Fish-Catching Tips

Tournament bass fishermen like O.T. Fears have preached the gospel of catch-and-release fishing for years.

For them, putting bass back to be caught again is a way of life. But even a bass fishing pro likes a plate of tasty fish fillets once in a while. Fears is no exception.

When he's hungry for fish, though, Fears goes after crappie and other panfish. These panfish species are far more prolific than bass and can stand the pressure of sportfishing harvests much more readily.

Crappie, bluegill, redear, green sunfish and other panfish can provide a lot of delicious meals without doing damage to the resource. "That's why I fish for them," says Fears. "Not only are they prolific, they're fun to catch."

And when Fears goes "meat fishing" for crappie and bream, he relies heavily on Zebco closed-face spinning reels, especially the 444 TriggerSpin.

"It's a dandy reel for a lot of applications," says Fears, winner of the 1987 Red Man All American title and the $100,000 prize money that accompanied it. "The 444 is lightweight and has a fast retrieve speed."

Fears lives in eastern Oklahoma in Cherokee Indian Country. That's appropriate, since Fears is half Cherokee and proud of his Indian heritage. Near Sallisaw, his hometown, are numerous small streams filled with sunfish, smallmouth and spotted bass. And the area has many ponds and small lakes teeming with crappie and big sunfish.

Each year, similar bodies of water throughout the country produce giant crappie that can be caught in the spring by anglers walking the banks and fishing shoreline brush-piles, flooded buck brush and willow tree thickets.

"I do as much crappie fishing as I can between tournaments from January through May," Fears says.

"Early in the year, I fish deep structure for crappie— submerged creek channel edges, especially bluff-type edges. They might be 40 feet deep or more. The crappie can gather up in big schools on places like that."

As the water starts to warm up, the crappie gradually work their way toward the shallows. Then, Fears looks for brush-piles and other cover.

The dark-colored males will move in first and you can catch them near the shoreline. The bigger females will usually hang out a little further from the bank.

"When you can catch males in the brush near the shore, you can often catch the bigger females by putting a cork on your line above a jig and swimming it through the area a little bit farther out," says Fears.

"Experiment until you find the depth where the fish are holding. It can change a lot from day to day, depending on the weather. A cold front or a heavy, cold rain can make crappie that were up shallow turn around and move back to deep water in just a few hours. But you'd be surprised how shallow the fish might be, even when the weather's still pretty cold."

Fears' best trips for crappie occur a bit later in the spring when surface water temperatures climb into the mid-50's and the crappie, big and small, move into very shallow water in preparation for spawning.

Not only is fishing good then in major reservoirs, it can produce eye-popping stringers of slab crappie in the old river oxbows. Rivers impounded with a series of dams to create navigation systems are especially good places to find this kind of fishing."

The chance of hooking a lunker largemouth while angling for crappie is another reason Fears uses Zebco TriggerSpin reels for this kind of fishing.

"These reels have a smooth, efficient drag system," Fears says. "You can fight a big fish on light line with them. If a fish doesn't get wrapped around buck brush, you can probably land the bass."

Fears also uses TriggerSpin reels when he and his young son, Daniel Hawk, go to fish for big bluegills. The reels handle the light monofilament—four- to eight-pound test—he prefers for such fishing without a lot of twisting and tangling, he says.

Although he uses them the majority of the time while panfishing, he also includes them in his bass fishing arsenal when he's wading or floating clear, rocky streams for smallmouth and spotted bass.

"They are just about the ideal reel for fishing tiny jig-and-grub baits, wee crankbaits or similar ultra-light lures that are

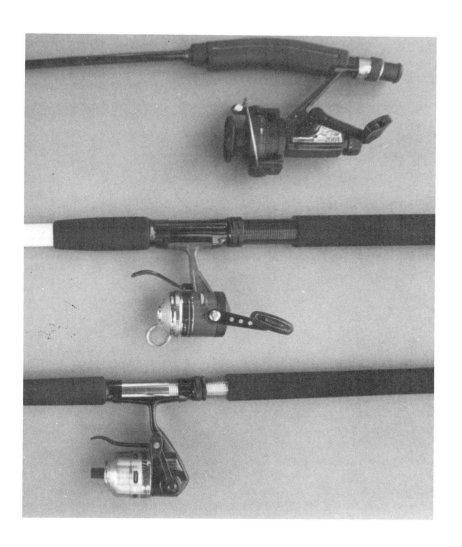

so effective for fishing small streams," Fears explains.

It surprises some folks to see a professional bass fisherman like Fears using a spincast reel. But Fears has no qualms about using a type of reel that some people think—merely because of its ease of operation—is for beginners.

"It doesn't bother me a bit," says Fears. "I use the reel I think is best for the job."

B 'n' M Team catches crappie.

Add Meat to Jigs and Spinners for More Panfish

If you can cast a lure in a hole in the cover, you'll likely land a crappie.

Traditionally, there are good panfish anglers who catch more crappie and bream with jigs and spinners than with live baits in some lakes, during certain seasons and under specific weather conditions. Conversely, there are throngs of astute panfishermen who frown on all the artificials, insisting their best results come from enticing strikes with real nutrients.

Regular success probably lies somewhere in between the two philosophies and techniques for most panfish enthusiasts, and they would do well to combine and refine the art of both systems. Perhaps the most realistic way to succeed, and fill a stringer with gourmet slabs, is a combination of artificial with the natural bait on the hook at the same time. In other words, add meat to catch more meat.

Perhaps no better example of this adaptation that leads to limit catches can be recalled than one in which my wife and I were fishing a big hole in the spatterdock lilies of Central Florida a few years ago. It was about mid-morning, and we had dropped minnows everywhere in the territory trying for a few speckled perch (crappie) since safe light. Only two had succumbed to the inviting morsels that flitted and squirmed on the hooks under a tiny cork on the surface. At that pace, we wouldn't even have a mess for lunch with the company we had on hand.

"Let's alter the offering a little," I suggested, and Lucile was perfectly willing. She had already lost hope, marked the morning off as an angling disaster.

With 8-pound test monofilament line on the B 'n' M, 12-foot fiberglass poles, I tied a tiny gold Mepps spinner on her line and a Super Jig on mine. Then I searched through the minnow bucket, and culled two of the smallest live minnows we had. I impaled each through the eyes behind the lures. I removed the corks, but left a small shot on the line about a foot above the baits.

"Now flip that spinner near the other side of the open hole near the lilies, twitch it a time or two, and then drag it slowly back toward the bow of the boat," I instructed my fishing wife, who was no novice.

She complied amazingly well, and on the first retrieve she came in with a 1-pound speck that hit the spinner like there was no tomorrow. He was vicious.

Taking my own advice, I flipped my jig and minnow combination a few yards away and likewise had a strike. Another slab speck went on the stringer. Without belaboring the technique, we caught all the fish we could use in a couple of hours, and were back at the dock in time to dress the catch, and start lunch for our friends that were waiting expectantly. They were agape at our success.

It was a concrete example of how adapting the system to a combination of two attractors paid off. I have watched it happen like instant replay many times since.

It doesn't necessarily have to be a minnow-jig or minnow-spinner combination. There are many other live baits that bring good results when tipped on the hooks behind the hardware. Meat even works on small crankbaits too.

Throughout the South where freshwater shrimp are plentiful in the grass, and can be caught easily with a small-mesh dip net, there is no better tipping meat than this inch-long crustacean. The immediate week or so prior to spawning when the males of the species maraud in the cover searching for bedding ground, the shrimp-tipped spinner or jig is dynamite. The small, hand-size daddies seem to fight the combination with a passion seldom witnessed with either the artificial or the natural bait alone.

There are many other good tipping meats. The mealy worms that you can raise yourself or buy at many bait shops, (Georgia Mealies, Route 7, Box 50, Tifton, GA. 31794), is an excellent tipping meat. This larvae is about one inch long, white when fresh, and these "maggots" wriggle and move when impaled through the center section. Few self-respecting, hungry panfish can refuse such a morsel when it is slowly led past their noses around cover.

The original fish bait virtually all over the world was the common old earthworm. It's still a fine meat for tipping. While all of the various sub-species will work, the snake-like squirming worm about five inches long that has come to be known as a "Georgia Wiggler" is probably the most effective of the worm tips. These should be hooked through the mid-section, not threaded on the hooks as old-timers of yesteryear impaled worms. There's a lot of appetizing attraction to a long-dangling worm pulled through the water at the end of a spinner or jig bait. It brings a lot of specks a-runnin' with their mouths watering.

Equally as great as a natural tipping meat, is the larvae from unhatched wasps from nests that often hang on limbs draped along lake and stream shorelines in the fall. The buzzing parents do not appreciate your kidnapping their young, and it is a good idea to cover up with a poncho, then slap water on the nest before trying to abscond with the young wasps. Once you have the guardians wet down pretty good they are not much of a threat. They can't fly very well, and you can cut off the "Mexican Hat," as some anglers call the paper-like nest, carry it a safe distance away, and dig out the white baby wasps. It is among the very best meats for tipping.

Other tried and true additives to crappie lures are catalpa worms that have been turned wrong side out, resembling something soaked in buttermilk. It is so white that it can be seen from many feet away in reasonably clear water. It obviously helps the panfish find a meal.

Sapheads, a white grub-like worm found under the bark

of decaying pine trees is a fine, tough, natural addition for lure hooks. They usually are white with a red head, and look appetizing to a fish in the water. They are long livers too.

Bonnet worms live in the stalks of the cow lilies. You can find them simply by looking at the leaf tops, and where there are holes in the stalk, there will almost always be a worm or two not far down. Break off the lily, and the worm is easily captured. Some Florida natives swear by this bonnet worm bait, declaring it the best tipping meat of all. You have to beat the birds to these worms. Red-winged blackbirds and grackles walk the lily pad areas relentlessly from dawn to dusk pecking out the worms. A good meal for the birds is also a good meal for the panfish. You compete with the birds for the live meat.

Crickets, grasshoppers, snails and even tiny lizards are the favorite tips for many devout crappie anglers. Almost anything alive will give your technique an added dimension that pays off on the stringer.

There is an additional bonus. If you are not dead-set on catching only one species, just crappies, you'll be pleased with a stringer of big bream. . . bluegills, shellcrackers, warmouth perch and punkinseed, among other panfish. You may even pull in a few yearling largemouths that take a liking to meat on the hardware. Almost every fish that swims likes the looks of a man-made attractor with some real meat on it. They will often compete with the crappies for whatever you flaunt in their faces.

And if you are like most American fishermen, simply looking for a mess of fish while having fun at the same time, you won't be overly concerned when you have a bream on the line instead of another speckled perch. After all, the fight in the bream ounce for ounce is unbelievable, far greater than in the crappie. It's not the size of the fish that counts. It's the size of the fight in the fish that counts. And while it is controversial, there are just as many devout, veteran anglers who prefer bream on the dinner table as crappies. Either way you win by tipping your jigs and spinners with a bite or two of real nourishment.

Try it! You'll be glad you did.

Go Natural—Put Panfish on the Table with Real Baits That They Cannot Resist

From the Canadian border of North Dakota to the tips of Texas and Florida, up the Atlantic coast past Virginia and all points in between, panfish are sought by more anglers than any other species. Those informed fishermen who know how to find them and what natural baits to put on the proper hook and line, will fill stringers and the dinner table skillet with a gourmet fish that is truly finger-licking good.

Crappies and bluegills are the primary panfish sought in these Southern and Midwestern States, although there are several lesser species that thrill many cane pole and light tackle fishermen in these regions.

Bluegills are fighters every inch of the way from the time they gobble down your bait until they flounce over the gunnels to the deck or at your feet on the bank if you are not boat fishing, and millions are caught by men, women and children from the hills and the bridges every year. It's truly an all-American species that thrills the very young, the novice, the senior citizen and frequently is the fish that originally introduced professionals to the adventures of freshwater fishing.

How do you locate bluegills so that you don't waste time with a bait in the wrong place? Use your senses and learn what sights, sounds and smells are made by hordes of this species that inhabit almost every lake, stream, pond and reservoir that isn't overly polluted.

You may see some aquatic growth bump and shake where bedding bluegills are working or a quivering twig from a half-submerged tree top. You may hear and see a "titty size" bluegill (one so big you have to hold him against your chest to get unhooked) suck in a mayfly, junebug, mosquito, caterpillar or some other insect that was too reckless and fell in the drink. Or perhaps the best bluegill-finding sense of them all—smell—will lead you to schooling or spawning fish. When they are congregated in sufficient numbers, and particularly when nesting, they exude a musty, ripe-watermelon smell that is easily detectable by experienced panfish anglers. Follow your nose and put a bait in their faces and often you'll catch limits without moving another step. When there's no wind, the instant you smell the fish, you may be on top of them. If there is some breeze, you may have to head into it until you lose the scent, backtrack and pinpoint the school.

What are the best baits for bluegills that are available to almost all fishermen? Go natural with the same creatures the bluegills find, eat and grow on in your neck of the woods. They gulp the morsels down without having to make the mistakes of artificial enticers. If they have nosed around for worms on the bottom all their lives, they have little reason to suspect that such a juicy morsel with a hook impaled through it is lethal.

The age-old earthworms are still good bluegill baits everywhere. It is the nearly universal natural bait. They are available commercially in every state, but for the energetic, a pork and bean can full can be spaded up in moist dirt in shady spots every month that the ground isn't frozen. You can make an area super-productive by sprinkling corn meal, flour, cattle food or some other nutrient around the area. Cover it with boards, sacks or an old piece of canvas, wet it during dry seasons, and you have a low budget worm hatchery.

One of the best places to fish earthworms is in spots where fast-rising water from freshets covers new ground. Bluegills by instinct know that this flooding will bring worms out of the earth and they come from great distances to forage on the bottom. Worms are likewise productive in brushpiles, lily and grass pads, around stumps and logs, bottom structure, often in deep water, and in creek mouths.

Earthworms fished for bluegills should be lively, four or five inch wigglers, impaled through the midsection on a long shank, No. 4 hook. A single worm is sufficient. Eagle Claw, TruTurn and others make these hooks with small diameters that will bend easily. That helps to retrieve the hook when it is swallowed to the stomach by a big gripper-size fish. It also assists in getting the hook back when hung on the bottom, as you will many times in cover. Few panfish are large enough to straighten the hook and come unbuttoned. A clear monofilament eight-pound test line will get more strikes than a heavier one. A single small shot six inches above the hook will get it down quicker. A tiny bobber no larger than a dime rigged to allow the bait to barely touch or float just off the bottom helps relay the bluegill attack

Mavis Coleman smiles with speck.

and seeing that cork go down is one of the great thrills of panfish angling. You can use a light or ultralight rod with this earthworm bait if you choose, but most of this panfishing is with a 10- or 12-foot cane pole or B 'n' M telescopic fiberglass poles. It's not as awkward and distance is not an advantage.

You need not set the hook. These fish hang themselves. You can play the fish or horse him in. Once he gulps down the bait, he isn't likely to get away. Even small children laugh and struggle as this gallant species ounce for ounce equals any fish in strength and determination.

While earthworms are widely accepted as the bluegills' natural bait, there are others that often are more productive during various seasons and in some areas.

Once the weather warms enough for insects to stir, crickets fished with tiny lead shot on the line, a No. 6 hook and a thimble-size bobber that allows the kicking cricket to suspend a foot or two below the surface, will attract any self-respecting bluegill in the neighborhood. It looks like the real thing. Instinct plays a part in fishing crickets or their first cousins, small grasshoppers. Bluegills do not seem inclined to bite these insects early in the season. Only when they hatch and are plentiful along the shore and tree line, are crickets attacked regularly by bluegills. They are not a bottom bait. They should be fished close to the surface regardless of the water depth. Wild black crickets are just as good for fish bait as the pen-raised gray variety but it takes a lot of effort to catch enough for a morning's adventure. They are sold throughout much of the country by bait shop operators. Cricket cages are available that make these baits easy to retrieve for hooking. They are wire-meshed and open and you must protect them from ants and other predators. If you have crickets left over from a fishing trip, they will live for weeks in a small cage if they are fed a few slices of potato, apple or other vegetable. A water-soaked sponge will provide the needed water supply. There are other naturals for bluegills popular in specific areas but not always available in every state.

Freshwater shrimp, tiny translucent crustaceans, are abundant in all the warmer states from early spring until fall. They can be caught with a fine mesh dip net dragged along the bottom where there is any kind of aquatic growth, grass, weeds, coontail, hydrilla, dollar lilies, etc. Impaled on a No. 6 hook with no shot, no bobber and allowed to trickle near the bottom, this "nothing" pole bait is great. Often bluegills will strike it when ignoring everything else. It's the natural food supply of bluegills in at least a dozen states. If you have shrimp left over at the end of the day, wrap them in newspapers and store in the refrigerator. They will often live overnight and maintain their natural color.

Other fine naturals for bluegills include catalpa worms, maggots, sapheads and fuzzy oak worms. Catalpas are available only a few weeks of the year from the leaves of a tree by the same name. Maggots or mealy worms can be hatched and grown in wet meal or animal feed when open to flies that lay eggs in the goo. The maggots are the larvae and they are not nasty as the word implies. Sapheads are the white, red-headed tree-boring creatures found under the bark of dead pines. Oak worms eat the leaves off hardwoods in the fall in many states. Gathered and fished under trees that lean over the water where they fall when early frosts hit, they are unbelievably successful. Bluegills come a-runnin'. All these baits are best fished on light lines, tiny hooks, little or no lead and a cork that offers almost no resistance when the bluegills run off with the morsels.

Black and white crappies abound in virtually all of the contiguous states and, like the bluegills, they are easy to catch and pleasant to the palate. While they can be caught with an assortment of artificial lures, the great harvest of this species by sportsmen is with natural baits.

Live minnows are the standard for crappie anglers. Millions of the small fish are commercially hatched, raised and shipped from Lonoke, Arkansas, among other places, to bait and tackle shops throughout the nation. They are sold to fishermen at prices ranging from five dozen for a dollar to 65 and 75 cents a dozen.

Minnows are best kept alive in styrofoam buckets with tight-fitting lids with a few ice cubes dropped in occasionally in hot weather. With the water temperature kept below 70 degrees, several dozen minnows will often survive in a small container for a week or more. A little Catch and Release chemical from Jungle Labs in the water will also help the minnows to remain healthy. Some fishermen use floating metal or plastic containers tied over the side of the boat to hold minnows when they are fishing. This is cumbersome and is a drag when you are on crappies and losing baits.

During spawning seasons when you locate crappies, again by using your senses of sight, smell and sound, catching limits of the species often is easy. If the fish are congregated in aquatic or brush cover, they are in such a frenzy that almost anything dead or alive in their area will be gulped down. Crappies may bed in a foot of water or in ten times that depth. They are not as selective as bass and bluegills. They do not guard the bed with the intensity of other panfish but are often found by the hundreds in a small area for several days at a time as they compete for nesting grounds.

Once they observe this bedding frenzy, crappie anglers will profit from the fish's semi-protective attitude and apparently constant hunger. Using a light monofilament line in the 10- to 12-pound test range on a cane pole, a No. 2/0 TruTurn or other gold-colored, small diameter hook, a medium size shot eight inches above, and a cork barely large enough to float the hook, lead and bait, the fisherman is in business. If you are fishing from an anchored or still boat, crappies are most likely to hit a minnow in the cover that is impaled under the dorsal fin and allowed to play. He is more active hooked there than through the lips or behind the eyes. Just drop the live morsel in the holes in the cover, let it wriggle near the bottom, and be ready to fight the fish through the obstacles when the cork pops under, as it often will when you are on the fish.

Do not set the hook on crappies. Give them a three count after the cork goes down, and then pull steadily to the boat. The tissue-like mouths of the crappies will not stand much of a jerk, but firm pressure will keep them hooked and coming toward you. Don't let the fish play under the water or on the surface. That's when he is the strongest. Out of the water you have only the weight of the fish and you'll do better by horsing the crappie to the gunnels. Most veterans use nets when the fish gets within reach. It saves some of the livelier, heavier slabs but it also takes time to un-foul the hook, lead, cork and line. Nets are for those who are chagrined over losing a fish or two that dropped off short of the gunwale.

Often crappies are scattered in cover and it is not advisable to tie up or anchor the boat. You may be able to catch more fish in this instance by using your trolling motor or a paddle and moving slowly from one hole to another in the grass, lilies, log jam or bottom structure, by hooking your minnow through the lips or eyes, attaching a little more weight, and dropping it in every tacklebox-size opening you pass. Many times your cork will go right on down almost without stopping as the stalking crappies hit the minnow as it tumbles toward the bottom.

There are periods of high temperature and cold snaps when the crappies will slip back out of cover and loll around almost dormant in deeper holes. They will still bite a live minnow. Using your depthfinder or a less sophisticated hand line or pole, locate the drop-offs and let your slightly weighted minnow flutter in the face of the fish. There is no weather too hot or too cold to stop them from feeding when a tasty morsel is so convenient. Only high wind reduces your catch.

There are some impoundments almost covered with stumps in deep water. A system of "stump jumping" is often the best way to catch crappies in these areas. Veterans with small outboards or trolling motors go from one stump to another, circling it slowly while dangling a minnow 20 feet deep or more near the base of the wood stickup. Crappies hang out around these tree trunks and you can catch them. Some veterans use rods and reels with two or more hooks on the line with a slip lead on the bottom. Minnows hooked through the back will attract attention. You may double frequently. If you are stump jumping with a cane pole and a cork, it's important to fish with intensity and alertness. If the cork moves even a smidgen, bring up the pole tip quickly. Crappies will still bite at this depth with the adroitness of a magician. Some say the fish must have hands to get the bait off so softly. Don't let the boat bump the logs. It's the crappie home and they will leave when a man-made shake is felt.

Many lakes have a lot of open water with little cover and guides and avid locals with the time and patience make their own crappie hideouts, burying trees, tires, brush and other materials. Crappies will frequent these hideouts because forage fish gather there. Pinpointed with a depthfinder or a fix on horizon structures, fishermen can drop minnows within inches of the man-made cover and bring home fish the year around, while the uninformed are often skunked.

While fishing for crappies in cover is the easy way to catch this species several months of the year, you can almost guarantee success in the open water of shallow lakes and streams by trolling every month that you can get your boat on the water. Minnows hooked through the eyes with enough shot clamped on the line every eight inches above the hook to carry the bait down eight or ten feet, will catch fish. A cork on the surface, preferably a three-inch oblong styrofoam bobber, is an advantage even though it will sink from the shot if the boat is still. If you troll or drift at the right speed, this cork will surface while the hooked

J.M. Strickland admires a nice crappie.

minnow follows near the bottom. You try to troll at a speed that will keep the line at 60 degrees to the surface and the poles in holders off the gunnels perpendicular to the boat. Hand held poles will not do as well. You need enough holders to set the legal limit of hooks off the bow and stern of your boat. Keep the wind on the stern of the boat and troll away from the wind. It's the best way of catching limits almost any season and any place. It's revolutionary summer crappie fishing in many states.

Few natural baits other than minnows are regularly successful for crappie anglers. You can catch some fish near the bottom with common grasshoppers and a little lead on a light line with a tiny cork in the cover. You can catch some crappies with live crawfish in the cover. Crickets occasionally will attract a crappie as will several freshwater shrimp threaded on a 2/0 hook in the aquatic holes. But there is no substitute for the time-honored live minnow about 2 1/2 to 3 inches long.

While bass fishing makes the headlines, it's the crappies and blue gills that make the menu of more homes than any other species. More people go fishing to put food on the table than for any other reason, according to a reliable poll. You can bring home that delicious protein in virtually every state month after month when you go for the two most prominent panfish species— crappies and bluegills. And while that gourmet meat is reason enough to fish with natural baits, there is still plenty of thrill from a plunging cork, a tug on the pole tip and the sing of a line as it splits the water with a lively flatfish surging for the other side of the lake. Few outdoorsmen can deny the excitement of natural bait fishing for panfish.

Slow Crappie and Fast Water
Often Great Fun for
Summer Anglers

White water rattled around both sides of a cypress log lodged mid-stream in the Lumber River in Southeastern North Carolina. It was late July and the thermometer hovered in the high nineties at noon. By most authorities, this was neither the time nor the place to catch crappies. But it turned out to be a panfish bonanza with both black crappies and slab-size bluegills unaware it was inappropriate to make fishermen happy here and now.

Harry Bell, a Tar Heel native and veteran river panfish angler, slipped a bell anchor to the bottom a few steps upstream from the half-submerged obstruction that was splitting the white water of the desolate and scenic Lumber. His 12-foot plywood boat quickly headed into the current as the anchor held. He picked up his spinning tackle and began talking. "You see that slow swirling eddy behind that log? And then that other one to the right between the rapids and the bank? I'll bet you money that we can catch some nice fish in both those places. This time of the day, they like to hang around close to the fast-running water because it is much cooler than the pond water around here.

"Crappie are lazy. They like to make a living using up just as little energy as possible. They won't get out in the current because it works them to death just to keep from being swept downstream. That's why most fishermen seldom go after these panfish in the fast water of the rivers. Like it or not, these fish have to survive in the river, and they can only do that by eating. They have learned that they can huddle up on the upstream edge of these eddies, and stalk a belly full of food, even in the hot weather.

"The current picks up insects, worms, minnows and other flotsam and carries it past the obstructions. Crappies, and bream too, pounce on this forage when it circles in the eddies. You can toss a few chips or blades of grass in the water and you'll see it rush past the log, then circle for a minute or more before dashing on downstream. It's that action in the water that has helped me catch summertime crappies in all the rivers around here for a lifetime. They like to stalk easy-to-catch food without doing much work," Bell shared some of his river-fishing expertise.

A moment later, the old sportsman flipped a hook with a tiny minnow impaled under the dorsal fin, a single lead shot eight inches up the line and an oblong yellow cork a foot above that, into the fast-running water. It scampered toward the log as he played out line, tightened it ever so slightly, and watched it ease into the calm retreat near the obstruction. Bingo! The cork went down and Bell reeled in a flouncing, 14-ounce crappie that parted the current on the way to the stern of the boat. He lifted it over the side and grinned. He seemed to be saying, I told you so.

"I fish like this all up and down the river. There are dozens of places like this where there is calm water just a few feet from the rushing rapids. Almost always, there are three or four panfish holding in these eddies. I fish the Waccamaw, Pee Dee and Black rivers here in the Carolinas this same way, and when I get to Florida in the fall, I catch a lot of fine speckled perch in the eddies behind logs, grass and rocks in the St. Johns and Oklawaha rivers.

"I call this kind of fishing letting the bait find the fish instead of hunting for the fish. You can use a strong trolling motor and fish some of these honey holes along the shoreline and behind obstructions, but in most places the water is too shallow and too fast to hold the boat. Then if you try to drift with the current, you pass most of the good spots because you move far too fast to hit all the likely-looking eddies. By anchoring upstream from the obstructions and letting your bait float around the logs, it moves like the trash and topwater stuff, eventually easing right to the spots where the fish hold up," Bell explained his system. "The bait hunts the fish for you." Bell then tossed his re-baited hook a few feet nearer the shoreline, and the current grabbed it. It dashed downstream. The cagey old veteran tightened the line and pointed his rod tip toward the bank. Almost as if it had eyes, the cork danced toward the bank, and calmly circled in another eddy. The cork disappeared. It was instant replay. Bell came in with another summertime crappie that was after an easy meal.

"You can catch them with Betts and Super Jigs, Beetle Spins, Hal-Flies, among other artificials in these same eddies. But when I use those lures instead of minnows, I like to fish with a 14-foot B 'n' M fiberglass pole. I anchor close to the honey holes, and then jig the bait slowly up and down near the obstructions. It's a productive way to catch crappies in these river havens," Bell revealed additional secrets.

"You need to be aware of a few other things if you go after these panfish in fast water. Sometimes one or two big crappies will come around the obstruction, and then lie flat against the log or rock on the upstream side. The current flattens the fish against the log, and he needs to use little energy to stay there. He waits until food dashes by and then pounces on it. I believe these upstream fish hunt out that position when they feel that there are too many others behind the obstruction. There is too much competition for the floating food in the eddy. So a fish or two will get the jump by holding in the fast water. That may be giving the fish credit for too much intelligence, but that seems to be what I have observed," Bell again shared his expertise.

He had one other bit of advice. "Sometimes there will be a tussock of grass or weeds out in the stream. You may see only a few stalks, but there may be a sizeable obstruction of roots submerged. I always fish these grass obstructions. They seem to attract crappie even more than logs and rocks in some rivers," Bell said.

On that middle-of-the-day adventure in the hot weather, Bell put a dozen nice crappies in the boat. He caught a fish or two at every obstruction he fished, and even managed to pull in three nice copperhead bream that were stalking food behind the logs and grass the same way the crappies were.

There are other situations where crappies can be caught in fast water. Many tailraces behind hydroelectric dams in the Carolinas are great for panfish. On the Great Pee Dee River that flows through the Piedmont section of North Carolina into South Carolina, there are half a dozen dams where crappies feed around obstructions near the fast current.

One of the best of these is Falls Dam, near Badin, North Carolina, where stringers of fine white and black crappies have been caught for a generation. They loll behind the huge boulders here where eddies may be as large as your living room. Minnows floated near the bottom in these choice rest havens bring crappies a runnin'. Unfortunately, in this particular area the crappies are not as large as they once were. They are plentiful, but few reach 1-pound size today. Other tailraces still have slab-size crappies. Most such spots are unsafe for boating. You either wade or bank fish from some of the boulders that jut out into the rapids.

While crappie fishing is generally considered a lake adventure, you can carry home plenty of tasty panfish for the dinner table, and have a lot fun doing so in the rivers and streams. You just have to outfox the species and "let the bait find the fish." Harry Bell knows how to catch slow crappies in fast water in the summertime.

Trolling along the woodline in rivers
is a good way to catch crappie.

Real Crappie Roundup on S.C.-GA. Border

It was summer and sportsmen fishing the rivers and tributaries of Lake Hartwell on the Georgia-South Carolina border properly surmised that the plentiful crappies in this giant impoundment would likely be found in deep holes. They were right. A nocturnal experience when an armada of boats rounded up the schools in covered-wagon fashion proved the point. Haskell Curran and Joe Snyder, Greenville, South Carolina, fishermen, had scouted the narrow waters of Coneross Creek in its upper reaches on a Tuesday night a few days before the full moon during the Dog Days of August.

They were pleasantly rewarded when they anchored about 30 feet off a high, rocky cliff shoreline and dropped their minnows, impaled on 2/0 hooks, near the bottom in 22 feet of cider-colored water. While there was no visible bottom cover, the depthfinder showed a jagged, rocky complex where fish could hide and escape the hot weather.

Snyder almost had his open-face reel jerked from his hand as soon as his bait touched bottom. He reeled in a fine black crappie that put a good bend in his 5 1/2 foot limber graphite rod. "If I had been fishing tandem hooks, and if I had hooked two this size I would have had a real struggle getting both of them to the surface in this deep water on my ultralight tackle and six-pound test line," Snyder observed.

Before he got the words out, Curran pulled in a hand-size crappie from the same side of the boat. "I believe we have found the mother lode, and we might as well rig up our Coleman lanterns and plan to stay right here awhile. If we can get these fish to bite that quickly, there must be a bunch of them down there, and we won't have to scout any more trying to locate them," Curran said.

They hung bright gasoline lanterns with reflectors that focused the beams on the surface over the side. The light attracted insects, then minnows and served to concentrate crappies near the boat.

Curran prepares a fish for the skillet.

Carolina outdoorsmen had used lanterns for years. This portion of Coneross Creek was no more than 200 yards wide as it narrowed sharply from many times that width when it left the Tugaloo River. The Tugaloo and the Seneca rivers merge to form the Lake Hartwell impoundment, and it is the border between Georgia and South Carolina. It has long been a popular fishing lake for hybrid stripers, largemouth bass and crappies.

Curran and Snyder had volunteered to look for a hot spot on the lake so that a group of fellow churchmen could join them on Friday night and hopefully pull in enough crappies for a community fish fry on the weekend. All during the night Curran and Snyder fished the same deep hole, pulling anchor at daybreak with a fine stringer of crappies, mostly small to medium size, but with an occasional lunker like the first one that Joe pulled in.

"I don't have any skepticism about bringing our fishing buddies here Friday night. With the full moon and the hot days, these fish ought to be right here all week and maybe longer," Curran said. "Night fishing will be fine here for quite a spell." The fishing partners spread the word about the deep hole in the rocks off the 40-foot cliff at Coneross Creek, and late Friday afternoon a convoy of vehicles pulling boats headed down Highway 184 near Clemson University and on to SR 24 that went to Friendship Shore and the U.S. Corps of Engineers' public launching ramp. Haskell had stopped off at a bait shop on the way to buy minnows. He didn't get them by the dozen as they are generally sold. He bought three pounds of minnows that flipped and flitted in pure oxygen that filled plastic bags above the water. They would stay alive for hours even in the torrid Dog-Day weather. At the ramp, Curran divided the minnows, and the fleet roared off toward the honey hole in Coneross Creek, about three miles northwest of the landing.

They reached the rocky cliff area about 9:00 P.M. And the story unfolds. The boats formed a complete circle around the area where Curran and Snyder had caught fish on Tuesday night. There were ten bass boats of assorted sizes plus one big pontoon that had half a dozen fishermen aboard. They encircled the area like covered wagons on the journey West in pioneer days. They tied up to each other. It truly was a crappie fishing roundup.

Immediately the anglers started reeling in nice crappies. There were thrills enough for everyone as the night wore on and a steady splashing of fish on the surface broke the silence of an otherwise peaceful night. At dawn they counted. The group had put more than 300 crappies in the coolers, a noteworthy night of fishing anywhere.

A few evenings later the church membership enjoyed a freshwater fish gourmet supper. Coneross Creek had provided the food, rounded up by outdoor enthusiasts who love nocturnal fishing during Dog Days, and any other time.

Mitchell Carter gets an open-water crappie in Badin Lake.

Crappie Capitals of the South

Although crappie are found in almost every state in America, Southern panfish anglers are blessed with a wealth of excellent crappie-producing lakes, both in terms of size and numbers of fish.

We are about to share the wealth.

To list the number of good Southern crappie lakes would take several pages and include a multitude of lakes, man-made reservoirs, rivers and streams. In the South there is plenty of water that provides the prime habitat necessary for these prolific creatures and the result is an excellent crappie spawn year after year in every Southern state.

While there are many fine crappie lakes in both the North and South, four bodies of water stand out above the crowd. These are lakes that produce such phenomenal numbers or impressive trophy fish (sometimes both) that they have become renowned as some of America's best crappie factories. Call them the Crappie Capitals of the South.

Although each has differing physical characteristics and other dissimilarities, all share the common denominator of offering the kind of fishing that a true crappie enthusiast craves. Whether it be catching a crappie worth mounting or limiting out day after day, these four hot-spots are the perfect destinations for a fishing vacation.

And we'll provide you with information for planning what could be the crappie vacation of a lifetime. Enjoy this sampling of the best.

Kentucky Lake

The most renowned crappie waters in America has to be Kentucky Lake, a 40-year-old, 160,000-acre impoundment that runs 185 miles through Kentucky and Tennessee. While this reservoir produces outstanding numbers of papermouths, it is most famous for the sheer size of its aquatic inhabitants.

"Although I think people enjoy filling up their freezers with fillets, most people come to Kentucky Lake because of the size of our crappie," says ten-year Kentucky Lake crappie guide Steve McCadams, perhaps America's best-known panfish guide and author of two books on crappie fishing. "Our crappie probably average 3/4-pound, which is an excellent average. Two-pound crappie are not unusual and we have three-pound-plus crappie caught each spring."

As with most crappie waters, spring is prime time on Kentucky Lake. Crappie are easiest to locate and most cooperative from February to June when they move up shallow. When spawning, crappie can be found along shoreline cover like stumps, bushes and willow trees in less than eight feet of water and catching a quick limit is often easy.

A standard Kentucky Lake rig is an eight- to ten-foot fly rod or telescoping pole with a 1/16 or 1/32-ounce plastic jig that is usually teamed with a live minnow.

A resourceful guide, McCadams is just one of many Kentucky Lake crappie specialists who have learned to follow crappie and catch them during other times of the year when the fish are deeper and more difficult to locate.

For fishing stump rows and other deep bottom structure, McCadams uses a special rig that utilizes two hooks set at different depths. Crappie are notoriously depth conscious (and reluctant to move very far vertically to take a bait), so this rig allows him to cover two different depth ranges in search of his prey. The rig consists of 40-pound-test line from the reel to a barrel swivel. On the other side of the swivel is a four-foot leader of 30-pound line with a one-ounce bell-shaped sinker on the end of it. About 18 inches up from the sinker is a 2/0 hook on a six-inch drop loop. Eighteen inches above the bottom hook is a second hook. In addition to providing a minnow or jig (sometimes both) at two different depths, the heavy bell-shaped sinker allows you to feel the deep water structure, so you are able to consistently keep the rig in contact with the fish-holding cover.

McCadams' favorite part of the big reservoir is near Paris, Tennessee, where the Big Sandy River meets the Tennessee River. This is the widest part of the impoundment with an average depth of 12 feet. It has an abundance of cover, as well as several tributaries that are excellent creeks to fish, harboring crappie that are easy to locate.

Kentucky Lake is a trophy-hunter's dream.

TRAVEL INFORMATION: Recommended lodging: Paris Landing State Inn, Rt. 1, Buchanan, TN 38222 (901) 642-4140.

The lady shows off a fine fish.

Recommended guide: Steve McCadams, 41 Anderson Drive, Paris, TN 38242 (901) 642-0360. An autographed copy of his excellent book *Crappie Wisdom* is available at that address for $11.95.

Tourism information: Greater Paris and Henry County Chamber of Commerce, P.O. Box 82, Paris, TN 38242, (901) 642-3431; Northwest Tennessee Tourist Council, Box 63, Martin, TN 38237, (901) 857-4213.

Fishing information: Tennessee Wildlife Resource Agency, Fishing Education and Information, P.O. Box 40747, Nashville, TN 37204, (615) 360-0500.

WEISS LAKE

Another prime crappie lake is the 30,000-acre Weiss Lake, an impoundment of the Coosa and Chattooga Rivers on the Alabama-Georgia border (about 75 miles northeast of Birmingham). Although its most recent crappie spawns have been below normal due to drought conditions, Weiss is a storied body of water with a reputation for providing both good quality and quantities of crappie.

"Weiss is a real shallow lake that has a bunch of feeder creeks coming into it," explains guide Andre Reynolds of Centre, Alabama, who was born and raised on Weiss Lake, where he has a 4-pound crappie to his credit. "I think those two factors are why crappie fishing is so good on this lake."

Indeed. Weiss Lake is a crappie's fantasy with an abundance of relatively shallow water and bottom structure, including old creek channels, river channels, ledges and drop-offs. Most of these areas are decorated with stumps or brush, which makes them even more attractive to the fish. And knowledgeable Weiss anglers add to that natural structure with well-placed brushpiles that become their own private fishing holes—at least for awhile.

"I do a lot of planting—putting cedar trees out on creek channel edges, off points near creek channels, or right in among stump beds adjacent to a creek channel," Reynolds says. "Planting these trees is a lot of work, but it really pays off beginning with the first full moon in April when the big fish start moving in from the deeper water. You start catching the big females off these trees in 10 to 20 feet of water."

The premier crappie months are March and April, when spawning season provides an AVERAGE of 100-plus fish a day, according to Reynolds. The average size is about a half-pound, and 2-pounders are almost commonplace. Weiss is also an outstanding winter crappie-producer as well.

The weapon of choice among Reynolds and other Weiss regulars is the standard mini-jig, which is often coupled with a live minnow. Reynolds uses a colorful jig without any live enticement, fishing it on a bobber when in water less than 15 feet deep. For fishing deeper, he does not use a cork, preferring to bounce the jig off bottom structure.

Weiss Lake can be productive regardless of the season. It is a remarkable crappie lake.

TRAVEL INFORMATION: Recommended lodging: Bay Springs Motel, Rt. 3, Centre, AL 35960, (205) 927-3618.

Recommended guide: Andre Reynolds, Rt. 1, 333 Sherry Drive, Centre, AL 35960, (205) 927-8522.

Tourism information: Alabama Mountain Lakes Association, 400 Wells Street, Decatur, AL 35601, (205) 350-3500; Cherokee County Tourist Association, P.O. Box 193, Cedar Bluff, AL 36959, (205) 779-6533.

Fishing information: Alabama Game and Fish Division, 64 N. Union St., Montgomery, AL 36130, (205) 261-3471.

LAKE OKEECHOBEE

Although it can't compete with Kentucky, Weiss and other lakes in terms of growing trophy crappie, no lake in the country can compare to Florida's Lake Okeechobee when it comes to producing sheer numbers, according to recently released catch statistics.

Lake Okeechobee's extensive fishing industry bills the 763-square-mile natural lake as the "Speck Capital of the World" (Floridians refer to crappie as speckled perch) and it has good reason to stake that claim.

In the winter of 1987, Florida Game and Fresh Water Fish Commission biologists were able to document the catch of ONE MILLION crappie in the Big O. Based on that evidence, the estimate that the catch documented in the creel survey accounts for just ten percent of the enormous lake's total crappie population.

That means Lake Okeechobee is home to about TEN MILLION crappie.

"Actually, we've got so many crappie in the lake that we

may have a stunting problem," claims biologist Steve Miller, who points out the average crappie in the creel survey weighed a half-pound.

A pound crappie is a big Okeechobee speck. A 2-pound is a monster. But obviously, the massive lake makes up for that lack of individual size with outstanding quantities of specks easily available to panfish anglers.

Although Lake Okeechobee is a nationally renowned bass factory, speck fishing steals the spotlight in the winter months (late November through March) when the seasonal influx of crappie fishermen infiltrates the region. Crappie fishing is big business in the winter and early spring when Big O specks are spawning and simple to catch. "The speck fishing is good year-round," Miller emphasizes. "But most people don't fish for them during the hot months."

Although speck fishing is productive throughout the lake, the northern end of Okeechobee is especially good, so it is heavily fished. That doesn't matter much, though. It is common to see 50 to 100 boats anchored in the mouths of tributaries that enter the lake and every one is usually catching fish. One of the prime areas is the Taylor Creek-Kissimmee area of the north end.

The majority of the speck fishermen in this part of the lake drift and troll several lines at the same time in search of specks, particularly bedding crappie. This method is called a "spider rig" because the multiple poles used make the boats resemble legs of the real thing. Plastic jigs and/or minnows are the common bait.

During the winter spawn, some Lake Okeechobee crappie anglers take their sport especially serious, chartering an airplane to fly over the lake for an hour or so scouting for beds. "The beds are easy to see from the air," Miller says, "and it's not that expensive in relative terms when you consider a guide will charge you $150 a day."

Still, considering the size of the Big O, hiring a guide for a day or two is a good idea.

Lake Okeechobee is the perfect winter vacation fishing spot. The weather is usually cooperative and with ten million crappie, the fish are certainly plentiful.

TRAVEL INFORMATION: Recommended lodging: Lakeport Lodge, Rt. 6, Box 801, Okeechobee, FL 34974, (813) 946-2020; Calusa Lodge, Rt. 2 Highway 78, Lakeport, FL 33471, (813) 946-0544.

Recommended guides: Glen Hunter, Rt. 6, Box 862, Okeechobee, FL 33474, (813) 946-1569; Jim Fowler, P.O. Box 1254, Okeechobee, FL 34973, (813) 467-2052.
Tourism information: Florida Division of Tourism, 107 West Gaines St., Sollins Building, Room 505, Tallahassee, FL 32301, (904) 488-5606.
Fishing information: Florida Game and Fresh Water Fish Commission, 620 S. Meridian St., Tallahassee, FL 32399 (904) 488-7326.

Lake Arkabutla

It doesn't have the reputation of Kentucky or Weiss or the name of Okeechobee, but Mississippi's Lake Arkabutla certainly has the trophy-size crappie.

Located on the border of DeSoto and Tate counties (about 45 miles south of Memphis, Tennessee), Arkabutla is a 30,000-acre impoundment at full pool that provides excellent habitat for crappie with countless acres of old farm fields, flooded timber and brush. Although it is subject to fluctuation and heavy run-off, which reduces the size of its annual crappie spawn, Arkabutla consistently produces big crappie—some of the largest in the country.

"One of the very best crappie lakes I've ever fished is Arkabutla," claims Bill Dance, television show host, who lives in Memphis. "It doesn't have much quantity, but it produces a surprising number of 3- and 4-pound crappie.

"It is a wide flood plain reservoir that was built, primarily, for flood control. It's a muddy reservoir that produces big crappie—despite the fact that it never really clears up. My most productive technique is a shallow pattern and spring is the best time. I fish objects and fish vertically as much as possible with a tight line and a cork around visible cover. A jig or minnow works well.

"In the spring the crappie spawn last in Arkabutla because of the muddy conditions, so April and May are the prime spawning times. The fish are easy to locate. There is a lot of dead water from week to week because of the fluctuation of the water. Crappie born in Arkabutla soon learn that they have no residence. They're constantly on the move as a result of water fluctuation. Crappie found today are gone tomorrow, but you can follow them by moving with the falling water, which is what they do. They are structure-oriented. As the water level falls, they follow the ditches and the channels. So that's what the better crappie anglers do."

There is easy access to Arkabutla. The Army Corps of Engineers has built 10 public launch ramps.

There are no crappie guides on Arkabutla. And very few bait shops. but that is almost a blessing. It means the big crappie on this 20,000-acre impoundment haven't been discovered. Discover it for yourself.

TRAVEL INFORMATION: Recommended lodging: Howard Johnson's, 501 E. Main St., Senatobia, Mississippi 38668, (601) 562-5241.

Recommended guides: There are no guides on this reservoir. The best source for current information on the lake is the Resource Manager, Rt. 1, Box 572, Coldwater, MS 38618, (601) 562-6261.

Tourism information: Mississippi Department of Economic Development, Division of Tourism, P.O. Box 849, Jackson, MS 39205 (800) 647-2290.

Fishing information: Mississippi Dept. of Wildlife Cons., P.O. Box 451, Jackson, MS 39205, (601) 961-5432.

A lonesome tree or brushpile in a lake will often hold feeding crappies.

My Most Unforgettable Crappie Fishing Experiences

Two crappie fishing experiences stand out above all the hundreds I have lived while fishing in many states for half a century and catching at least 250,000 of these wonderful panfish that thrill old and young on a line and delight the palate on the dinner table. While they do not dance on their tails, make the line whine like the devil has been hooked, or challenge the endurance of plastic gears on modern reels, the crappie species continues to have a society of followers everywhere who thrill when the cork goes down, smile when the big slabs flounce on the deck, and talk about the day's catch for hours at sunset at the 19th hole.

I began fishing for crappies that we called "white perch" for lack of better biological information, on The Great Pee Dee River where the muddy waters flow past the Uwharrie Mountain range between Stanly and Montgomery counties in the Piedmont hills of North Carolina in the late 1920's. In that era when hydroelectric dams had just impounded four or five deep stretches of this big river within a few miles of each other, there were almost no sport-fishing boats. There were a few old homemade bateaux used by catfish and carp trappers, and a lawyer or doctor or two had enough money to own a crude fishing boat. But generally the crappie and even the bass fishing was done from the hill. I never saw a rod and reel until early in the 1930's. I fished with 14-foot cane poles cut from the river thicket, a cotton line, big cork, wrap-around lead, 3/0 steel hook, and I always used creek-caught native minnows impaled under the dorsal fin. I never had the money to buy minnows, and they were for sale at very few places then. I would find a cove along the shoreline where there were willows draping over the water, a grass bed, brush pile, log or some other cover close enough to fish around from the bank. I would bait the hook and set two or three poles in the area, lean back against a tree trunk, and wait for a crappie to come along and find my baited hook in the cider-colored river. Oddly enough, the fishing was good even with that humble style. Often we caught a stringer full of big fish without moving two yards from

Mitchell Carter gets a big crappie from Lake Tillery

where we started. The fish came to us. We didn't go hunt the fish. They were plentiful.

The tall Falls Dam had been constructed across the Pee Dee near Badin, North Carolina, a few years before I started fishing. At that time, it was illegal to fish for crappie or bass before May 10. The state protected the fish during the early spring spawning season. When May 10 rolled around, just about every family headed for the river "before the fish all get caught out." To get to the base of the dam you had to crawl down a steep, rocky cliff at least 70 feet high. It was treacherous, dangerous, and only a few fishermen would challenge this precipice. But we knew that when the water was turned off the electricity-making dynamos at night the crappies gathered in the small pockets at the tailrace of the dam and you could catch them like mad until about 8:00 in the morning when the water rushed out and rose rapidly around the huge boulders below the falls. That stopped the fish from biting.

We always reached the dam about 4:00 A.M. and made the precarious crawl down the cliff before daylight. There was a path of sorts, but the rocks were slick and the hand-holds inadequate. With both hands free it would have been difficult. But when you had to carry a water-filled minnow bucket, a shoulder full of long poles, a little tackle in a box, plus a dim lantern and a few sandwiches, you almost had to be a trapeze performer to safely make the descent to the few flat rocks at the water level where you could stand without holding onto something.

I started this crawl one May 10th with the minnows and had gone only halfway when I lost my grip, dropped the bucket and spilled the dozens of minnows in the rocks. I had caught the bait in a tow sack, homemade seine pulled through Little Bear Creek the previous afternoon. All the minnows were scattered and flouncing on the rocky cliff ledge. I scrambled in the dark, picking up the bait, finally found a couple of dozen, rushed on down the rocks, scooped up some water, and managed to save a few of the scarce and precious live baits. We had no jigs or lures of any kind. We had driven 15 miles to get to the dam, and to lose the minnows was a disaster. Embarrassed over having been so clumsy, I apologized to my companions, and we decided to make the most of what we had as dawn began to peek through the trees on the horizon. We would use what we had.

It was a bonanza morning. The fish had come up the river

to the dam as if they were attending a national crappie reunion. You could see them breaking in every pool, and even when the water rose, they were still plentiful. It made no difference whether we had dead minnows or lively ones, pieces of bait or whole fish. The crappie were striking everything. By mid-morning we had strung 42 crappie on a heavy masonry cord, and all the rescued minnows had served their purpose. We headed for home in the old A-Model Ford, hanging our fish out the back windows so they almost dragged the ground. We were really showing off. That was one of those days fraught with disaster that was unusually successful. All's well that ends well.

My other most unique experience fishing for crappies happened 30 years later when I was fishing with my brother in Lake Okeechobee in Florida one February morning. We were still using cane poles and minnows, but we did have an outboard motor by then and had rented a boat at Joe and Wanda's Fish Camp at the mouth of the Kissimmee River. We chugged out the river to Kings Bar where a lot of aquatic growth flourished in the shallow water where we had caught speckled perch (crappies) for several years when they spawned in Florida. This was during an era when it was illegal to trap crappie and bluegills in the Big O. Traps were marked everywhere in the shallows with floating corks, bottles, jugs and the like. But the traps presumably were for catfish, a species that has always been legal to catch and to sell. You could not legally net or trap game fish then as you can at Okeechobee now with proper permits.

We often watched the commercial trappers pull their chicken-wire traps and take out the catfish. They normally had dozens in the same big trap, and as far as I know they were releasing any gamefish that accidentally entered the cone-shaped snares about the size of bean hampers.

We fished for crappies with a cork, a little lead, a Missouri minnow hooked through the lips and allowed the bait to wriggle around near the bottom. No real self-respecting speckled perch can refuse to strike such a live morsel in his face, and we regularly caught our 50-fish limits per person within a few hours. The river was wild then. Redwing blackbirds always cleaned the crumbs from the picnic tables. Grass beds obscured the river banks. Mosquitoes swarmed in droves. Encampments along the river banks were like wilderness areas, desolate and intriguing. Speckled perch were caught by every novice with little or no experience or patience. But catching crappies at Okeechobee that February in great quantities is not what made the trip memorable. It was the unbelievable coincidence I witnessed that happened to my brother Mitchell, a snowbird from North Carolina, who was enjoying a winter vacation week in the tropical Florida paradise.

Mitchell had put several fish in the boat shortly after sunup, and we were marveling at the bluebird weather. It was warm, fair and calm. He dropped his hook and bait through a hole in the lily pads in about six feet of water and watched the cork slowly bounce and submerge. He knew it was a strange strike. He set the hook gently and thought he was hung. But he could still feel the quiver of a live critter struggling on the bottom. Slowly he put more and more strain on the line, and he could feel the hang-up giving, coming slowly toward the surface. Minutes later the rusty end of a chicken wire fish trap with two-inch mesh came into view. He took hold of the wire and lifted it to the gunnels. It was amazing! Crappie were thrashing around like chickens with their heads cut off. The two-inch mesh wire was large enough that his hook and minnow had gone through it and into the trap. Obviously the trap had lost its marker weeks before, and even its owner didn't know where it was. But a crappie inside the cage gulped down the minnow. That was Mitchell's strange bite. When he felt the strike and tried to pull the fish up, it would not pass through the wire. But the gentle firm pull raised the whole trap from the sandy bottom to the surface. It was half filled with muck. He quickly counted seven nice speckled perch in the abandoned trap, one of which had swallowed the bait and hook. He opened the trap door and put his imprisoned fish in the livewell—seven nice specks with a single bite.

That was almost unbelievable. Decades of crappie fishing and nothing like that had ever happened to either one of us before. But the tale didn't end with that one-chance-in-a-million miracle. An hour later and a mile from where that incident happened, he dropped another minnow in a hole in the aquatic grass. Again the cork eased under He pulled and was hung on something again. Firmly he grasped the line and pulled it hand over hand to the top. Another rusty fish trap broke the surface. Flouncing fish shattered the stillness again. They were wild with fright. He opened the trap lid. Five nice specks were inside this time, one with his hook in its mouth. Like the first strike, the hung fish was too big to pass through the hole in the chicken wire. He had caught a cool dozen nice fish with just two strikes, hanging two lost fish traps and their prey in the same morning. It was a coincidence almost too much for Robert Ripley's Believe-It-Or-Not. But it happened exactly that way.

Was it illegal for us to keep those speckled perch in the traps? Should we have just kept the two that took the bait and released the other ten? The verdict was not available then and the jury is still out now. But we sure enjoyed telling about the excitement when we fried them on the bank for lunch that morning.

Another 2-pounder gets caught.

Crappie Things I Remember

While some people say you can't catch speckled perch in Florida except during early spring and late winter months when they are spawning, the biggest stringer I ever landed was in June when a German tourist, who couldn't speak English, and his wife fished with me in Lake Lochloosa. We trolled the open water with jig and minnow combinations and had 142 fish in about four hours, running out of minnows three times and leaving the fish biting just as well when we left as when we started. Insects were all over the surface that morning and the fish were filling their bellies.

In 1984, again fishing in the open with a trolling motor and the same system, J.M. Strickland of North Carolina, and I pulled in 56 specks and quit at 10:30. After **dressing** these fish, scaling, gutting and de-heading, the stringer weighed 40 pounds, including four pounds of roe. That's a lot of fine meals for one morning.

In October of 1984, a companion and I trolling a Southern Lit'l Hustler and minnow combination in Orange Lake, landed 18 crappie that weighed 32 pounds.

Then there was the Sunday morning when I found the specks in the lilies. My wife and I dropped minnows in the bed and wrestled 91 fish over the side, carried them to camp, dressed them and cleaned ourselves up enough to be in Sunday School at the Baptist Church at 9:45. We caught the whole stringer without moving the boat.

Outdoor painter Charles Frace,
of Brentwood, Tennessee, and his family are ready for
Cross Creek fishing adventure.

126

Florida's Wintertime Crappie

It is times like these that Bill Johnson thinks of his relatives in Indiana. Or his best friend in northern Alabama. Not to mention his former fishing buddy in Tennessee.

Sitting in short sleeves, having long since discarded a light jacket worn to cut the early-morning chill, Johnson opens the homemade livewell on his johnboat and tosses in another fat and feisty black crappie—or speckled perch as Floridians call America's favorite panfish. It is still early, but Lake Okeechobee has already yielded his limit and we're working on mine.

It is late December and that is the 60th speck

Small bass lures will catch crappies too.

of the morning. It is such a beautiful morning and the bedding specks are so cooperative that Johnson's thoughts are with other crappie enthusiasts he has known. "They are probably cutting a hole in the ice to reach the fish about now and freezing to death," Johnson says of his Indiana relatives. He has been told of snow and freezing weather that have made some crappie outings tests of endurance for friends in Alabama and Tennessee, as well.

In the colder regions of the country, crappie fishing might test your stamina. But in Florida, the winter is fine and serves as a prime time for crappie fishermen. Florida is definitely the place to be for wintertime crappie.

December marks the beginning of the spawning season

for the native specks in Florida, which will bed through March in many cases. When the water temperature reaches that magical 65- to 68-degree range, the specks go on the beds, leaving the deeper, more open water for shallow-water vegetation and shoreline cover.

As a result, reaching the state's 50-fish limit can be ridiculously easy during the coldest times of the year when Northerners are braving the winter in search of a few willing crappie.

And Florida has an abundance of crappie that become easy to locate and very accessible when the cool winter temperatures begin to intermingle with periodic warming trends that keep the specks in a spawning mode. Although no statistics are kept on such things, Florida has to rank near the top for its sheer numbers of black crappie.

Massive shallow lakes like Okeechobee, Kissimmee, Tohopekliga, Lochloosa, Orange, Crescent and George produce impressive numbers of specks each year. They may not grow to the size of a Kentucky Lake or Weiss Lake monster, but the Sunshine State can certainly hold its own in the number of crappie it produces annually.

Consider Lake Okeechobee, that 763-square-mile dishpan-shaped lake that serves as the liquid heart of South Florida. Tourism officials have long called the Big O the "speck (crappie) capital of the world"—with good reason.

In the winter of 1988, Florida Game and Fresh Water Fish Commission officials tabulated the results of an extensive creel study and estimated that Lake Okeechobee is home to more than 10 million specks. That's 10,000,000 crappie—in one body of water. The creel study actually documented more than one million crappie that were caught in the winter of 1987 alone.

The Big O has long been known as a major-league crappie factory, but commission biologists have been documenting a phenomenal growth increase since 1984 and expect that the numbers will continue to climb. The biggest problem facing the Big O's speck fishery is an overabundance that could begin stunting the population.

"The best fishing for specks usually starts in December with the spawn and continues through March and April on Okeechobee," says Steve Miller, a commission biologist who concentrates his efforts on the big lake. "The biggest problem when the fish are bedding is keeping two poles in the water at the same time."

Lake Okeechobee crappie are not large; a 2-pound speck is a rare wall-mount in this part of the country. During the commission creel survey, the fish averaged a half-pound each.

The extensive fishing industry along Lake Okeechobee's shores has long taken advantage of the winter speck season, which surpasses the lake's famed bass fishing in terms of participation. It is common to see 100 to 200 boats anchored in the mouth of any of the tributaries that feed Lake Okeechobee when the specks are bedding heavily. And Big O crappie fishermen are serious about their sport. "They sometimes charter an airplane to fly the lake for an hour or two looking for beds," Miller adds. "They're easy to see from the air and it's not that expensive when you consider a guide will charge you $150 a day."

Many of the hundreds of Lake Okeechobee bass guides double as speck scouts in the winter when the demand greatly increases. One of the best is Jim Fowler of Okeechobee, who knows the big lake and its canals as well as most people know their backyards.

Last winter, Fowler defied logic with one school of spawning specks he located on the northern end of the lake. He and his son caught 15 specks that weighed about 2 pounds each, fishing mixing vegetation in shallow water. As usual, Fowler caught the Big O trophies on a tiny pink grub, using a fiberglass telescoping pole.

When he isn't working as postmaster for the city of South Bay, Thomas Williams can be found fishing Lake Okeechobee's canal system throughout the winter. He has consistently outstanding success fishing vertically, dabbling jigs of his own making along the grass-lined drop-offs and holes in the canals.

Few fishermen have been as successful as Belle Glade's Thomas Wilson in terms of catching plenty of crappie when it counted.

Wilson has won two Speckathon events held on Lake Okeechobee (with two different partners) and qualified for two Crappiethon USA events. Using an 11-foot fiberglass Crappie Stick, Wilson uses the small, skirted tube jig made by Mid-South Tackle of Jonesboro, Arkansas.

The Mini-Jig, which comes in every color imaginable, ranks with the live minnow as the number one crappie bait throughout Florida. Wilson prefers the chartreuse Mini-Jig, which he fishes on 8-pound test line in the various types of vegetation that thrive in Lake Okeechobee.

129

The key to catching wintertime crappie on the big lake is quietly approaching the shallow spawning specks. "You have to approach quietly and carefully fish the small openings and potholes (in the vegetation)," Wilson explains. "You want to ease the lure into the water and lower it two or three feet and then jig it up and down with a smooth motion."

With its overabundance of crappie, Lake Okeechobee provides Wilson with plenty of opportunity to sharpen his fish-catching skills.

In terms of size, the Big O must yield to some north Florida lakes, which produce Florida-type trophies on a consistent basis. Three superb crappie lakes are located near the city of Gainesville and each produces an impressive number of 1 1/2- to 2-pound specks each winter.

Orange and Lochloosa lakes are connected by famed Cross Creek, where Marjorie Kinnan Rawlings penned her Pulitzer Prize-winning novel, *The Yearling*. Orange (12,000 acres) and Lochloosa (8,000 acres) are large, shallow bodies of water with an abundance of aquatic vegetation, particularly lily pads and hydrilla. A few miles north sits Newnans Lake, a shallow, open 5,800-acre lake where John McGilvray caught the state record speck back in 1964—3-pounds, 12-ounces. He caught it on December 29 of that year.

The most common method of fishing those three north Florida lakes involves slow trolling mini-jigs and/or live minnows. The most advanced crappie fishermen in this region mount several strategically-placed pole holders on their boat, giving the craft a spider-like appearance as they troll the open water looking for specks. Once they locate the fish, most anglers will toss out a marker buoy and concentrate on the school of fish, which are likely spawners during this time of the year. Bedding specks will school up so closely that you can quickly be well into your limit using tiny jigs, in-line spinners and spinnerbaits like the Beetle Spin—without ever moving the boat.

One of the most productive lures in these waters is the 1/16-ounce Beetle Spin that will run about 2 feet deep on a moderate retrieve. Some local panfish anglers place a 1/4- or 1/2-ounce bullet weight above the small spinnerbait to make it run deeper. The combination of a tiny, vibrating spinnerbait running deep enough to reach the fish pays off with remarkable consistency.

Florida speck fishermen utilize live bait, probably more

than artificial lures, although the aggressive nature of the spawning specks eliminates the necessity of using live creatures. Minnows, grass shrimp and even nightcrawlers fished near the bottom are regular producers in Florida waters.

On Lake Kissimmee, 35,000 acres of shallow, weedy, waters located next door to Mickey Mouse, live-bait fishermen outnumber others, with Missouri minnows and grass shrimp being the most prevalent bait. The grass shrimp, which will attract every aquatic creature that swims in these waters, can be bought or easily netted along shallow weedlines.

This is a typical Okeechobee speckled perch

Kissimmee regulars drift or troll the open water unless bedding crappie can be found along the endless miles of cattails and bulrushes.

One idiosyncrasy of Florida crappie differs significantly from the species found in other states. Precise depth for the lure presentation doesn't seem to be as critical as with crappie in colder climes, according to knowledgeable fishermen who have experience in several states. Florida crappie have a tendency to travel upwards farther to get a bait or lure than they do in other states.

Not only is crappie fishing outstanding during the Florida winter, the weather is almost as good. Overall, it is truly a winter wonderland for crappie.

A bass strikes instead of a crappie.

Run-and-Gun Fishing Method Has Specks in Grave Situation

As a rule, Lake Okeechobee speck fishermen are a laid-back bunch.

In contrast to the fast-paced world of bass fishing, local speck enthusiasts prefer the slow and steady approach. You see them fishing out of pontoon boats and old wooden skiffs that survive the long ride southward each winter. And always, they are anchored into position, willing to out-wait the black crappie that Floridians call specks.

J.R. Graves doesn't fit the same mold. He is South Florida's run-and-gun speck man.

After spending an average of 150 days speck fishing on the Big O for the past 31 years, Graves has as much knowledge about the plentiful panfish as any angler. Through the years, he has developed a system that consistently produces limits, yet seems unorthodox to many.

"The biggest mistake people make on this lake is sitting in one spot too long and not looking around more," said Graves, a long-time speck guide on a lake that is home to an estimated 10 million crappie. "Most people who have caught specks in a certain spot will return there for several days and sit there for hours before they realize that the specks have moved.

"Specks are like bass in that they will move from time to time. You have to constantly be searching new water to either find them again or find a new school of fish. There's a heck of a lot more to speck fishing than simply sitting in one spot with a cane pole."

Slow Trolling

The most consistent way to locate schools of specks involves slowly trolling both the open-water areas (which often have submerged vegetation) and along the grass-lines. Graves trolls with eight to ten rods protruding from his boat, giving him the appearance of a gigantic spider floating across the water. The lines on his rods are set at various lengths to cover a considerable range of depths.

133

After a couple of strikes on one rod, Graves adjusts all of the lines to that length. Crappie are notoriously depth-conscious. The species will not swim significantly upward or move down to hit a bait, but once you determine their exact depth, you can usually pattern them throughout that part of the lake.

"Ninety percent of the fishermen in this lake stay in shallow water," Graves said, "and that is their main mistake. The majority of the specks are only shallow part of the year. I prefer to fish the deeper water where most of the specks are and I know I'm fishing for mostly unmolested fish."

Graves has enjoyed his most consistent success in deep water. Typically, he leaves the mouth of the Kissimmee River and runs about 7 miles offshore. Using a sea anchor to slow the boat, Graves begins drifting back toward shore.

Once he gets a couple of strikes—signifying that his boat has run through a school of specks—Graves throws out a marker buoy to pinpoint their position. He then becomes more of a typical Okeechobee speck fisherman, slowing down and thoroughly working the school of fish.

For Lake Okeechobee specks, Graves uses six- to eight-pound test line and a handmade lead jig with a feather skirt, similar to the old No-Alibi jigs. The most productive colors are white and chartreuse.

Productive Trick

A little trick that has paid off handsomely involves the way Graves ties the jig. After tying it, he moves the knot down the eye of the jig until it rests in the middle of it (instead of at the top).

"This makes the jig fall through the water in more of a horizontal position, which really makes it dart from side to side," he said. "It falls more naturally this way."

Graves' approach to speck fishing is slightly more sophisticated than most. He utilizes three different outfits for various situations, in contrast to the average crappie fisherman who fishes strictly with a cane pole.

For situations in which he is making long casts to locate specks, Graves uses a light spinning outfit. When fishing deep water offshore, a long rod coupled with a small closed-faced spinning reel is a better tool (because the trigger on the reel allows him to easily adjust the depth of his jig). And for situations in which he is jigging holes in the vegetation, Graves uses an eight-foot custom-made graphite fly rod, which is used more like a cane pole.

Crappiethon Classic V

Texas High School Freshman Exemplifies Good Life Hooking Fish, Not Drugs

Many 15-year-old high school freshmen experiment with drugs and alcohol, but Shane Allman, Denton, Texas, gets his kicks from trying new jigs, flies and tackle that will put more crappie in the boat.

The youngest contender among the 196 qualifiers for Crappiethon Classic V in Chattanooga in June of 1988, Shane is an avid, dedicated professional who spends 50 days or more each year stalking this popular panfish. When not fishing, studying or in the classroom, he can be found duck hunting or training retrievers on his grandmother's 750-acre Texas ranch. The ranch was once a hunting resort, but now it is the bonanza outdoor paradise where Shane enjoys the out-of-doors and shuns any suggestion that he get involved with the myriad of drugs that harass the world.

Shane's Crappiethon Classic partner was James Spangler, a 36-year-old McKinney, Texas, paper hanger, who teamed with the talented teenager to take first place in the Lewisville Lake Crappie Tournament, north of Dallas in '88. The odd couple partners landed 21.38 pounds for top honors. The win qualified the pair for one of the 96 couples contending for a $30,000 prize at the Chattanooga extravaganza. Each of the winning partners got a new Lowes boat, 45-hp Mercury and split a $15,000 cash check.

"Shane camped out nine straight days on the river bank at Lewisville, and learned how to find the crappies on the tournament day. His scouting helped us take first place and qualify for Classic V," Spangler revealed at Chattanooga.

"Shane is a good student, but he loves the outdoors too. He duck hunts with a lot of grown-ups, and that's how we got acquainted. The hunting experiences led to our combining our skills in crappie tournament fishing," Spangler says.

Shane's father passed away in April of '88 and the young

photo by Doug Hannon

fisherman was, of course, distressed. But his father was not a
fisherman or hunter. Shane learned to love the outdoors from
friends and relatives until Spangler took him in tow.

"My young partner almost lived on Hickory Creek at the
Lewisville Lake crappie tournament site studying the habits and
movements of the schools of fish in the early spring. It was on his
spring break from school that he learned what was directly

responsible for our stopping right on a big congregation of crappies, and catching the winning stringer no more than 400 yards from where he camped. We caught the whole stringer without moving ten feet," Spangler said.

Spangler and Shane caught all their fish on a Shiney Hiney jig made by Arkie Lures, Springdale, Arkansas. The young angler tried a live minnow, but the fish would only strike jigs on that March day. It was enough to convince this partnership that jigs are big for them in all tournaments now.

"That was our first tournament, and we won it all. Much of the credit is Shane's, but that Shiny Hiney helped too. We use a colored jig head with a tinsel body and two gold and silver streamers. It's a neat lure, and we vertically jig it on a two-piece, graphite B 'n' M pole equipped with a B 'n' M fly rod-style reel. I think this tackle by B 'n' M that's made in West Point, Mississippi, is the best crappie rig on the market," the senior member of the Spangler-Allman team declares.

Those winning fish at the Lewisville Lake were abnormally large. Seven were heavier than $1 \frac{1}{2}$-pounds, and the giant size made their stringer a winner. All their big fish were caught on jigs. The Shiny Hiney caught most of them, but some were pulled in on Betts jigs. These are made in Fuquay-Varina, North Carolina.

"We don't have any sophisticated fishing equipment. We don't even have a trolling motor. But we are dedicated fishermen, and nobody tries harder than we do to catch fish and win," says Spangler.

Crappie fishing competitively is exploding all over the U.S. There are more than 20 million avid crappie fishermen in the land. In 1987, 240,000 bought tickets and fished for the tagged crappie that brought hundreds of cash and merchandise prizes. One crappie tournament in Arizona in '87 had 408 entries, and all 32 events averaged 230 boats with two anglers to the boat. A total of more than 16,000 fished those events, including men, women and even children. Qualifiers for the Classic were the top three finishers in each of the 32 tournaments.

Shane and Spangler didn't win the Classic in '88, but they had fun, and both have many years to compete in the future. Meantime, an outstanding young man is not being tempted to try drugs. He is happy with a fishing pole in his hand or a duck gun on his shoulder. This is an All-American kid who is an example for today's generation. Life looks a little more promising after you talk with Shane Allman.

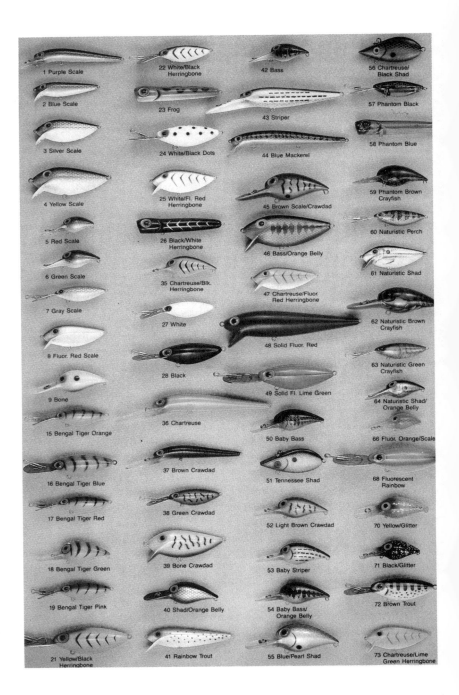

1 Purple Scale
2 Blue Scale
3 Silver Scale
4 Yellow Scale
5 Red Scale
6 Green Scale
7 Gray Scale
8 Fluor. Red Scale
9 Bone
15 Bengal Tiger Orange
16 Bengal Tiger Blue
17 Bengal Tiger Red
18 Bengal Tiger Green
19 Bengal Tiger Pink
21 Yellow/Black Herringbone

22 White/Black Herringbone
23 Frog
24 White/Black Dots
25 White/Fl. Red Herringbone
26 Black/White Herringbone
35 Chartreuse/Blk. Herringbone
27 White
28 Black
36 Chartreuse
37 Brown Crawdad
38 Green Crawdad
39 Bone Crawdad
40 Shad/Orange Belly
41 Rainbow Trout

42 Bass
43 Striper
44 Blue Mackerel
45 Brown Scale/Crawdad
46 Bass/Orange Belly
47 Chartreuse/Fluor. Red Herringbone
48 Solid Fluor. Red
49 Solid Fl. Lime Green
50 Baby Bass
51 Tennessee Shad
52 Light Brown Crawdad
53 Baby Striper
54 Baby Bass/ Orange Belly
55 Blue/Pearl Shad

56 Chartreuse/ Black Shad
57 Phantom Black
58 Phantom Blue
59 Phantom Brown Crayfish
60 Naturistic Perch
61 Naturistic Shad
62 Naturistic Brown Crayfish
63 Naturistic Green Crayfish
64 Naturistic Shad/ Orange Belly
66 Fluor. Orange/Scale
68 Fluorescent Rainbow
70 Yellow/Glitter
71 Black/Glitter
72 Brown Trout
73 Chartreuse/Lime Green Herringbone

138

Formula for Success in *Field & Stream's* New Crappie Video

Catching crappie can be done at any time of the year, with any type of equipment and by any angler, young or old, making crappie one of America's favorite gamefish. But there's a difference between just catching crappie and catching them consistently.

To help anglers catch more crappie consistently, *Field & Stream* Magazine and 3M now offer "Formula For Success: Crappie," the sixth video in the *Field & Stream* Video Library. "Formula For Success: Crappie" covers the concepts and techniques crappie experts have developed over the years. Since crappie fishing is a family sport, this video features ordinary people doing something they love, catching crappie.

Introduced by Ken Schultz, associate fishing editor for *Field & Stream*, this video teaches how to catch more crappie consistently by using the three-step formula of location, behavior and presentation. Knowing where to find crappie, how they react to weather, light and water conditions, and what type of lure presentation is best at various times are all covered. Using these three principles, anglers can catch more crappie, making the most of their valuable leisure time.

"Formula For Success: Crappie" also teaches anglers the different tactics necessary for lakes and reservoirs and how to vary tactics to be successful in both spring and summer. The best types of equipment for successful crappie fishing, and how equipment can affect the angler's success, are also discussed.

At $19.95, "Formula For Success: Crappie" is available at fishing tackle and sporting goods stores, through a special offer in *Field & Stream* Magazine, or directly from 3M by calling 800/383-6501, ext. 6850.

The video is produced in association with OMC Power Group (Johnson Outboards and Evinrude Motors) and OMC Boat Group (Sea Nymph and Lowe). Normark/Blue Fox Tackle Company and Zebco provided additional technical support.

For more information on "Formula for Success: Crappie," part of the *Field & Stream* video Library from 3M, contact: 3M Leisure Time Products, 3M Center, Bldg. 225-3N-04, St. Paul, MN 55144-1000, or call 800/383-6501, ext. 6850.

Small Storm crankbaits catch crappie.

Three Well-Kept Secrets for Jig Fishing

Bob Tindal had only an hour to fish. He had to get back to Pelion, South Carolina where he was busy making tiny boats for swamp fishermen. But he loved the spring of the year for crappie fishing, and he rushed to get his boat in the water. Quickly, he moved under the old I-95 bridge a mile north of the tiny town of Santee in the low country. Before he dropped his first jig into the 30-foot water around the abutment, he knew he would catch fish. Mayflies were covering the cement pilings from top to bottom, many tumbling into the ripples on the Santee-Cooper, when the breeze swished under the structure. After all, this was May. Weren't the mayflies supposed to be mating here this month?

Bob tied on a small Super Jig made by the Phillips family in Jonesboro, Arkansas. It was a tiny plastic jig with several half-inch long tentacles that wriggled life-like in the wind, and they would have that same movement in the slight current under the bridge.

Then came the first of Tindal's long-discovered jig secrets for catching crappies in relatively deep water. His palomar knot in the 8-pound test monofilament was jacked tight and the 1/8 ounce leaded hook with the jig threaded all the way to the eye was carefully slipped so it was at right angles to the line. When he turned it loose, the knot was tight enough to hold it in that perpendicular position.

Using a long limber rod with an open-faced ultralight reel, Tindal dropped the tiny jig in the water a foot from the concrete abutment, and it trickled down in the yellow water toward the bottom. It never made the fall. A big slab crappie gathered it in and dived. Tindal methodically reeled the fish to the gunnels and lifted it over the side. It was a 2-pounder.

Hastily, Bob slid the hook back to its right angle position and dropped it again among the mayflies that were drifting past the abutment as the breeze picked up, and more of the insects lost their hold and took a swim. Every eddy place in sight had the

141

mayflies circling on the surface and fish were in a frenzy gulping them down. All the positive signs of a lifetime of fishing relayed the message to Tindal that this was the day you dream about.

Within the hour, Bob landed 20 nice crappie under the Santee River bridge, and for good measure added two yearling bass and three hand-size bluegills. He caught them all on the same style jig that had to be replaced several times because the fish tore it up when they frantically fought to escape this phony mayfly that had fluttered down halfway to the bottom.

Bob Tindal's success that May morning revealed the first of three important secrets. Spotting the mayflies was just an added bonus. The secret was tying the jig on perpendicular to the line and using a light test line to begin with. The falling Mini-Jig was so real that the crappie couldn't resist it. With the jig tied in the normal position where it dangled vertical to the line, Tindal could not entice a strike. Obviously, this was a secret worth remembering. His long stringer of panfish that he plopped in the back of his pickup as he headed for home was proof of his expertise and his well-kept secret.

In the far reaches of this same river near the hamlet of Elloree, South Carolina, Billy Vaughan and his fishing partner son, Tommy, live on a shady shoreline where they can look out over acres of water with bushes and floating cover that piles up in the calm coves around weeds and grasses that reach the surface. For a generation Billy has caught long stringers of big crappies around those bushes, and in the flotsam debris that often is several inches thick on the surface.

They are exclusively jig fishermen for crappie and today use a custom-made, hairy little phony insect that Tommy makes and markets. He calls it "Rooty-Tooty 309," and it catches fish in an unorthodox manner that amazes many veterans.

Observers call it Pandemonium panfishing. That's a pretty good description. In their metal johnboat, Billy and Tommy putt-putted with their 25-horsepower outboard right into the middle of this floating debris. It's their flotsam pattern. With the boat snuggled in the debris, Tommy pushes the engine out of gear and lets it idle as they pick up long cane poles or rods and reels and tie on Rooty-Tooty 309's.

Billy grabbed up a long piece of one-inch PVC pipe that has a one foot bend at right angles in the end.

"This is what we call our 'holy rod.' You can't get a jig down through this topwater junk unless you make a hole. So we made this PVC into a tool for getting us through the floating stuff. We just jiggle the crooked end around until we work out a hole about the size of your hat or a little bigger. Then we drop the jig on a light line, about six or eight pound test, into the hole and let it settle. The crappie can't stand it," Billy Vaughan said as he dropped the 309 into a hole.

With the motor running and the hole-making creating chaos, both Vaughans landed hand-size crappie within minutes and kept the instant replay going until they had a live-box overflowing. Some of their catch was slab monsters in the two-pound class. They had moved a few yards several times in the debris, but always they left the outboard running and jiggled out two more small holes in the flotsam where they dropped the jigs.

This is the second secret of catching crappie with jigs. Fish the close places, and make a lot or noise. The Vaughans say that the throbbing vibration of the outboard and the jiggling of the holy rod shakes insects, small shrimp and minnows loose from the cover. They start falling toward the bottom, and the crappie are waiting for them to move. A jig fluttering down at the same time entices the crappies to strike. They do not spook and run when there's a fuss on top. Indeed, it brings them running to gulp down the dislodged food. It's like ringing the dinner bell.

This second secret reveals that noise is not a culprit. Fish the places where the fish hide in the shade and stalk food, even if you must make your own entry through the floating stuff. It may make your fishing better, and certainly it will not spook the crappie, as the Vaughans will testify.

The talented Bob Tindal unveiled the third secret when he drove down to Lake Newnans in Central Florida one winter day to fish around the shallows that lace the shoreline where giant cypress trees and knees grow 100 feet or more out into the lake. He had tied his tiny one-man boat on top of his pickup and he had no outboard or trolling motor, just a one-handed paddle that he could use adroitly as he moved slowly among the trees and fished a 12-foot B 'n' M telescopic pole with a foot and a half of line. He had several colors of Betts Jigs, fuzzy little insect mimickers, with a No. 10 hook halfway covered up and some Hal-flies. He dropped the jig vertically around the cypress trunks. It was almost weightless, slipping below the surface ever so slowly.

He fished holes where few anglers were ever able to reach before. His tiny boat, that rose no more than eight inches above the surface, could slide in between trees time after time, and the

At day's end. . . angler admires catch.

crappie seemed to have been waiting for him to get there. Sometimes they struck his jig before it sank, like it was a popping bug. At other times it dropped slowly in the tannic acid-colored water, and big crappie tried to take the pole away from him. He loaded the boat while many veterans on the outskirts of the tree line had little success. He put the bait where the fish were, and that was possible only because he had a tiny boat and a long pole with a short line that allowed him opportunity where none was available to the conventional crappie angler.

The one-man boat could be dangerous in big bodies of water, but just a hop and skip off the shoreline in waist-deep water with trees and stumps everywhere, Tindal was in no danger, and he had unlocked another secret for crappie angling.

Untold secrets for successful crappie fishing are myriad, but these three recounted here have been shared by their innovators. They work everywhere that crappie are found, and the purists who prefer jig fishing to live bait will often do much better in these situations than the bait fisherman who swears that there "ain't nothing as much like a minnow as a minnow."

144

Hannon catches a copperhead.

Even Trophy Bass Scholar
Likes to Catch Crappies

Many prominent lunker bass fishing guides wouldn't want to be found dead angling for bluegills or crappies with, of all things, a cane pole. But when these gourmet flatfish are biting, and you can entice one of the professional wall mount hunters to forsake his trade and go fishing with you on his day off, he quickly shows his enthusiasm. He has the time of his life.

145

That, at least, is the impression I got from a day of speckled perch fishing on Lake Lochloosa in Central Florida with Douglas Hannon, the remarkable black bass scientist and professional guide who works out of Odessa Florida, the "Bass Professor." The next day we enjoyed an adventure catching bluegills in the same unsophisticated way with cane poles. We call those bream "grippers" because they are so large it takes a huge man's hand to spread from dorsal fin to the fish's belly.

Hannon, a Winnipeg, Canada, native, lives at Odessa, near Tampa, where he is an astute student of the out-of-doors. Hannon has caught and released over 400 trophy-size bass, all over 10-pounds, during two decades of studying the Florida bass species, yet he enjoys catching panfish just as most youngsters of the country do when they start fishing.

While he has spent almost as much time on the water as he has on land since being introduced to fishing by his wife in Texas 25 years ago, he is a complete novice when it comes to catching speckled perch. At least he was unfamiliar with the how and where until he made a date to meet me at Lake Lochloosa to try his hand at these flatfish that attract more visiting anglers to the Sunshine State each winter than any other variety.

"Don't bring a thing but your fishing license," I told him. "The boat is in the water, the poles are rigged for specks, the minnows are in the bucket, and I know the fish are anxious to bite."

It was early fall. You find many speck fishermen who believe you can only catch these fish when they are bedding in early spring. That's erroneous. Speckled perch will bite every month of the year if you can find them. Some of the best crappie fishing in Central Florida is during May and June. But, like all kinds of fishing, the days you come in with 50 flatfish limits, you see others pulling boats up to the fish camp docks muttering that they had no luck, the specks had lockjaw or maybe there just weren't any fish in the lake any more.

Doug arrived about noon, and soon we were in my Bassmaster boat and making the five minute run from the Twin Lakes Fish Camp to the very heart of the 8600 acres of Lochloosa. The boat is equipped with strong pole holders on both sides of the bow and stern, a couple of feet from each end of the boat. Some people try to sit on their 12- or 14-foot poles or hold them in their hands while fishing for speckled perch. You can get away with that if you are fishing with a single pole or maybe even two, but when you fish with three poles or more, you will catch more specks with pole holders. Specks will definitely bite better when poles are affixed to the boat, and you are moving than when you attempt to hand-hold a pole.

I lowered my Motor-Guide variable speed electric trolling motor into the water. I cut the engine in the middle of the lake and picked up the first pole.

"I'll fish the front and run the motor. You bait up four or five poles and fish the stern. The first thing we will do is take this red plastic worm and cut it into half-inch pieces and thread them on the hook, all the way up to the eyes. They must be kept pushed high on the No. 2, thin, gold-colored hook. Then right behind this piece of plastic, impale a small minnow. Hook him right through both eyes and he will live longer than any other way," I told Douglas. (This was a substitute for a manufactured Super Jig.)

"You must be going to troll these baits. That's almost the way I hook a shiner when I'm fishing for big bass," Doug said. "But I don't put the plastic on the hook."

"Yep, that's the idea. The specks will see a minnow apparently swimming along normally when we get started. I discovered some years ago that you will get about 50 percent more strikes with the piece of plastic in front of the minnow. I believe it helps attract them.

"I discovered this plastic bit by accident almost. I was out here alone one spring day and not catching any fish. I looked through my tackle box for something, and saw this little No. 4 hook with a piece of purple plastic on it. I think it cost about 35 cents. I put the hook on one of my speck lines, and I hadn't gone 20 feet before it was being yanked hard and bent all the way into the water. I pulled a 1-pound speck out with that little hook. It was a repeat performance all that morning on that one hook while I scarcely caught anything on the other two," I told Doug.

After that experience, I bought several of those hooks and caught fish regularly with them, but I found it could be done easily and cheaper by simply slicing up the jelly worms I used for bass fishing. I have used purple, blue, black and red worms since that memorable morning, but have now settled on red. Maybe it is just superstition, but I'm convinced I do better on red.

"Another thing you have to remember about baiting up that took me years of fishing these waters to learn is, don't use big minnows. When I buy minnows, I immediately throw out all of them that are more than two inches long. That is not to say you won't catch a speck with a minnow that size now and then, but I am sure you will not catch as many. I saw this demonstrated to my satisfaction in Lake Griffin, near Leesburg, Florida, about 25 years ago. We were catching fish regularly when we ran out of bait. There was a vendor in those days who stayed out on the lake who brought minnows for sale to the boats. He brought us some minnows and they were much larger than what we had been using. We couldn't buy a bite with them. We dumped them over the side, returned to the camp, got some small ones like we had previously, and when we dropped those lines back in that honey hole, the specks seemed to be just waiting there with open mouths. We started catching them again immediately," I said.

"You going to fish out here in the middle of the lake?" Doug asked. "I thought the crappie fishing was done around the lily pads, grass patches or the cypress roots and knees along the shoreline."

"When specks are bedding, often you can catch them in those places with just such cover or anywhere else that there is a structure on the bottom. Oddly enough, most often when you can catch them in those up-close places, you can also catch them in the deep water. This fish is just as likely to bed in ten inches of water. We are looking for feeding fish today.

"You can be almost certain there are some of the species right here where I stopped the boat. The bait fish are plentiful. They are out here feeding on the mosquitoes and other insects that you can see on top of the water. These insects were unable to fly this morning because of a heavy fog that moved in and didn't clear up until nearly noon. It forced them into the water, and the crappie and bream are feeding on them now. You can see and hear one breaking every minute or two," I said.

"Yeah, I have seen several breaking since we stopped. That's much like the way I locate bass in the open water. When I find the bait fish, I'm pretty sure there are some lunkers around, and I troll big shiners through the area. I'm sure you could catch some bass right in here where you are going to fish for specks if you would put out some shiners," Douglas opined.

He was undoubtedly right. Some of those fish tearing up the water's surface were too big and too aggressive to be crappies. But we were out for the flatfish at that moment, and the bass could wait for another day.

"There's a little wind blowing out of the south this afternoon, Doug, and my system for speck fishing dictates that

I head north. That puts the wind directly on the stern. We not only get a little push from the wind that sometimes is enough to propel us without the electric motor, it keeps us floating smoothly. Now some good speck fishermen drift for these fish with the boat broadside to the wind. You can catch some fish that way, but it keeps the lines and hooks rocking up and down in a most unnatural way, and I cannot land fish nearly as well trolling into the wind either, even though I can make the proper speed with a wind as light as this is now," I said.

We now had our poles out perpendicular to the boat. I do not troll lines directly off the back of the boat, but at right angles to the boat, both in front and in the rear. There are times when lines out the stern will do well, but with a wind as light as we had that afternoon, I prefer to fish alongside the boat.

"Doug, you will note that I have three medium size shot above the hooks. I spread these about six inches apart up the line. Then I have the smallest styrofoam cork that will only partially support the hook, bait and weights. I like the corks to be about two inches long and small. These specks will often turn a hook loose if you have one of the big old snap-on corks. These offer entirely too much resistance for the fish, and even though a speck doesn't spook easily, he will often turn away when he pulls on a bait tied too securely to a float. My corks will sink from the lead shot if the boat is not moving, but when I pull them slowly with the trolling motor, they will ride on the surface.

"Here where we are fishing now the water is about ten feet deep. We will troll it slowly at about eight feet at first. If we don't start picking up some fish, we will try faster speeds and different depths. I find that the specks here bite better when we are trolling a couple of feet off the bottom, but I have seen the time when they would bite in this same water only two or three feet deep," I continued.

We hadn't moved the boat 50 feet before one of Doug's lines was taut, and his cane pole was bent and shaking. He pulled in a 14-inch speck that was in the 1-pound class, probably a two or three year old fish. They have a life span normally of five to six years, and they are catchable from ages of six to nine months until they are adults in four years and occasionally reach weights of 3-pounds and more. The world record is 6-pounds. Most of the specks caught in Lochloosa weigh from 10-ounces to 2-pounds, but we have put some in the cooler up to 3-pounds.

Douglas had landed the first speck with the finesse of the

angling expert that he is, although the expertise had never been exhibited before on speckled perch. He had simply picked up the pole after the speck had struck and hung himself, and lifted the flouncing fish into the boat. Some inexperienced crappie anglers lose more fish than they land by jerking the hook out of tender mouths too viciously. Beginners almost always lose crappies by jerking too hard.

You can't do much hanging the specks yourself when trolling in these deep waters and using this method. They either strike and are hooked, or they get the bait and are gone. Often they will follow right along, and take a second or even a third bait if they don't hang themselves.

When we had slowly trolled with the wind for a mile and were nearing the north shoreline, we picked up the poles, raised the electric motor, cranked up and motored back to our starting point. We wanted to put the wind on the stern again and repeat the route. We had caught 25 specks on the first drift, and had thrown out a plastic jug with a weight on it to mark the spot where we had landed more than one fish in a short distance. I never throw out a buoy after a single strike or catch. I wait until we have two or more strikes at the same time or almost the same time.

Once I have a school pegged with such a marker, I often make figure eights trolling around the jig in giant "S's" as some fishermen call them. When the specks are really congregated, and the wind is no factor, you can catch all the fish you want without any further hunting.

By the time the sun was low on the horizon, Douglas had smiled and laughed all afternoon, and we had nearly a cooler full of what we call good eating-size fish. They were just right for frying without having to cut them in two or slice. I do not filet small flatfish. It is a waste of good meat, and if you don't mind eating with your fingers, you can save every morsel of protein in a speckled perch by simply stripping the meat off the bones after the fish is cooked. There is no way to save all the meat by cutting a strip off each side of the backbone when the fish is raw.

"How are you going to get all these fish dressed?" Douglas asked.

"I have been catching, dressing and eating specks for a lot of years, and it is no trouble to me. I believe in saving fish, and sharing them with the neighbors in the Cross Creek community, many of whom are old and unable to fish. I have dressed so many that I think I am pretty good at it. I can dress any small speck in nine seconds. The larger ones may take as much as 15 seconds. That includes scaling, gutting and de-heading," I told him.

"This has been a really fun afternoon. Have you ever been a professional guide for these speckled perch? I'm sure there must be many people who would pay good money to go with you," Doug said.

"I have helped a lot of youngsters and senior citizens catch them, but all for free. I enjoy seeing people happy when they fish here. There was one time when a young man from Kentucky, his name was Bud English, I believe, who had fished out here for a week or so and hadn't caught any fish. I was bringing in near limits of flat fish every day. On his final day here he wanted to know if he could go with me that morning. I told him I'd be glad to have him. We caught a nice string of fish, and were back at camp and had them dressed by about 10:00 a.m.," I said. "He had to leave for home that afternoon."

"English was really happy with his fish, and said he was going to carry them back home for his wife and children to enjoy at meal time. He asked me how much he owed me. I told him there was no charge, but he reached in his billfold and handed me a $5.00 bill. I tacked it on my den wall here at Cross Creek, and it's still there. It's the only money I ever made fishing," I laughed.

In that my system has proven successful, I have carried numerous people out in quest of specks for years. On one occasion I remember taking Bill Cook, a Baptist preacher from Morganton, Kentucky, the manufacturer of the "Bill Bug" that is an excellent bluegill and trout bait. Cook had fished all his life, but not like I fish for specks. He was delighted with the 50 speckled perch we caught the afternoon he fished with me.

"But the most pleasure I ever enjoyed from helping novices catch fish was some years ago when two school teachers and their wives from Perry, Florida, needed some help in catching fish. They had fished an entire afternoon right near me in a grass patch, and while I loaded the boat, they hadn't caught a single fish," I rambled on to Douglas. "I showed them my system of catching fish, rigged some poles for them, and the next day they all caught their limits. A week later I received a nice "thank you" card from the teacher who said they fed the whole Perry neighborhood with the fish they carried home."

While my trolling technique for crappies with Hannon was in Florida, the same system is productive in open water anywhere if there is a good population of these panfish. It is a near sure-fire way of putting a gourmet meal on the table any month of the year.

Bass Professor Doug Hannon baits a bream hook on a cane pole. He loves to catch panfish.

Lochloosa Crappie-Jigging Secrets Revealed

Bob Tyndal pushed his small one-man boat down the ramp at Twin Lakes Fish Camp and putt-putted out the mouth of Cross Creek into the 8,600 acres of Lake Lochloosa in Alachua County. This spring-fed natural Central Florida lake adjacent to U.S. Highway 301 on its east bank near Hawthorne, long has been an acknowledged leader in speckled perch production and catch success despite acres of hydrilla that prohibit any kind of fishing in much of its area.

But Tyndal loved the hydrilla and any other dense aquatic growth that left a few holes where he could get a weighted jig near the bottom. He was sure of catching a stringer of specks with a technique he had perfected and documented dozens of times in previous experiences on Lochloosa.

He eased his boat into a thick island of the "green peril," as many call the obnoxious hydrilla, and he didn't need to anchor or tie up to anything. With the calm, overcast day, he would stay put. He could see a half dozen hat-size holes in the weeds where he was confident speckled perch lurked and stalked forage fish virtually trapped in the cover near the bottom in seven feet of clear water.

Bob tied on, in his very special way, a pink Super Jig, made in Jonesboro, Arkansas, a tiny lure with a No. 4 gold hook that had proven productive for him in a lot of Florida streams and lakes. The tie-on was his big secret.

"You can't catch many specks in these holes with a jig that hangs vertically on the end of the line. For some reason they will reject it most of the time, even when it is flitted right in their faces. I think it looks phony.

"I tie the jig on with a Palomar knot that will allow me to twist the jig horizontally to the line. I never use a minnow or anything else on the jig. But when it juts out at 90 degrees from the line, it looks more like something alive than a jig that is on the end, and it goes down tail first in the cover. I believe specks look at a jig, think it is edible and strike. They don't rush for a fake

153

minnow flitting down with its head toward the surface," Bob rationalizes. "They are suspicious.

"Of course, when you catch a fish, the jig is pulled downward. You jack it back horizontal. It's ready to go again."

Tyndal uses nothing heavier than 8-pound test line and likes the 1/8th ounce leaded jig hook. He fishes with a long, limber composite rod and an open-face ultralight reel. His jig floats toward the bottom, and if there is a speckled perch in the territory, it strikes and this old veteran outdoorsman reels in another slab to the gunnels.

Tyndal has his best luck in Lochloosa from early February through June, but in the deep water, you can jig specks successfully every month of the year. It's a matter of tightening the jig at a right angle and letting it fall slowly in the heavy cover. Some jig speck anglers use a tiny bobber. Tyndal believes that is unnecessary, and he doesn't want any weight on the line other than the lead on the head of the jig hook.

While most astute speck fishermen have learned that the species is harder to spook than many other game fish, few deliberately create chaos to attract the specks to the boat. But that is the technique used by Billy and Tommy Vaughan, a father-son team who fish Santee-Cooper and many other lakes of the South in the annual Crappiethon competition.

The Vaughans carry a ten-foot length of PVC pipe with them when they launch their flat-bottom skiff. They run their small boat into thick cover on the surface, push the outboard out of gear and let it run in idle. Tommy picks up the pipe that has a one-foot, 90-degree bend on the end. He sticks it in the cover and wallows out a hole, hopefully clearing a spot about waterbucket size. That's what they call their "holy rod."

With a little clearing in the hydrilla or water hyacinths, they drop minnows or jigs or combinations of those baits into the hole with either long, limber flyrods or cane poles. They set the depth with a tiny cork so that they are fishing less than a foot from the bottom. Usually, they have a single BB shot clamped on the line a foot above the bait. They catch fish with this novel approach that often puts the quieter speck anglers to shame.

Billy, the father on this team, says, "We leave the motor idling because the vibration shakes grass shrimp and insects off the aquatic growth, and it wriggles toward the bottom. It draws the specks to the spot and when we drop a bait right in the hole where the other stuff is going down, the specks just can't leave it alone."

The Vaughans' favorite jig is called a "Rooty Tooty 309," and it's an invention of Tommy's. It is a hairy little phony insect that catches a lot of fish for these unorthodox crappie fishermen. Santee-Cooper is one of the best lakes anywhere for this Pandemonium panfish technique.

The third speck-catching secret now in vogue on Lochloosa is a hand-me-down from the late Catfish Ludwig. Ludwig passed away in 1987, but he taught his jig-bobbing to Ron Gilyen, an Indiana transplant who lives at Fin-Way Fish Camp on Highway 301. The camp is owned by Wade Boggs, of Boston Red Sox baseball fame, and is run by the Boggs family. Ron often assists around the camp.

"I marveled at the stringer of specks that Catfish brought in here day after day for years, often when everyone else said the fish just weren't biting. Finally, he invited me to tag along and I learned his secrets and mastered his technique. Now I have tourists around here wondering how I catch those long stringers of specks," Ron smiles. "I inherited the secret from Catfish."

He does it with a technique he calls "jig-bobbing." He uses Mini-Jigs of several colors, and fishes two long B 'n' M fiberglass rods at a time, one two feet longer than the other. He holds the poles about 18 inches from the end, and lets the butts rest in a concave plastic brace at each elbow. With a dime-size sinker and the least lead shot he can find, he drops the jig in holes in the cover, usually letting it fall about six feet when he is fishing in water eight feet deep, He fishes one jig a foot or so deeper than the other, and once he finds where they are striking, he sets both corks at the same depth. By having poles two different lengths, he can fish spots at different distances from his boat.

Most specks hit his jig on the way down and that lifts the little cork so that it doesn't stand up on the surface. Any time the cork flattens, he sets the hook with a little flip of the pole tip and comes in with fine specks. He is among the most consistent speck catchers in Central Florida, and Lochloosa is his home base.

Four good fish camps serve Lochloosa fishermen. On Highway 301 there is the Fin-Way Fish Camp with bait, tackle, snacks, licenses, cabins, boats, motors and guide service. It is open the year 'round.

On Cross Creek, directly on the opposite side of the lake from 301, there is Twin Lakes Fish Camp, Cross Creek Fish Camp and Permenter's Fish Camp. All are full service facilities with everything speck anglers need from lodging to rental boats and motors.

The award-winning Yearling Restaurant is also located on the Creek and serves a variety of local seafood from Lochloosa and the sister Lake Orange on the western end of the creek.

With new jig techniques now being adopted by locals and tourists, speck fishing has taken on a new dimension on Lochloosa. The hydrilla put a stop to trolling jigs and minnow combinations. You stay hung up too much. But the vertical fishing of jigs is still bringing success to speck fishermen who have accepted change and are glad they did.

The Vaughans make noise and load the boat.

Crappie Anglers Earn $20,000
Catching Slabs

Alan Padgett (L) and Bobby Martin (R) winners of the 1990 U.S. Crappie Association Championship display their winning stringer with Doug Poe (C) the association's tournament director.

How would you like to make $20,000 for a weekend of crappie fishing? That was the payday Alan Padgett of Kathleen, Georgia, and Bobby Martin of Warner-Robins, Georgia, realized after fishing and winning the Zebco/U.S. Crappie Association National Championship Tournament held on Lake Wylie, South Carolina, on May 5, 1990.

Padgett and Martin are not newcomers to the world of competitive crappie fishing. In 1986 they earned over $30,000 and their first world championship in the sport of papermouth angling. But they said this year's win drew on all of their accumulated knowledge and experience at finding and taking crappie, particularly their abilities to read weather and water conditions as well as their knowledge about migrational habits of papermouths.

157

"During the practice day, when the water was calm and slick, we found crappie holding on brush-piles located on the tops of underwater humps in four to seven feet of water," Padgett said. "On the morning of the tournament, however, the weather took a turn for the worse as the wind blew. We returned to the humps to fish but found the crappie weren't there."

From past experience, Padgett and Martin understood when the wind blew and the surface of the water became choppy that crappie inhabiting shallow water would move out to deeper water. They also knew the fish still would suspend at about the same depth where they had been in the shallow water.

"We followed the crappie out of the shallows and away from the humps into the deeper water," Padgett explained. "Then we trolled 1/34- and 1/24-ounce Hal-Fly jigs at a depth of four to five feet over a 15-foot bottom and took our winning stringer."

Padgett and Martin mentioned that crappie holding in shallow water often are not visible on depth finders. Therefore, a sportsman must use his instinct to fish for papermouths, based upon his knowledge of where the fish should be under specific water and weather conditions—as Padgett and Martin did to win the tournament.

In claiming this year's Zebco/U.S. Crappie Association Championship title, Padgett and Martin defeated 57 other two-man teams who traveled from around the country to compete for the tournament's $40,000 in cash and prizes. As champions, Padgett and Martin received $9,000 in cash and a fully-rigged Astro boat with a 90-horsepower Mercury motor, a MotorGuide trolling motor and complete electronics. The second place team, Terry Rutherford of Martinez, Georgia, and Gary Stephens of Cropwell, Alabama, took home $3,5000 in cash and a fully-rigged, 16-foot, Fisher Marsh-Hawk boat with a 40-horsepower Mercury motor.

The championship tournament was the culmination of a five month, 17-lake, competitive circuit which pitted the skills of some of the nation's best crappie fishermen against one another in one-day lake tournaments. The top five teams in the two-man team category, adult-child category and husband-wife category at each one-day tournament qualified for a berth at the national championship, which was sponsored by Blakemore Road-Runner lures, B 'n' M Pole Company, DuPont Power Lines, Hal-Fly Jigs, SparklScales, MotorGuide, ZEBCO Rods & Reels and Brunswick Marine.

158

Carolina's Lake Tillery Crappie

Clinton Shinkle cast a minnow hooked on a black and white Super Jig 40 feet into the dingy water. It quickly sank in Lake Tillery two feet below the colorful snap-on cork, and settled around the bare limbs of a half-submerged sweetgum tree that had succumbed to Hurricane Hugo several months earlier.

The cork shuddered a moment, came alive and headed out into the vast expanses of the Great Pee Dee River that separates Montgomery and Stanly counties in the heartland of North Carolina, the Piedmont as the middle of the Tar Heel State is known.

Shinkle's smile broadened, his dark eyes flashed, and he instinctively twitched the tip of his 7-foot rod with the ultralight open-faced reel. He knew it didn't take much hook setting to catch the bountiful white crappies that thrive all along the hundreds of miles of hilly shorelines.

His line was tight, the cork surfaced, and moments later he retrieved a healthy, splashy, 14-inch panfish to his precarious perch on the sweetgum log. He pulled it out of the water. Moments later he had his lunch swimming on a stringer tied to a myrtle bush on the bank.

"I have caught some 2-pounders right here around this same tree. There's a deep hole about 12 feet from the bank. The crappies gather in that hole in April and May, and sometimes stay around until fall. I can usually catch a mess any morning with a jig-minnow combination. You can catch them from the bank with a cane pole or rod and reel. But I like to sit on this old log with my boots dangling in the water, and cast along the tree from the tip-top branches back to where I am sitting.

"I live in Norwood, about three miles down the road. I park my pickup on the highway bank there, walk a couple of hundred yards through the woods, and have a lot of fun dragging these big old slabs out of this hole. I've been fishing it for years, and I seldom go home skunked," the old veteran panfisherman versed us on his fishing experience.

The giant Lake Tillery impoundment was created by

Carolina Power and Light Company when it constructed the Norwood dam half a century ago. It backs up water over farms and hills and dells around the Uwharrie mountain range. Some water is well over 100 feet deep, but there are hundreds of sloughs, coves, branches and cracks where panfish feed and spawn. Shorelines along the shallows glisten with dead mussel shells, slick rocks and gravels that are ideal habitat for bedding crappie, bream and bass.

Panfish anglers converge on Tillery from far and near from the first warm day of February until the cold of November drives them indoors. Generally, they catch fine crappie limits.

While originally fishermen fished solely from the rocky, wooded banks with cane poles and a live minnow impaled under the dorsal fin, change has come to Tillery since World War II. Many natives still fish from the hill with poles and minnows, but the majority of panfishermen today move along this shady shoreline with trolling motors, and flip jigs on poles or rods and reels in the shadows of overhanging flora. Some veterans combine a small minnow with a many-tentacled white, pink, black or chartreuse-colored jig. Yet, there are many successful crappie fishermen who insist they can do better with a jig alone—but some say they catch more with a minnow without a jig. It's a matter of confidence, and expertise in getting the feel for the system you prefer.

Pier fishing has become the rage in the last two decades. Once the shoreline was desolate, rocky and covered with trees and pastures. Today, luxury resort homes cover almost every lot on the Stanly County side of the river (there are some on the Montgomery shoreline too) almost every home not only has a boathouse, it has a walk-on pier jutting out 30-50 feet into the lake. Buried Christmas trees and other debris are piled around the pier cover. Crappies trap forage food around these implants, and fishermen put a lot of tasty meals on the dinner tables.

Some of these Tillery homes house full-time residents (not vacationers). Working at public jobs in the daytime, these waterfront fishermen burn lights near the surface over the brush piles after dark. The lights attract the insects that in turn draw gambusia minnows that provide forage food for marauding crappies all the warm months. Some of the best catches have been made by the night pier fishermen.

But bank crappie anglers have stories to tell too. While most crappies caught in Tillery range from about one-half pound

Hack Curran with Lake Tillery crappie.

to a pound and a half, two ladies fishing minnows under corks on cane poles just below the Highway 24-27 bridge five miles east of Albemarle, struggled with slabs on the line one May morning. They dragged two crappies to the shore, and put them on stringers. Two hours later, they weighed their twin crappies on the Minnow Pond Tackle & Bait Shop scales. They weighed exactly 3 1/4-pounds. These Goliath-size panfish were unusual, but there are stories of crappie exceeding 4-pounds being reeled in from Tillery.

The Minnow Pond Tackle & Bait Shop is located on Highway 24-27 two miles west of the Pee Dee River bridge. You can get minnows, jigs, poles, fishing licenses, snacks, gas and crappie-fishing advice there the year around.

Several good launching ramps are available on the Stanly side of Tillery. One wide ramp just east of the bridge allows more than one trailer to load or unload at the same time.

The Indian Mound Road turns south a mile west of the Highway 24-27 bridge. It connects with Highway 52 at Norwood. Branching off Indian Mound Road is Lakeshore Drive. A good single-trailer, hard-surface ramp is at the end of the drive, about one mile. This ramp puts boats within two or three minutes of some of the best crappie tributaries—Cedar & Jacobs creeks. In the spring, these shallow waters attract a myriad of spawning panfish, and thousands are caught from boats, the wooded shoreline and the Indian Mound roadway shoulders that are often filled with families fishing shoulder to shoulder at Easter time.

Shinkle pulled in his stringer of big crappies and with his rod and reel over his shoulder, he looked back at his favorite log and fishing hole.

"I've got to go to work. But I'll be back," he promised, and you didn't know whether he was talking to the fishermen in the nearby boats or if he had a personal relationship with his cherished honey hole that understood his farewell. It was clear that this hole of muddy water around a fallen tree was his claim to a little piece of heaven. Indeed, he would soon be back.

Stanly County Anglers Land Slabs

Fishing in a private pond, crappie-fishing veterans Pete Sides and Earl Simpson of Stanly County, pulled in two real giants of the species in early spring of 1990 that they will not soon forget.

Sides hauled in a 3-pound, 8-ounce crappie from the pond, and Simpson landed one that weighed 2-pounds, 11-ounces in the same area just a few days apart.

While it was not quite monster size, Pat Parker weighed in a 2-pound, 8-ounce crappie caught in another lake the same week that Sides and Simpson recorded their catches. It was a period when the big crappies were biting all over Lake Tillery and Badin Lake.

The North Carolina state crappie record is 4-pounds, 15-ounces. The national record weighed 6-pounds, and was caught from the bank with a cane pole in Louisiana.

163

Nice crappies from the Waccamaw.

Poor Man's Fly Fishing Pays Off in Swampy Carolina Rivers

A wide-brimmed, weather-beaten old straw hat shaded the eyes of a swarthy preoccupied fisherman riding alone in the bow of a homemade plywood bateau that quietly drifted with the current around a bend in the desolate, scenic Waccamaw River that winds its way through the Green Swamp in southeastern North Carolina. It crosses the border into the sister state, and on to its destination in Winyah Bay at Georgetown, South Carolina. The serious angler hardly noticed us as we slowed the outboard, and eased upstream past his wake in our sophisticated bass boat. We were scouting these blackwater, low country swampland flats for largemouths that often live to ripe old ages without having had the opportunity to reject the best laid lures of modern man. It truly is a picturesque Southern river with cypress-clad shorelines and dangling Spanish moss that makes every turn in the narrow stream another picture postcard that you could write home about. We were aware of this uniqueness, but the presence of this old native stoically situated in his boat with a limber cane pole and unusually long line got our attention quickly when we saw splashing on the surface beneath a willow bush, heard an envied noise of a fish in distress, and then the finale when the angler lipped a two- or three-pound bass. He quickly lifted it over the side and into his live-box built into the center of his tiny boat right behind where he sat on a six-inch pine board that was his bow sea.

This drama transpired in a matter of moments as we had simply intended to ease past this old timer on our way to alleged greener pastures a few miles north where some of the natives who live off the water at the village of Curuso Island land fine bream and crappie the year around. Perhaps there was a lesson to learn here, and from a distance we watched, holding on to an overhanging myrtle bush as the native angler's boat floated on toward the next oxbow in the Waccamaw.

With expertise obviously gained from years of experience on these river flats with overhead, surface and underwater obstacles arrayed as far as you could see, this veteran knew what he was doing, and his humble innovation from the normal fly fishing technique was the way to put fish in the boat. This was apparent as he put another crappie and two fine copperhead bream in the boat before he floated out of sight 200 yards downstream. We just observed with mouths agape. We knew we must learn more about this fisherman's method that was obviously successful, yet without outboard, trolling motor, rod, reel, net or anything electronic. He was really back to the basics with a two-foot "one-handed paddle" keeping him 30 feet from the bank and straight in the slow-moving water.

I turned loose of the limb that was holding us in place, cranked the motor and with more than the normal courtesy, we pulled near the old fisherman, passed along a friendly "hello" and attracted his attention.

"Sir, can we talk with you a minute?" I asked politely.

He glanced up, pulled the paddle a couple of times through the water, put his pole down in the boat, and grasped a limb from a sweetgum tree top that was half submerged on the west bank.

"Whatcha want to talk about?" he asked in an almost hostile tone, or at least it seemed so.

I introduced myself and my companion. "We have been impressed with how you are catching fish, and just wanted to see if you would share your experience and know-how with us."

"Oh, I don't know all that much about fishing. I just live up the swamp apiece. Born there. Fished and hunted this old Waccamaw all my life. I farm a little patch or two, but I makes a living fishing and hunting. Mind you, I don't do nothing against the law. I do sell some catfish, but these other fish I eat just about every day of the year. I do some whittling of dough trays, and once in a while I chop out another boat from a big cypress log. They's always a market for those log boats. My name's Dodo Clewis. Ever'body knows me around here," he said, and there was an unspoken hint that perhaps sometime in the past he had had run-ins with game wardens.

"We know something about fly fishing, and we catch our share of bass with that system and with rods and reels, but you seem to have unlocked a secret here with your cane pole. You are using it like a fly rig but without a reel. Can we take a look?" I asked

"Ain't nothin' to it. I just got some of this old plastic line, and tied it onto a 14-foot pole. I use a white bug for bait. You can see that this river is narrow here, no more than 40 or 50 feet in places, and if you tried to use one of them fly rods like I see on TV, you'd stay hung up half the time. With this little old boat, I kind of slip up on the fish, and I can flip that bug under the bushes where the fish are lying out. On cloudy days and early in the morning, you can catch a mess of crappie and bream just about every time," he revealed.

That was it. With an 8-pound test monofilament line about four feet longer than the pole, this veteran could hit a pork and bean can at 30 feet under the overhanging shoreline bushes. He was amazingly accurate, and convinced that unless you can "put the bug within about six inches of the bank" you won't catch any fish. He emphasized that just about every fish he caught struck the bug just a hand's width from the swampland shore in the darkest shade he could find.

He had a preference for colors. White was number one, but he liked that "light green" (chartreuse) bug too. He was using a medium-size popping bug with red eyes, and black hair sprouting out from the No. 4 Eagle Claw hook in that cork body. Four white rubber legs about an inch long protruded from around the bug's eyes. His technique was much like that we had experienced many times with more conventional fly gear. He put the bug in his honey hole, let it float motionless for half a minute or more. Then he flicked it a time or two with a twitch of the cane pole tip. If nothing happened, he snatched it out of the cover, let it buggy whip out in the open, and back it went within seconds to another likely-looking fish-hide under the bushes. His speed and accuracy were uncanny, made possible by years of trial and error, and no doubt many cuss words vibrated through this swamp from snarled lines on both sides of the river before he became the expert that he is today.

"Sometimes there's a spot under the bushes that's hard to get to with flipping the bug across the bow like I usually do. But it may be just the place where a big old copperhead or slab crappie might be looking for something to eat. I take the bug in my fingers, make a bow out of the pole, aim it right for the spot and let it go. Most times I get it where I want's it, and I get some big 'uns out," Clewis said, demonstrating his technique of sling-shotting the morsel into tiny openings along the bank where no normal fly-fishing expert would dare to tread.

"Do you ever use any other kind of bait for these fish with that fly-fishing system?" I asked Dodo.

"Yeah, sometimes I use a spinner, a gold'un. If the fish just ain't going after my bug on top, I knows they are there somewhere. I put on a shiner and maybe a cricket or worm, but sometimes nothing but the spinner. I flip it in the same holes as I do the bug, and I catch some good bream and goggle-eye (black crappie). I have some baits that look like a caterpillar worm on a gold hook, and it floats a spell, and then sinks kind of slow. It'll catch some bass and bream, too, on this old river," he said, and it was apparent that this old river rat was getting more talkative and sharing all his secrets.

"Is there any time of the year that this kind of fishing is better for you?" I asked.

"Yep, it's better in the summer and fall. You can catch some when the frosts quit in the spring, and a few crappie will strike even in the coldest days in the winter, but most of the fish hide under the bushes when the sun's bearing down. Then in the fall when the insects are plentiful and topple off the bushes, the bream bite real good. I think the fish know they can get something to eat when these insects get cold and fall off the leaves. They just hang around in the morning 'til the sun comes up and the skeeters and bugs start losing their grip on the bushes. Then I flip my little old bait right where the skeeters fall, and the fish are ready to swallow it," Dodo said.

"Until a few years ago I never saw one of these bugs that I bought at the hardware store in Tabor City. I just dug me a can of worms or caught some grasshoppers and crickets. Bream will still bite them too, but it's easier to get these bugs. They don't cost but about a dollar, and I can use them a day or two if some old mudfish or jack don't come along and take everything with him," Clewis acknowledged.

"Did you ever fish this way at any other place?" I questioned this expert again.

Yeah, I fish Lake Waccamaw sometimes. That's the headwaters of this river. The river is hard to get to up the swamp because of the trees that are all over the place and block the water. But you can put in at the lake apiece off the highway that goes from Whiteville to Wilmington (Highway 74). They's some good ramps up there, and fishing is good around the cypress knees all around the lake and the grass patches in the water at the river mouth are full of crappie and grass perch (punkinseed). I use this same old pole and same baits. I just pop it along the grassline or around the cypress stumps and stuff where it's not so light. The water's clear in Waccamaw, and you got to be quiet, and put the bait on the other side of the tree or somewhere that the fish don't spook. It's good to have a little boat like this then. It's hard to get in some of the close spots with a big boat like you fellows have, but you can fish the grass lines, and you can use those fly rods and reels there without getting hung up much like you would in the river," Dodo shares some of his know-how.

He was right on just about every count from the good months of the year, to the dark spots in the cover, to the fishing in Lake Waccamaw. We learned that on subsequent adventures when part of the time we adapted to Dodo's unsophisticated gear and caught limits of bream and crappie in the river after we learned to manipulate that bug into dishpan-size openings along the shoreline. But we were even more successful when we went to the lake that Dodo talked about. Lake Waccamaw is the largest freshwater lake created by nature in the South, except for Okeechobee in Florida. It was formed by a meteor centuries ago that blasted a five by seven mile hole in the Columbus County low country. Averaging about eight feet in depth with a pure white sand bottom, it has long been a fine freshwater fishing haven for many species.

We went there with fly rods and reels, tapered lines, wet and dry flies and all the sophisticated equipment in a new bass boat. The fish cooperated, and we had a thrilling adventure. We shifted to casting and spinning rods and reels and likewise put middle-size largemouths in the boat in quantities of bragging proportions. They loved spinners, crankbaits, topwaters and plastic worms. We had a ball more than once in that North Carolina fishing hotspot.

Reflecting on the experience, we owe Dodo Clewis some gratitude. He helped us find a good fishing hole, and showed us the way to use humble fishing gear and still taste success. As a matter of fact, we find ourselves back up that narrow, desolate river frequently now. It's a nearly undisturbed Paradise where neither the fish nor the fishermen are so refined that yesteryear's methods are frowned upon. And how can you imagine a more thrilling moment for a fisherman than that instant when he slingshots a man-made bug into a dark hole in the cover, and then feels like minnows are flouncing in his veins when he has both sight and sound tickle his senses as a fish explodes on the surface after the offering? It's a moment you'll remember up the Waccamaw.

169

Crappies love stick-ups and this one hit a jig in a brushpile.

Bass and Crappie Feed in the Holes When Hydrilla Thins Out

Lake Lochloosa was a veritable meadow with hydrilla as thick as 150 stalks to the square foot and more. The green peril discouraged even the most patient fisherman from forcing his outboard to push his boat through the surface wilderness that often choked down the prop and made escape from the aquatic

jungle of exotic greenery extremely difficult. Many veterans with expertise had to pole out of this thick mess when their motors could not produce enough power to put their boats on plane. Other less knowledgeable boaters burned up water pumps and ruined dozens of outboards.

While biologists and lay fishermen are acutely aware that

aquatic growth is necessary for a healthy population of bass and other species, when it reaches the epidemic proportions evident in Lake Lochloosa on many occasions in the last decade, it is such a nuisance as to make even the most avid hydrilla proponent question its value to the resource and the angling public. But from that chaos has come a ray of light that is making every student of the obnoxious plant, and its dominance in shallow lakes sit up and take note. It has its good and bad influence on fish and fishermen.

It's a pity it can't be present in reasonable quantities, but that's one of the tragedies of hydrilla. Generally, it's feast or famine with too much or none at all. In the twin lakes of Lochloosa and Orange in Alachua County, Florida, where there was great fishing before the advent of hydrilla in 1976, and times of great bass fishing since then, the plant has often covered almost all of the 23,000 acres in the area, and hundreds of fishermen gave up catching any species in the watery wilderness. You just couldn't get the hook down with natural baits, and even topwater lures fouled on the dense surface growth and gave the fish little chance to strike. When you did hang a nice fish, you didn't know whether it was a 1-pound yearling or a 10-pound giant because she buried in the thick hydrilla, and you had to hunt the fish like a needle in a haystack when you finally pulled all the greenery to the gunnels of the boat.

It must be noted that a few diehards fished even the bad years when the hydrilla was thickest. Some found a few holes in which they could float shiners and catch big bass, or they dropped lures in small openings and pulled fish in with the hay. But for most anglers, native and tourist, the fishing in these once prolific waters was not worth the effort. Fish camps suffered and many families who moved here for the once excellent angling, packed up and moved away. It seemed tragic, comparable to the 1954 sinkhole that opened in Orange Lake and sent the whole 13,600 acres of water plunging into the bowels of the earth, and Lochloosa became a shallow pond.

In the spring of 1986, the St. John's Water Management District was appropriated enough money to treat a small portion of Lochloosa with the newest S.O.N.A.R. chemical spray. It had helped three years previously when it was used for the first time, but the plant came back more vigorous and stronger than ever. The agency sprayed a few hundred acres and some fantastic events transpired within weeks of the treatment. Fishermen again smiled on Lochloosa, and when they tied up their boats in the Cross Creek marinas to show off their catches.

One old-timer who has fished these lakes all of his life explained why he thinks the catch success was so astoundingly good.

"The bass and the crappie are hungry, real hungry. This hydrilla was so dense over so much of the lake for so long that the forage fish had too much hiding habitat. The predators had not been able to feed like they normally would. They could not get to the food fish. Then holes of a couple of hundred acres appeared in the open, deep water off from the shoreline that had been unfishable for months because of the hydrilla. Some of the shad, shiners and gambusia minnows were out of their hiding places. The predators filled their stomachs. They chose to catch their prey in the open. The big fish came out of the woods, and literally were as thick as flies in this opening free of the aquatic jungle. It was a heyday for anglers.

"For the first time in a long time, the novices and the experts caught fish. Largemouth bass struck about any lure you threw at them. And the big speckled perch were right out there with the bass—and hungry. The crappie even went after the bass lures and, as a matter of fact, the bass anglers couldn't keep the specks off their hooks long enough to give the bass a chance to strike. Obviously, there were more specks than bass, but there were plenty of both.

"I believe that for the first time in many months, the predators caught all the food fish they wanted to eat. I think the thick hydrilla had been starving them, and now they are taking advantage of the clearing to gulp down anything that looks like a meal," the old veteran said.

He may have been right! Definitely, the bass and specks did bite in the open water the fastest they had in three or four years. While there was some problem fighting your way through the ring of hydrilla all around the lake, once you reached the open water where the chemical had temporarily knocked the weeds down, you could anchor the boat or troll along slowly, cast in any direction, and come in with some fine fish. One local angler caught a cooler full of mixed bass and specks in two hours, and didn't get out of an area larger than half a football field. The specks weighed up to 2-pounds, and he had three bass up to 8-pounds. He even had a couple of yearling-size sunshine bass, the hybrid stripers released in the lakes a few years ago.

Most of the fish being caught in the open water after the S.O.N.A.R. were hitting Rat-L-Traps, the small one, or Lee Scissoms midget deep-running crankbait that is about half the size of most minnow-style lures. But Mepps Spinners, Uncle Josh pork rinds and even brightly colored small spoons were fantastically productive.

Perhaps because the thick hydrilla absorbed much of the nutrient in the lakes, the water was almost as clear as a spring run. This clearness may be the reason why the specks and bass were biting best in the late afternoon, at dawn or on heavy overcast days. That trait suited the fishermen just fine in that most of the summer days in Central Florida are too hot for some anglers to stay out in the middle of the day. The striking habits of the fish made it possible to catch a nice stringer full in the cool of the afternoon and even at night, the time when some of the fishermen with daytime jobs are off duty, looking for recreation and meat for the table.

Of course, the hydrilla came back and filled these holes within a couple of years when the spraying stopped. But as long as the open water acres remained uncluttered, the fish swam out of the cover to where the food was plentiful.

Ironically, in the midst of this area cleared of hydrilla, is a man-made fish hide constructed by the Florida Game and Fresh Water Fish Commission before the weeds covered the lake. It is about a quarter acre of weighted, submerged tree tops. This cover became an attraction for the forage fish coming out of the much more dense hydrilla. It is marked with a buoy, and focuses in exactly where anglers can find a honey hole. While the catchable bass and specks seemed to be everywhere in this clearing, the bigger predators were caught around these tree tops. You'll still cuss some lure hang-ups in these trees, but it is not to be compared with the obstacles of dense hydrilla.

This phenomenon in the hydrilla-infested lakes in Florida may be a lesson for biologists in many of the other states where the exotic weed has spread since its unfortunate introduction in Florida some 20 years ago. It just may be possible to spray small portions of lakes when funds are not available to treat the whole area, and give fishermen at least a few months reprieve from the bondage of the weed when it is so dense that whole lakes are unfishable. It will grow back, but it generally takes a year or two to choke the surface so boats and fishermen cannot get to the fish. Control, not elimination, is the goal of the wildlife biologists where hydrilla is concerned.

Some fishermen mistakenly believe that cold weather kills hydrilla. That's a fantasy! It grows well in South Dakota even in lakes that freeze over two feet deep and more in the winter. The hydrilla is back healthy and growing as fast as the ice melts in the spring. Mechanical harvesting of hydrilla on the Rapid City water system lake has been going on for years. It grows back fast.

Others who live where lakes are deep believe they have no threat from the hydrilla because it won't reach the surface. It would be great to have it on the bottom where it would provide excellent bass and crappie cover. But it doesn't work that way. It has often been discovered growing to the surface in 30 feet of water, and there are places at Crystal River in Florida where it has grown to the surface in water that deep. This hardy plant will grow in almost all water that isn't salty. It grows in muddy or clear water and requires only two candlepower of light to thrive. It grows in shade or sunshine, and establishes tubers on the bottom that will sprout and replenish the crop even when a drawdown exposes the ground for years. Chemicals that destroy the weed growth in an area like that in Lochloosa do not kill the tubers. They will soon sprout new, healthy stalks that some say are even more vigorous than the original.

Areas along coastal streams where there is a tidal current have been able to accept and live with the hydrilla better than the natural lakes with little current and no outlets. Unusually high tides sometimes bring in saltwater that kills the plants and the weeds also may be broken loose by mechanical means and may float with the tide out to sea.

The beloved manatee eats hydrilla like man goes after strawberry shortcake. It is a delicacy for the old sea cow, and at Homosassa Springs, Florida, where manatees are nursed back to health when captured after being wounded by outboard motor props, they have eaten every stalk of the weed in the river where they are confined. The Homosassa State Park Attraction management has had to haul truck loads of hydrilla to the manatees to keep them well fed. They will eat their weight in hydrilla daily. But manatees will not survive in water that cools to 50 degrees or below.

Grass carp (white amur) have been introduced in some areas and this species eats the hydrilla with a passion. But most biologists disapprove of the weed-eating fish except in small lakes with no outlets to other public waters. It has been used in some states in limited quantities as a hybrid, usually sterile and

unable to reproduce. Biologists fear the grass carp will destroy too much of the friendly aquatic growth and root out the native gamefish species. The jury is still out on this controversial weed eater.

Controversy is rampant over whether hydrilla is a curse or a blessing, trash or treasure. Wherever two good fishermen get together, you have differing attitudes and ideas about this plant. One thing, however, is agreed upon by everyone. Hydrilla is a great thing for the fish, but not always for the fisherman. It would have the blessing of all the populace if it could be controlled. Unfortunately, it is uncontrollable and being spread by man and waterfowl. It becomes a menace, directly responsible for the deaths of several swimmers. It has clogged and choked hundreds of lakes and streams, and often deprives anglers of fishing opportunity. When there is insufficient money to spray a whole lake, maybe funds can be found to knock the weeds down in a sizeable opening in lakes so that fishermen can reach and bring home a mess of fish again. If it works at one place, perhaps it will work elsewhere, and make chemical treatment affordable. There are a lot of anglers happy that at least there are holes where you can catch fish after a S.O.N.A.R. treatment even when it doesn't destroy the exotic weed

Louisiana's Black Lake-Clear Lake Is a Paradise for Serious Crappie Fishermen

More than 35 miles of watery wilderness filled with standing cypress trees as far as you can see, interrupted only slightly by boat-trail channels, describes the unique complex of lakes near Campti, Louisiana, known as Black Lake-Clear Lake. It's a single body of tannic-colored water that joins under Highway 9, five miles east of Campti, and veteran panfishermen challenge anglers from everywhere to name a better honey hole for "white perch," the Cajun moniker for black crappie.

First-time visitors to Black Lake in the northwest corner of Louisiana in Natchitoches Parish, 100 miles from the ever-popular Toledo Bend reservoir, suddenly are agape when they emerge from boring miles of roadside pine and oak forests to eyeball an enticing jungle of cypress trees reminiscent of coastal Georgia, Florida and the Carolinas.

Even novices recognize a fishy lake when looking north from the bridge to Black Lake and south to its twin Clear Lake, identical fishing holes with water ranging from about 14 feet deep to three or four along the bush-covered shoreline. It's the classic crappie condo habitat, and anglers are usually in a tizzy to get a boat in the water. They launch at Black Lake Lodge on the eastern bank, a modern facility with lodging, food, tackle, bait, guides, licenses and friendly advice. In a matter of minutes, many start drowning minnows (they call them "shiners") or twitching tiny jigs around the cypress trunks and knees that seem to be growing everywhere. At Black Lake, there is no need for long boat rides. You can start dragging in slab-size crappies within rock-throwing distance of the landing. Indeed, some bank fishermen make fine catches from lawn-chair comfort with cane poles fishing around the riprap that supports the embankment of the low-level bridge.

Crappie do not spook easily in this jungle of trees. The water is mostly ten feet deep or more once you are a few yards away from the bank, and with the bottom literally covered with trunks, brush and roots, fish apparently feel they are occupying a safe haven. A motor putt-putting overhead causes only a momentary pause in the feeding frenzy.

Experienced Louisiana natives like Richard Childs who grew up fishing with his father near Shreveport, and now enjoys crappie stalking with his wife when he isn't guiding, says, "Crappie fishing here is a year-round sport. You don't have to troll for them in the open channels like some people used to do. If you can fish a small jig, and stay out of the limbs and bushes, you can take in a fine mess of big white perch (as he insists on calling crappies) every day you have time to fish.

"You do have to fish often enough to keep up with where they are holding. In the dead of winter, they are almost always suspended around some of the trees near the bridge where the water is the deepest. A little later on when they start looking for nesting grounds, and their bellies are full of eggs, they sometimes will move a little nearer the western shoreline, away from the launching ramp and road traffic. They do not spook easily with all this cover, but when they are in a spawning mood, they do search for a little more peaceful water," Guide Childs believes.

"In the spring, if I start around the trees near the channels and don't get some strikes quickly, I move toward the four-foot water nearer the shore. Often you can see the big spawners lolling just under the surface around the cypress trees. They hang around and spew out their eggs in the sand. That's a fine time to catch some really big crappie in the 3-pound class. You can even see them bite. Many of that size are also caught in the deep water after the spawn and throughout the winter. There are so many crappies here and the lake is so under-fished that even the novices usually carry a mess of fish home all year long," says Childs.

Shiny minnows that are sold at the Black Lake Lodge bait shop at the east end of the bridge, are great for crappies when impaled under the dorsal fin on a 2/0 gold hook and floated under a cork a foot or two off the bottom around the cypress tree or shoreline cover. A single lead shot eight inches above the hook keeps the minnow down, and light test line 4-6-pound test gets the most strikes. You'll lose some of the giants in the cover on this light line, but the extra strikes make it the most productive.

Almost all the professional guides and better lay anglers on Black Lake use fiberglass, 10-12 foot poles, although cane poles are still around. The Lew's Bream Buster is a favorite, as is the B 'n' M telescopic fiberglass marketed in nearby Mississippi. They are easy to handle in the trees. They store in the trunk of your car, and that makes them easy to transport. They seldom break, even with the largest panfish on the line, and one young man last spring dragged an 8-pound largemouth bass over the gunnels on an eight-pound test line and ten-foot B 'n' M pole.

"People here who fish for white perch (crappies) almost all use small jigs in the 1/64, 1/32 and 1/16-ounce sizes. They are marketed by Armstrong Cricket Farm in West Monroe, Louisiana, and the Black Lake Lodge store keeps a good supply of these jigs. They also sell crickets and artificial lures.

"I especially like the 1/32-ounce jig, in the clear color. I tie it on a six-pound test line, and when I am fishing the deep water out here in the woods, I want the line to be the same length as the pole. I use no lead or bobber. I just flip it around the cypress trees, and let it fall slowly to the bottom. Most of my hits come on the fall. If I get no strike on the fall, I keep jigging it from the bottom back to the top, letting it fall back a little after each twitch. There are not many times when a crappie doesn't hit it before I get it back to the surface. Slowness is one of the secrets to jigging for crappies. You can't be too fast. Take your time. Let the jig filter down real slow, then twitch and fall back, always retrieving slower than your instinct tells you," Guide Childs reveals a Black Lake technique.

"You asked me why I didn't fish with minnows. Well, economics plays a part in my fishing, and with most other natives here. If you fish with minnows, that's a nickel every time you bait your hook, and you are going to lose quite a few over the course of a day out here. A jig costs 65 cents retail, and I can fish day after day with it unless it hangs, and I break it off. It's a matter of money, plus, I think I can catch more crappie around these trees with a jig than I can with a live shiner," or so says Richard. "Many locals here live on fixed incomes and they want to save every penny they can. They don't buy live bait, and they can paddle their small boats out here where the fish are. That means they don't have to buy gasoline and outboard oil, either. This is a lake where you can fish economically."

Fishing a mid-March morning when a cold front pushes the thermometer down near freezing, it's easy to lose interest in crappie fishing even when a nice one gets on the jig every now and then, and you thrill to the tussle of fighting him around the

Mepps Double Cross spinner is a tried and true crappie catcher.

myriad of trees to the net. But it is made even more exciting by the uncertainty of what you have on the line until you eyeball the fish. Black Lake is full of nice bluegills and shellcrackers, and these plentiful species like the tiny jig as well as the crappies. There is even a larger, more challenging fish that strikes too, called a "barfish" by Richard. The name comes from the black horizontal stripes from head to tail. These fish are really striped bass and white bass or hybrids. Mostly they are one and two-pound size, but they are challenging on a light line and limber pole. Crappie fishermen sometimes stop where these are grouped up and fill a cooler with their so-called barfish.

"Bass strike these little lures, too. It's nothing unusual to land three or four in a half day of crappie fishing in the early spring and winter. But when the crappies are spawning, they bite so fast you don't have to worry about other species. You can catch 50-60 or more in half a day and have all you want.

"You may not believe it, but in the fall when the shad school on the surface here, largemouth bass are so thick that they will bite everything you throw at 'em. I've seen good bass fishermen here come in with 70 a day, many of them in the 6-7-pound class. Black Lake is really a great place for almost all the freshwater species found in the South. It's kind of remote and it does not have the fishing pressure that most great fishing lakes have," Richard Childs testifies to a truly great place to catch crappies, bream, barfish and even largemouth bass.

You can reach Black Lake by turning north off Highway 84, at Clarence, Louisiana, onto Highway 71. Eight miles up 71 is the village of Campti. Turn right on Highway 9, and Black Lake is five miles down that road. Full service facilities are located there. Chandler's Camp and Black Lake Lodge are on the lake, owned by Bill and Jean Baker. They have cottages, motel rooms, trailers, bait and tackle, boats, guides, a store and meals. You can contact them at P.O. Box 240, Creston, LA 71070. Telephone 318-875-2288

Crappie May Move When Pressure Disturbs Their Feeding Zones

Author catches a yearling crappie.

One hundred and twenty boats were within slingshot distance of each other in the open water of Lake Okeechobee in south Florida. All were slow trolling or drifting for speckled perch (crappies) in some of the deepest water of the lake where this gourmet species can be caught in all seasons with minnows, jigs, small crankbaits, spinners or a combination of the artificial with trailing live bait. Looking over the armada of boats, you were keenly aware that a lot of fish were being pulled over the gunnels. There were standing anglers in at least half the boats almost constantly and that's reason to know fish are being pulled in even if you can't see the silvery creature fluttering on the line. Most would be sitting down if the fish were not biting.

With so many boats moving over a relatively small area of the lake, an observer would know from a quick glance that the specks were concentrated. And once a few boats come close together, it attracts all the others within eyeball range. The assumption is usually true, there must be some specks biting at that spot or the boats wouldn't be congregated. Thus, most of the boats in the lake eventually converge on a relatively localized hotspot and fish so close together that they sometimes get lines tangled. They are often close enough to fish in each other's live-wells or wire baskets hung along the side of the boats. It rankles the short tempered to be crowded but he can't do much about it. If he objects, he might have to listen to invectives or at least a redneck yell "you think you own this damn lake."

What the crowding of a hot area does is greatly reduce the period that the fish will be there. If they are not bedding in the open water, which they often do, then they are feeding. It is a hotspot for the crappie as well as for the fisherman. It has bottom aquatic growth or cover or maybe structure from an old creek channel. Some reason makes it more desirable for the foraging fish than other areas of the huge lake, impoundment or stream.

Open water fishing today normally means that trolling motors or small outboards are pushing the boats along. They may be almost noiseless but when more than 100 are focused in a small area, it still creates unnatural currents and noise and may spook the schools from the immediate honey hole. They may be there for two or three days despite the chaos, but often they will move overnight and the anglers have the chore of relocating the fish. It's the normal reaction of a fisherman to return to the spot where he caught fish the day before, the week before or even last year. That observation has validity but when more than normal human pressure is pinpointed, crappie may decide there is better pasture elsewhere.

Then what do you do next morning when the crappie have abandoned the hotspot of the previous day?

When the 120 boats spooked the speckled perch from Okeechobee that morning and not a bite could be seen the next day, it was obvious that they had moved; we had not caught them all, they were avoiding the boats.

I went to the north end of the lake at a spot the depthfinder determined was slightly deeper than the rest of the water in the area. I put the wind on the stern of the boat, put my trolling motor on slow speed, and headed for the south shoreline five miles away. I had traveled no more than half a mile when my Lew Childres & Sons Breambuster bent and the tip of the pole fluttered under the surface. It was a healthy strike that no little fellow could have conceived. I pulled the pole out of the holder and lifted the butt end. It tried to stay down and a real slab half-circled the boat, popped almost to the surface, turned and dived again. The white flash of the turn was enough to excite my companion in the boat.

"You got a real horse, this time!" he said.

And indeed it was. It made two other runs to the surface, popped my 8-pound-test line and was free. It may have been my biggest crappie hookup ever. The big ones truly always get away, as that one did.

Minutes later, and not a hundred yards from where the trophy speck escaped, my partner had two strikes at once in the back of the boat and I had another on the starboard bow.

"This is it! Throw the marker over!" I shouted. "The specks are here or we wouldn't be getting multiple hits at the same instant." He tossed the little H-shaped, orange buoy over the side and it unwound until the weight hit the bottom. The depth was just over six feet, about the same as that where the specks were congregated the day before.

We began circling the marker slowly. There was not another boat within hollering distance but many were still plying the waters to the south where the fish were biting the previous day. There were no standers in those boats. The action was nil. But we had found the mother lode. This newly discovered area was swarming with specks and we quickly began pulling in all sizes with a combination Mepps Spinner with a two-inch minnow impaled through the eyes on a 2/0 gold hook. That, and the ever-popular Mini-Jig, was the choice of the crappie that day and they lost no time striking whenever it was trolled a foot off the bottom with three shot up the line and a small bobber riding calmly on the surface when the boat moved at the proper speed. You knew the hook and bait were near the bottom when the line from the end of the pole to the water descended at about a 60-degree angle.

We discovered something else trolling that morning. With the poles all held in rod holders mounted on the gunnels, the specks bit those poles best that had no more than 18 inches of line between the pole tip and the bobber. Those that had more line apparently didn't give the bait the proper life-like action. Those with shorter space between the tip and the bobber perhaps had action that frightened the fish.

One thing was for sure, these fish had been frightened, spooked or disturbed the day before. They had not accepted the chaos of so many boats in the same area. They had moved during the night and were as thick as the proverbial hair on a dog's back in this new spot.

Noise is not something that will normally chase speckled perch away. As a matter of fact, many times I have seen Southern Florida natives fishing in grass, lilies or in brush cover splash water with their rods or poles or even a paddle all over their floating bobbers. Sometimes the crappies would strike the bait before the ripples from the splashing subsided. It indicated that the fish must have actually come to the melee, perhaps surmising that this was a place where fish were feeding in a frenzy and making unusual noise. Some crappie anglers even carry buckets of coarse sand with them in a boat and chum an area with this grit that allegedly attracts fish in the area.

But there is something about too much pressure in a localized area running the fish away, at least temporarily. Often they will return to that feeding spot later, but only when it has calmed down for a few days when the armada of fishermen has moved elsewhere in search of a concentration.

In shallows where crappie are nesting, it takes a lot of racket and water disturbance to stop them from returning. They seem to make up their minds where they want to spew out their eggs and if you don't yank the fish out of the water on a hook, she will lay or bust. Often you will catch a cooler full of specks in a lily pad nest without moving the boat, even when you have a host of boaters reaching for your hot spot. But open water crappie, feeding and frolicking with only bottom cover and no urge to spawn, may decide to move along when a large number of their school is caught and there are hundreds of baited hooks and lines being dragged through their playgrounds by a whirling gizmo near the surface. They may not have intelligence but there is some kind of instinctive prodding to move along.

The patient, astute crappie angler will not let this itinerant factor spoil his fishing trip. He will think and use his experience to decide where these fish might have moved. Then by trial and error he will again pinpoint the concentration and hopefully, with most of his competitor anglers far away, have a chance to catch his limit in comparative solitude until the word leaks out. And leak out it will. It's always just a matter of time until the best laid plans of mice and men go awry.

But the angler who gets there firstest with the mostest is likely to be the winner at day's end.

Veteran Lady Guide Freddie Tanner Uses Experience to Find Panfish

With the deck of her comfortable pontoon boat a beehive of human activity, Freddie Tanner, a veteran lady panfish guide on Orange and Lochloosa lakes in Alachua County, moves along the lily lines until she spots the tell-tale signs that make her successful. Then she either uses her trolling motor to stay with the fish or anchors on the honey hole while as many as a dozen novice anglers drag in specks and bream with humble cane poles that are far more practical than rods and reels on a crowded pontoon.

Long ago she learned how to detect schools of fish, and she uses that expertise to put panfish in the cooler today. But her earliest fishing experience was not as pleasant as most of her adventures today. Really, it was so traumatic that you wonder why she still loves to fish and guide.

She recalls that painful experience when she was three. Fishing with her mother, an avid angler all of her life, Freddie was fishing from the bank of a Brooks County, Georgia, creek near their home when a catfish came flying through the air, hit her in the forehead, and stuck there. Scared and hurting, the tiny girl screamed. Her mother, who had jerked the catfish out of the water only to see it come unbuttoned and zoom toward her baby, tried to pacify Freddie while jerking the dangerous, painful gill barb from her forehead. It burned like fire, as all such catfish stings do. Blood trickled down Freddie's tear-stained cheeks.

That was a bad start for Freddie's fishing career, but today the prominent lady panfish guide at Cross Creek, and her pontoon boat loaded with excited clients, is a frequent conversation topic when she docks on the canal behind her home and unloads the day's catch. The catfish spiking when she was a tiny tot is still remembered, but only as a novel occurrence of long ago.

The experience didn't dampen the enthusiasm Freddie had for fishing. She continued to stalk bream and crappies in the Georgia streams with her mother, father and brothers for years. It was a classic fishing family. (Her brother, Wilburn Folsom

185

guides bass fishermen in the Florida Panhandle lakes today with great success).

Another case of good and bad luck occurred after Freddie moved to Cross Creek. She was casting a broken-back Rapala from the bank into the canal behind her home. There was an explosion on the surface. Freddie set the hook and reeled in the largest speckled perch of her life. It weighed more than 4-pounds. Traditionally, record fish are eaten. She ate that big crappie that would have been a new Florida record if certified.

That was in 1982 when the short creek connecting Orange and Lochloosa lakes was almost dry. The fish gathered in the holes in the creek and the canals, and Freddie had some of her best luck then. Fishing from a small boat in the shallow water, Freddie caught 270 largemouth bass that summer right in her back yard, and loads of bream and specks.

Following that long drought, Freddie bought a 24-foot pontoon boat, and launched her panfish guiding career on the two lakes she had access to from her dock on Cross Creek—Orange and Lochloosa, about 23,000 acres of prolific water for panfish and largemouth bass. She has been occupied with guiding doctors, lawyers, Boy Scout troops, Sunday School classes, small business staffs, among others, at least 100 days a year since turning to professional guiding.

Primarily guiding for speckled perch (crappie) and bream (bluegills and shellcrackers), Freddie has unlocked the secret to finding and catching these panfish from her huge pontoon boat, proving you don't have to be cautious.

"When I am fishing the open water of these lakes, often trolling or drifting slowly, I look for the oily bubbles that rise and burst on the surface. These bubbles are formed when fish are rooting on the bottom, releasing gasses from the muck. Once I see several of these oily spots together, I anchor. I expect to catch bedding or schooling fish around these oily bubbles. I usually do.

"When I am fishing the aquatic cover, spatterdock lilies, tall grasses or weeds, I look for the fish bumps. If there are many crappies in the cover, they will make mad dashes for the gambusia minnows and other forage food. They are careless and slam right into the stalks of the lilies and weeds. You can see those bumps from 50 feet away. The shake is much like that you would expect if a submerged diver simply took hold of the stalk with his hand and shook it. It is a far different movement from that made by the wind or the current. The bumps are dead giveaways for panfish that I guide for," Freddie reveals one of her observations.

You can tell when something alive does the bumping. Crappie in the fall, winter and spring, and bream in the summer, are often betrayed by their own carelessness in recklessly ambushing food in their territory and bumping the lilies and weeds. It's a sure sign of fish.

While Freddie is coy about other secrets that help her find panfish for her clients, she observes the flotsam on the surface around the lilies and grasses. When she sees an accumulation of hair-like white roots in the cover, that's a proof in Central Florida that bedding fish are around. They root up the fibers from the bottom. These roots rise to the top and another Judas revelation is observed. The whiter the roots, the more recent the rooting. Stained or brown roots may mean the fish have spawned and left, but often the fish will hang around for days, the brown roots still betraying their presence.

"One of my ways of enticing speckled perch to bite is easy on a pontoon boat. It is what I call a 'bobbing bait.' We have poles sticking out from the rail with bobbers and baits. If it is calm and the baits are not moving, we rock the boat. Dancing on the pontoon or running back and forth across the deck makes the boat rock and roll. It gives the minnow, hooked through the eyes or under the dorsal fin, action. Often this brings strikes on both sides of the boat when otherwise things are quiet," Freddie reveals another of her successful tactics.

She has some advantages over many other guides in the lakes she fishes. She has lived on these waters so long that she knows where the springs are located that feed the lakes. These unmarked flows often attract crappie and bream. When the bumps, roots and other revelations fail to show, Freddie anchors in the spring runs. It's the place where fish like to hang out. The water stays at 72 degrees the year around, an ideal temperature for most freshwater species in Florida.

She remembers well the morning her clients pulled in 97 bream from the same hole. Then in 1986, there is the never-to-be forgotten day when she caught 15 big catfish that weighed 60-pounds. She seldom guides for largemouth bass, but when she does, she usually fishes live shiners. She has an 8-pound, 6-ounce largemouth mounted that she caught on a shiner.

There is a distinct difference in the panfish hooks Freddie uses compared to the conventional hardware. She insists upon the tiniest No. 12 shiner-bait hook she can buy. She says her minnows live longer on these small hooks and she seldom misses a bream or crappie strike because the fish gulp the hook down. There are few fish lip-hooked by Freddie's pontoon boat anglers.

When trolling the open water for speckled perch, Freddie has some lines with Beetle Spins and a minnow impaled through the eyes. On other hooks, she has only a minnow. She watches for results, and adapts all the lines to whatever seems to attract the most strikes. Normally the combination of jig and minnow is more successful than the minnow alone. Adding meat helps.

"One of the rewards for guiding on a pontoon boat is seeing the happiness in the eyes of my clients. I remember guiding seven doctors a few years ago. They had not seen each other since they were in school together 30 years ago. They scattered and practiced all over the country. They had a reunion on the boat, caught a few fish, cooked, ate and had a great time. You don't forget seeing people enjoy themselves like that," Freddie remembers a good day.

She has a gas grill on the boat that gives clients a chance to cook hotdogs or hamburgers, maybe even broil a fish, for lunch.

When the creek is low, as it has been several times during Freddie's guiding career, she sometimes uses her trolling motor to get the pontoon out of the creek. She doesn't like to see her 50 horsepower Mercury overheat from the silt that it picks up when the water is too shallow.

"I'm afraid of storms. When it begins to thunder and lightning, I head for home. I remember I was out fishing one day with my father. I saw some sharp lightning. We were on a bream bed, and catching fish every time the hook went down. Dad wanted to stay right there, but I cranked up and left that bed. I don't like fishing in a big, tall boat like this when there's a thunderstorm brewing," Freddie shows her safety standards that most clients eventually appreciate.

This veteran lady guide knows where to fish and how to catch them. She has a common-sense approach to guiding, placing fellowship and safety ahead of a long stringer of crappie or bream. Her hundreds of clients over the last decade approve of her tactics. They must. Year after year she has many repeat customers, proof of the pudding.

Clients are glad the catfish accident at age three didn't scare this lady away from fishing forever.

Garfish Betray Bream on Beds

While birds, bugs and worms reveal the presence of bluegills and other panfish during spawning season, and when they are congregated and feeding, some species of fish betray bream, too.

Roland Martin, the Clewiston, Florida, bassing professional who heads a stable of veteran guides on Lake Okeechobee, says he is reluctant to reveal the well-kept secret but his garfish pattern has led him to successful bass fishing many times.

Martin notes that when he sees several garfish milling around, and they are easily observed because they swim lazily near the surface, he has confidence in catching bass on that spot. They mingle with the largemouths.

The same is true of bluegills and other panfish. Gars will find the bream beds and stay there for days as they feed off the gambusia minnows, shiners and other forage fish that live off the bream eggs, fry and fingerlings. Any sighting of garfish by bream anglers is a promising sign and the area should be fished intensely. Somewhere close by the bream are nesting.

189

This veteran fishes the dense cover.

Living Fish Attractor

Christmas trees make good crappie hideouts.

Newnans Lake—Fisheries scientists for the Florida Game and Fresh Water Fish Commission have planted living fish attractors in this sprawling lake east of Gainesville.

"The concept of living fish attractors is basically planting vegetation on the lake bottom to improve the habitat and therefore improve the fishing," said Jerry Krummrich, fisheries scientist for the Commission.

"Experimental test plots of maidencane grass were planted during 1989 to determine survival in the overly enriched water.

The initial planting of approximately 750 plants have established and are thriving," he said.

Maidencane is a common aquatic grass found throughout the Southeastern United States from New Jersey south to Florida and Texas. The plant is thought to have possibly been introduced from Brazil. It reproduces from seed and through the spread of rhizomes. The plant supplies valuable cover and spawning sites around the root mass for game and non-game fish. In clear water lakes, maidencane grows from dry land out to a water depth of 8-9 feet.

Krummrich's opinion is that the maidencane will establish, but that expansion will be slow due to the limited light penetration in the fertile, turbid water. He feels that once maidencane is established, expansion could be accelerated through the use of drawdowns or a naturally occurring drought which would expose shoreline areas to seed germination. The plant grows faster on wet soil or in shallow water, and is stimulated to spread and reproduce under these conditions. This arousal of the plant's reproductive cycle is the natural way to expand the plant's range.

The transplanting effort involved moving approximately 10,000 stems of the aquatic grass from Palestine Lake in Union County to shoreline areas of Newnans. The stems were planted in an average of 18 inches of water along several miles of shoreline.

Newnans Lake is a 5,800 acre area located two miles east of Gainesville. The lake is designated as a Fish Management Area and a fishing license stamp is required of all fishermen between the ages of 16 and 64. Resident senior citizens and those certified totally and permanently disabled may obtain a free fishing and hunting certificate from the county tax collector. Children under the age of 16 do not require a fishing license stamp.

As the sun sets, crappie anglers linger for that
last strike of the day.

192

Many astute crappie regulars use cane poles.

Fishing on a Tight Budget

Fishing offers relaxation, solitude and a bonus of nutritious, tasty food for the table. Equipment can be as simple as a cane pole and bucket of worms and areas to fish are plentiful.

Fishermen without a boat can utilize fishing piers constructed by the Game and Fresh Water Fish Commission on Alligator and Watertown lakes, near Lake City, Suwannee Lake, near Live Oak, Koon Lake, near Mayo and the Jacksonville Urban Ponds throughout Duval County.

Bank fishing access in Florida is available to the Suwannee River from the Big Shoals Wildlife Management Area near the town of White Springs. The area has approximately 5 miles of river frontage. The Cypress Creek Wildlife Management Area, located in Hamilton County extends for 6 miles along the Suwannee. Both areas are open to fishing throughout the year. Access to fish is also available at most boat ramps on the river.

Other possibilities for the bank fisherman include: Sampson Canal between Sampson and Rowell lakes near Starke; Newnans Lake County Park, located on State Road 24 near Gainesville and Winsor Canal in Winsor.

In calm streams, canoes can be used to stalk **crappies**.

Escaped Slab Crappie
Taught Me a Lesson in Lake Okeechobee

Winds swept over the vast waters of Lake Okeechobee and waves swelled to white-cap proportions just off King's Bar where I bobbed along trolling for the speckled perch that is one of the most sought-after freshwater species in the country during the winter months. Miraculously, in that rough water I spotted my red and white, two-inch-long styrofoam bobber that a giant speck had wrestled away from me the previous day, breaking my 14-pound-test Stren monofilament line just inches from the end of my six-year-old, well "set" cane pole tip. That strike the day before had made the pole "set" multiply two-fold before the crack of the line parting spelled curtains for any chance I had of landing a real trophy panfish in that eight-foot-deep cove. I watched it disappear into the cider-colored waters for what I believed to be the finale of that episode. But it was not to be.

Here I was in that same general section of the 750-square-mile lake 24 hours later with a near gale wind brewing, and my old familiar cork was no more than 20 feet off the starboard bow. It was moving into the waves and wind. That critter that stole my hook, line, bobber and sinker was still around. Perhaps he had staked out this territory like largemouth bass do, and no little old hook in his mouth was going to run him away.

I flipped the Motor-Guide trolling motor toward the slow-moving bobber, and gave chase. In the wind it was not easy, but I closed in, and sure enough, it was my old bobber. I could recognize it anywhere, for who else would have jammed a round toothpick down next to the black plug in the cork so the line would be tight and not slide up and down when I set the depth? Ten feet before I reached my quarry, it suddenly took off, like a submarine diving, and it was gone, perhaps forever this time. I was never able to get my hand on that loose line that dangled above the cork to lift my elusive catch over the gunnels. So what? How does this true incident relate to catching speckled perch, as the black crappie is called in Florida?

The escapee speck provides some facts essential to every

open-water speckled perch fisherman, and a study of that particular situation enhances your chances of limit catches those seasons of the year when you have to do more than just float a minnow down onto a saucer-like indentation in the sand. That spawning season in Florida is usually from about the full moon in December until the full moon in March, but when you learn to observe the habits and life-styles of the speckled perch, you don't have to wait for pregnancy periods and the maternity wards. You can catch plenty of this gourmet species any time.

That cork on the end of a line proved to me that even in the open expanses of Okeechobee, and where there was only a sandy bottom without cover, specks tend to remain in the same place, albeit, this one was trying to digest a No. 2/0 gold hook and 11 feet of my line.

It was also noteworthy that when I trolled right past this loosely tied out critter with my boat, poles jutting out on both sides and with hooks baited for specks, the hooked fish was a cool customer. He was in no hurry to swim away from my intrusion. But, when I turned the boat and headed in his direction, he took off rapidly, sounding and fleeing the territory.

Numerous times over the past 50 years of my speck fishing, I have lost lines with fish on them. In the shallow water where the fish can sink the cork only by swimming fast and pulling the bobber under, not from just lying on the bottom, it is normal to see your cork surface a few yards from the boat. As you move toward it, it will generally move away, but not often in panic flight, just fast enough to stay out of reach, and eventually to pull the bobber under. Several times I have been able to get hold of the line and pull the fish into the boat hand over hand. It indicates that specks are not really much afraid of human predators in boats with lines dangling morsels of food in front of their noses. They don't head for the bright blue yonder in panic. They stay around the same spot even if they have a hook in their mouth.

Almost every speckled perch fisherman has heard some wag suggest that the way to catch these fish is to locate their schools by catching one, tying a balloon or other float to him, then turning him loose. In theory, the speck will swim to his cousins, and stay with them while you are able to keep track of his movement by watching the balloon. Have you ever tried such a trick? I have, not once, but several times. The floating cork in this episode is the same kind of gimmick. But you cannot find a school of specks by tying a marker on a hooked fish. The natural instinct of wildlife is to flee from any relative that shows up that is hurt or hampered. Fish know that an injured cousin is easy prey for the bass, bowfin, pickerel, alligator, garfish and other predators, and they will not allow a disabled member of the family to coexist with the school. The same thing is true of wild turkeys on land. An injured turkey will be run off by the healthy members of the flock. Geese won't allow a hurt goose to fly with the flock. Other species of wildlife are likewise hostile to cripples in their midst.

Observing the action of the speck with my hook, line and cork fastened to him, I came to the conclusion that as long as I drifted or trolled along hoping for a strike, even in that rough water, the fish lolled in my path and showed little or no fright. As a matter of fact, I am reasonably sure that they will frequently be attracted to the whirr of the trolling motor or the splashing of water with the tip of the cane pole. I have seen native speck fishermen in Lake Okeechobee beat their cane pole tips in the water around the lilies, and then get bites immediately when they lowered a minnow in the same spot. Similarly, I have tested their awareness of noise around the prop of my trolling motor repeatedly by dragging a lure and minnow within two feet of the spinning blade. Often I catch more fish on that hook near the propeller than I do on lines dangling from the stern or 14 feet out from either side of the boat.

While admittedly it is conjecture and derived just from personal observation and no scientific study, it appears to me that as long as the boat moves slowly and gently through the neighborhood of schooling specks, they have no fear. But, once you rapidly change direction or speed, they are, at least momentarily, spooked. That tied-out speck didn't even bother to flee when I trolled past that floating cork. But when I spotted it and turned to give chase, the fish panicked, and made a fast dash away from the boat.

A similar deduction is apparent when you watch any game fish in an aquarium. Shiners, bluegills, shad and other forage fish swim all around them hour after hour. The bait species seem undisturbed about the proximity of the predator that is nonchalant, too. But, if that predator suddenly turns from his normal course and eyes the forage fish, chaos reigns. The forage fish scramble to get distance between them and the predator. It indicates an instinctive impulse to survive by leaving the area. You can absorb these conclusions and become a more successful year-around crappie fisherman.

Troll with a bobber up the line at a distance that will allow you to fish a foot or two off the bottom. I use the Water Gremlin clothespin-type lead weights. They can be put on the line easily and removed easily, and it is important to be able to change the amount of weight to conform to the wind conditions. If the water surface is absolutely smooth, the wind calm, you may need no more than three sinkers. If it is very windy, 15 miles an hour or above, you may need five big shot. With just a little wind, five to ten miles per hour, three shot is the best number. These shot will pull the cork under if you are still in the water, but that's as it should be with my system for catching specks. I have refined that technique for crappies over the last 20 years and I know it is productive.

A trolled jig and minnow combination will virtually guarantee a catch of speckled perch in Florida where they are congregated. You will also hook all sizes of largemouth bass, even when you are speck fishing. You can get some of them out with patience. I landed one 5 1/2-pounder on such a rig. Most of the really big lunkers will break away. You will also hang chain pickerel, mudfish, bluegills and just about any other fish that inhabits the area where you are fishing. Some people fish Super Jigs, and other type jigs, without live bait added to them. In bedding season, there is no doubt you can catch the fish without the minnows, and to some extent during other seasons. But if you are looking for a way to catch specks regularly 12 months of the year, in the open water that is free from encumbrances, my advice is to use the jig and the impaled minnow. Hal-Flies and Betts jigs are good, too.

Once you have settled on the pole, the line, the bobber, the hook and the live bait, technique becomes all important. You won't catch a speck a week just running your boat out in the lake and tossing the hook in the water. You must properly secure that pole to the boat and then move with a pattern that is proven and foolproof. Good, strong pole holders should be bolted to the gunnels just forward of the seats in the bow and stern. Insert the poles into these pole holders so that they are almost parallel to the water and perpendicular to the boat. If you have a trolling motor, then move with the wind at a speed that will pull your cork to the surface, the line angling downward at about 60-70 degrees so that it is dragged just off the bottom. If you have no trolling motor, and if you can idle your gasoline outboard down enough, you can troll with it, but I have never found that as satisfactory as other speck fishermen do. For those who want to use spinner baits, the outboard motor trolling usually works pretty well. If you have a wind in the ten mile an hour range, and this depends to some degree upon the weight of your fishing boat and amount of freeboard, you can simply drift those lines and catch fish. Always put the stern of the boat to the wind so you don't have the corks jumping up and down with the waves like you do when the wind hits broadside. This stern to the wind and bow headed away from the wind is by far the most productive, whether you are trolling or drifting.

Strikes are easily recognized. Not only does the cork disappear, your limber pole will bend, often down into the water. It's your pleasure then, to simply pull, maybe after a slight twitch to set the hook in the thin membrane of the speck's mouth. The jig hooks are small and some fishermen find it necessary to net the fish or they may fall off before you get them in the boat if they are in the pound range or above. Most specks weigh less than 1-pound. If you are using the 2/0 gold hook and homemade plastic attractor, usually you can lift specks right into the boat without netting. Netting is a nuisance if you don't need it. Hooks, lines, leads, and bobbers get tangled in the nylon net webbing and if you are impatient to get the hook back in the water, you will experience minutes of delay that are irritating.

Basically that's it! Troll smoothly through the areas of deeper water where you believe the perch are schooling. They will not spook from your moving boat right over their homeland if it is not herky-jerky. That means your baits are going to be appetizing, and right in their faces.

If you get numerous strikes in the same area, mark it with a floating plastic jug or bottle, and then smoothly circle through that section of water time after time as long as the bites continue. The chances are they will stay right there for some time if you don't spook them with sudden turns and rapid acceleration of the boat.

That's the best way to put a limit of specks in the boat. You can get them any day of the year if your lake isn't frozen over or the temperature unbearable. And when you have a limit of specks in the boat, you have one of the finest gourmet meals for your dinner table that money can buy—and this simple system is perhaps the least expensive fishing you can do.

Try it. . . you'll like it.

Brenda Carter with a big speck.

Pandemonium Panfish—
You May Have to Stir 'Em Up

We never learned his name. We did inadvertently discover that he was a native of the area who was serving his third tour with the Marine Corps at Camp Lejeune in North Carolina. He was visiting his parents at Cross Creek, Florida, that fall week prior to an overseas assignment in West Germany. We also learned that this outdoorsman was a master at catching panfish, using some of the most unusual tactics imaginable. Ironically, they worked. We have used his unique techniques to catch crappie and bream ever since that memorable September morning.

Speckled perch (crappie) and bluegills were intermingled in the same beds in Orange Lake. This happens fairly regularly in the fall in Florida when the first crappie spawning occurs at the same time the bream do their egg-laying finale for the season. The previous day when we were fishing with live grass shrimp in this same cover, we did fairly well for the off season, landing a dozen dark-colored male crappie and eight gripper-size bluegills. They all bit the wad of shrimp stuck on a 2/0 TruTurn hook and dangled three feet deep in the holes in the cow lilies with a tiny cork and the smallest lead shot eight inches above the hook. The 2/0 hook is a little large for bream but anything smaller loses crappie in the dense cover. So we used the 2/0 and caught most of our strikes. We had plenty of fish for a backyard cookout for a few neighbors.

The pungent smell of frying fish attracted the attention of others along the country road at The Creek, as it will anywhere in the land where human noses work. We generously offered to repeat the fish fry the following day with additional invited guests who felt slighted that first afternoon. We had no doubts about catching enough for the outing. The lily holes where they were nosing out nests and spawning like there was no tomorrow had plenty of panfish. We had not calculated on a gale-force wind that blew all night from the west, piling up floating hyacinths and wild cabbage all over the surface. The lily pads that the fish had selected for their fall breeding spree were solid with floating stuff.

You could not get a baited hook in the honey holes where the fish were the previous day.

For the better part of an hour, we rooted out small holes in the flotsam mess and tried to get a fish on the line, any kind of panfish that would feed some of the expectant guests at the cookout. But the holes closed fast. We were having no luck.

That's when the Marine motored into the same patch of lilies. He had been there the day before. He knew the fish were bedding in this spot and revealed an I-thought-so grin when we told him we had caught nothing. The surface cover made it almost impossible to fish. Maybe the specks and bream had left the bottom darkness looking for sunlight that would be needed to hatch their eggs. Or maybe they couldn't see our baits in the deep shadows when we did occasionally get a hook through the flotsam and near the bottom.

"They are still here but the environment has changed since yesterday. We are going to have to change that and wake the fish up. That's easy. Just stay put and let me do my thing," the Marine fisherman almost commanded. Discouraged and about ready to give up, we leaned back and curiously awaited this confident angler's next move.

He cranked the outboard, turned the steering wheel hard left and gunned the engine. The boat went round and round in that one acre patch of lilies a dozen times. Hyacinths, wild lettuce and everything that was not fastened to the bottom was washed all over the place by the huge wake from the circling boat and roaring outboard. Anyone who has ever fished for bream and specks in Florida and witnessed such a fiasco would have been ready to take in the lines and head for home. It was over! But Yogi Berra made the classic remark, "It's never over 'til it's over." He was talking about a baseball game, but it's just as true in panfishing.

With the wild escapade over, there were holes in the lilies as big as picnic tables. Much of the floating aquatic junk plants that had covered the surface, washed completely out of the pads. A light breeze was carrying them out into the open water.

The Marine fisherman cut his engine, unwrapped his line from a B 'n' M fiberglass pole, impaled a translucent shrimp and dropped his bait in a wide-open space five feet in front of his boat. Then he leaned back, looked at us and began to talk.

"Move on over this way. Find yourself a clear hole and put your bait in the water. We have to wait a few minutes. When you

202

Despite stick-ups and hydrilla, this veteran lands his fish.

create all this uproar and turmoil, it takes the bluegills about ten minutes to come back to their beds. The few shellcrackers that are here won't come back for about 12 minutes. The specks will be the first to return. They will be back here in five or six minutes. Crappie do not spook as easily or stay spooked as long as the other panfish."

We will never know how this veteran panfisherman arrived at those spook time limits or even if he was accurate. We only know that in a few more minutes, maybe five or six, the specks were back. We had them on two hooks at the same time and pulled nice squirming slabs from the big holes. Within his time frame, both bream and shellcrackers also gulped down our baits and we fought them to the gunnels too. We were too busy catching fish to watch a time clock.

"You will notice that the blackish, male crappie bite the shrimp better than the lighter-colored females. Almost every one you catch on shrimp in fact is a black male. Later in the winter the males and females bite minnows better. They seem to know there are few wild shrimp in the cold water."

An hour passed and we had plenty of panfish for the afternoon festivities in the backyard. We had learned something and caught fish too. Panfish will return to a bed in a short time regardless of how much racket and noise you make. They have a driving instinct to spawn and populate the lakes with their species. If the cover was attractive for bedding before the surface stuff washed in, they will stay there until their breeding frenzy is finished. Man may help himself by doing whatever surface cleanup he finds will help get the bait in front of the fish. Then with a little patience, you'll have the panfish pinpointed on the beds again. They are indeed pandemonium panfish and the vacationing Marine helped us discover a pattern that has put a lot of specks and bream on the table for a generation.

I wish I had asked him his name.

When You Are Fogged In, Night Fishing Or Otherwise Lost, Crappie Still Bite

You don't have to know exactly where you are fishing to catch crappies. If you are in a lake where these fish are plentiful, as they are in virtually all of the lower 48, have the right lures, and understand their open water life-styles, then fish your lure slowly and properly, you may come home with enough of these gourmet panfish to feed the family, even if you didn't know where you were when they started flouncing over the gunnels.

Bubbles popped to the top at dawn that winter morning when I was fogged in tight on Orange Lake in Florida. Those bubbles probably meant that there were some fish on the bottom moving around and releasing gases from the muck. If they had been more than a dozen feet from the boat, I wouldn't have been able to even see the bubbles. I was fogged in so tight that I could see neither shoreline in this 13,000 acre lake, indeed I couldn't recognize my best friend in a boat 30 feet away. It was like being shut in a closet with white mist almost as thick as rain. It wet my hair and dripped off my cap bill. Obviously, if there was a special area out here in the 14-foot water where the speckled perch (crappie) hung out in greater numbers than in most spots, I could never locate them with a horizon fix. There were no visible objects to navigate by. So, how do you find the panfish species in the dark, especially when there is no structure on the bottom to find with a depthfinder? The truth is, you can't get off the lake unless you have a good compass and some experience navigating with it. You are trapped with your visual senses almost useless in such circumstances. All is not lost. You can still fill the live-box by patiently stalking the species that doesn't stop feeding simply because you can't see where you are.

Using the now-popular trolling system practiced widely all over the South, you may catch as many fish as you would on a clear day when you were not lost.

If you have some spoon plugs in various colors, flip one

out and let it move along near the bottom off the stern. If you have pole or rod holders on the gunnels, tie on several colors of Mini-Jigs (Midwest Lures, Jonesboro, AK), weight them down with three or four No. 6 split shot, thread an oblong cork on the line, and start trolling **with the wind**.

Move at the speed that will drag your cork to the surface, the leaded line and jig hanging down at about 60 degrees. If you keep the wind on the stern, move slowly with the spoon plugs and jigs flirting with the bottom, it won't be long before you'll see or feel some yanks on the rod or poles. You have located your prey. If you get more than one bump simultaneously, there may be a big school in your path. Start making circles, tight circles. Even if there is little visibility, you may hang close to your honey spot for some time by dropping out a marker. I like to have a one-gallon plastic jug with half a brick for an anchor. It's easy to see and has no value if you lose it. Keep circling your jug until the strikes cease.

If you have trouble getting strikes on the Mini-Jigs or Spoon Plugs, sweeten it up a bit by hooking on small minnows through the eyes or lips. Sometimes no added natural bait is necessary. At other times, specks are reluctant to make the mistake of hitting an inanimate object. The live minnow turns them on.

While everyone isn't sold on it, the gamefish Fish Formula sprayed on your jig and minnow and the spoon plugs, will bring strikes you might otherwise have missed. Even after talking for two hours with Fish Formula proponent Bill Dance, I was not sold on its productiveness in crappie fishing. Bill has long been sure it is a significant help when crappie fishing. Over the years I have scoffed at it, even though positive that Dance is a credible professional and trustworthy. I now feel sure that the scent does help, particularly when I'm not sure where the fish are schooled and I'm searching. Recently when the specks were scarce, I sprayed a single jig and minnow while leaving my other four hooks, baited similarly, alone. I was amazed that this scented bait caught five nice fish before I got a bite on any of the other lines. It was a convincing experience and too much to charge to chance.

Fogged in, sometimes until near noon in Florida, make the most of your senses other than sight. Listen! Crappie like to flip on the surface. You can almost always tell whether a break on the water was the action of a crappie.

The tail will pop when it comes over, as contrasted to a sucking sound made by bream. Bass make a bigger splash. Once you identify a crappie noise, head for it. They will almost always hit when they are frolicking on the surface. While it is true that once they flip on top they will dive back near the bottom, they will look up, suspend, and are poised for another rush to the surface if a meal is in sight. Listening and learning to identify surface splashes will make you a better speckled perch angler when you are blinded by fog or darkness.

Smell is important too, but not as much help as a flop on top. Specks will often give off a scent as distinct as a fish market. When you sense it, fish it. You may have located the mother lode. Unfortunately, the crappie smell may be confused with a school of shad or shiners. But if it is a strong smell and you dangle your baits in the area a few minutes without a hit, you may be smelling something other than your desired quarry.

I once thought I had a crappie school smell and was intensely fishing the spot. I was getting no strikes and neither was another boat a short distance away. I gave up and as I trolled away, I noticed a fisherman in the other boat was eating from a can of sardines. That was what I smelled.

On another occasion when I smelled something along the edge of a grass patch that was near the shoreline, I began searching for fish. Nothing bit, although the strange smell was strong. Finally, I got closer to the hill. There it was. A dead deer lay half covered with flies and other insects in the shallow water. It has been my experience that crappie congregations do not always smell the same. Wind, temperature and nearness to spawning areas often change the smell you detect. But I fish intensely every new smell my nose contacts when I'm blinded by fog or darkness.

Garfish are dead giveaways of crappie concentration. Even in the dense fog, you will often see the dorsal fins of gar fluttering on the surface. They are not there just for the exercise. They will gather where there is food and even half grown specks are forage food for gamefish that will swallow anything up to 1/4 of their lengths. Garfish get some of their oxygen from the air and surface more often than gamefish. Their flitting on top often is assurance that the fish you want are nearby.

Just make the most of your situation when you are fogged in. Don't crank up your outboard and race all over trying to find where you are. That's dangerous. Other boaters may have the same idea and collisions can be fatal. Stay put and fish where you are as you troll quietly with patience and astuteness. You may make a successful experience out of a day most people would not fish—fog creates hazards in visibility in which many will fear to troll. Often the weather doesn't look that bad when you leave the dock but fog rolls in once you are in the open. You can just sit there and grumble until it is blown away later in the day or you can start fishing. With a little luck and a few tips from fog fishermen with years of experience, you can fill the live-well and have a lot of fun pulling gourmet crappies into the boat while others cuss and fret about the elements. Fog doesn't turn the fish off, just fishermen who do not know how to cope with it

Anita Osterhage, lady guide in Florida
catches a speck at dark.

You Can Find Fall Crappies Feeding

Spawned out after the late months of spring, crappie usually return to deeper water and hide from the hot sun during the broiling heat of summer. Then skinny, flabby and hungry, they begin marauding along the tree and grass lines as the first cool days of autumn appear. They are seeking full stomachs of gambusia, insects, freshwater shrimp, and whatever other food supply isn't too big to swallow that moves near them. They are gluttons, and you can catch them in creel limits almost as well as when they are nesting in the spring. But it takes a little observation, and more expertise to put them in the boat in the fall.

They are not easily spooked in the fall when you find them in or near aquatic weeds and grasses. Often you can drive your boat with its outboard putt-putting right into the grass, let it idle out of gear, and catch crappie after hungry crappie on a redhead jig bounced near the bottom in a hole in the grass or along the open water a few yards from cover.

Two of South Carolina's finest crappie fishermen are Billy Vaughan and his son Tommy of Elloree, South Carolina. They catch fall crappie day in and day out with these jigs in four to six feet of water in a myriad of lakes and streams. And they never cut the motor off until their day's fishing is over.

"The vibration from an outboard that is out of gear will dislodge a lot of shrimp and tiny minnows from the moss and grass. Once these forage food creatures start falling toward the bottom, the crappie lying in wait of a gourmet meal will rise to take the scrambling critters, and they will take your jigs or live baits at the same time," Bill Vaughan says with confidence based on 45 years experience. He catches about 6,000 crappie a year in all seasons, and picnics with his neighbors at backyard fish fries.

But if you fail to find the crappie in the cover, you can still catch them in the fall by looking carefully for semi-deep water near cover, and by trolling for them. If you get your kicks out of catching crappie on light or ultralight spinning tackle, you can use that and bring home a meal for the family. But if you are less sophisticated and get a thrill from catching crappie on a cane pole or a Breambuster, it's just as good as the more elaborate tackle.

The almost sure way to catch these crappie in the fall is to ease your boat along through open water a few yards away from any normal cover using the jig and minnow technique previously described.

You can sit on these poles and catch some fish. You can hang on to them with your hands and catch some crappie. But you will do much better with some sturdy pole holders affixed to your boat gunnels so that you can troll with the poles perpendicular to the boat and parallel to the surface of the water. Your bait will move more life-like, and you'll do much better than you will sitting on a pole or even holding it in your hands.

Fall crappie to some degree are still much like those bedding in the spring in that they are schooling when they feed. When you get one strike and pull a keeper over the side, you'll do well to drop a marker on the spot, and circle it or make giant S's, criss-crossing that same area several times. Often the brothers and sisters of that first one you caught are still there waiting for the same attraction that caused their kinsman to disappear. If you have no store-bought marker, there's nothing better than a gallon Clorox jug with a piece of brick or cement block tied to it, and dropped over the side.

There are a few tricks that help bring the crappie running when you are trolling and not doing very well. In addition to that minnow on the jig that you have hooked through the eyes, you can take another small one and add him to the hook, impaling him just below the dorsal fin. That gives you a kind of cross on the hook and there are times when the fish will hit this dual bait when they refuse a single minnow and jig.

You'll also need to try several speeds, and that's why it's necessary to have a variable speed trolling motor. Depending upon the weight of your boat and its load, you'll find the right speed usually at three or four on a 12-speed motor. Remember, you want to move at a speed that just keeps your cork on top, the line dangling at about 60 degrees and the hook a foot off the bottom. Crappie cannot resist such a morsel and you'll bring home your share of fine gourmet fish in the fall in almost any of the freshwater lakes and rivers.

Fishing For Crappie?
(Watch). . .For the Birds

A great way to locate feeding crappies is to observe the purple martins diving for insects disturbed from their perches on weeds and floating debris on early foggy mornings in the Southland. . . .They truly become Judas birds for gamefish. If you locate them, you can catch 'em.

Splotches of leafless, half-dead hydrilla floated lazily on the surface of Lake Lochloosa and polka-dotted the calm, clear water of this Florida fishing Paradise on the early spring morning. A thick bank of greyish fog almost obscured the cypress-clad shoreline on this 8,600 acre panfish haven, long noted for its abundant populations of speckled perch (crappie), bream, warmouths and the renowned largemouth bass. The air was warmer than the water on this first real spring morning, and that caused the boiling cloud bank of fog that shrouded my bass boat, blacking out even the sun's rays that were fighting their way above the horizon and pounding the fog's upper layers. In time, the sun would win and the fog would submit to this superior force of nature.

Marveling at this maze of waterways lacing their way among the four-inch thick layer of hydrilla that had been uprooted by days of strong winds and a constant pecking and pulling of half a million coots during months of Florida's coldest winter in a hundred years, I was a little hesitant to guide my bass boat into the mess. But most of the hydrilla patches floating here were no larger than my living room, and there was plenty of water around them unclogged by this nuisance aquatic plant. I was certain I could weave my Bassmaster boat with its strong, variable speed Johnson trolling motor, near, but around, these tangled masses. I didn't wait to hang my lines and hooks that dangled from the half-dozen cane poles that sprouted from poleholders fore and aft, port and starboard. That's the way I fish for crappies. I troll slowly with 14-foot cane poles or 12-foot B 'n' M fiberglass poles, a small cork that rises to the surface despite the three lead shot that try to drag it under as I move along at moderate speed with jigs' hooks adorned with a small Missouri minnow impaled through the eyes. I learned years ago that a pink or purple jig with some live meat added is virtually irresistible to

211

crappies. Fished at the right speed and depth in waters where crappie populations are normal, you can catch them the year around. It requires a little knowledge of just how to rig the hooks, lines and sinkers and some know-how gained by experience as to where the fish are likely to congregate. I knew the more poles you have out, the greater your chances of enticing a strike. That's why my boat always looks like it is growing cane poles. Until 1980, Florida law prohibited an angler from using more than three fishing devices at one time, but the law was left off the books that year and unlimited poles can now protrude from adjustable holders on the gunwales of a boat. The law was changed back to three fishing devices per person for the 1981-82 season. (In some states it is illegal to troll any live bait).

I always troll these combination live and artificial baits about a foot off the bottom of lakes as shallow as the 12- to 14-foot Lochloosa. I generally hunt out the deepest holes in the lake, but on this particular morning when I saw those floating islands of hydrilla, I seemed to detect an inner voice prodding me to fish around that cover. After all, the water was eight feet deep or more, the crappie were full of roe, and on the prowl for a place to spawn and feed. The sandy bottom was attractive to them, and this species doesn't really care whether it spews out its eggs in ten inches of water or ten feet. It was worth a try. I turned my boat toward the area that was splotched with the floating stuff.

A hundred yards away, I noticed that a huge flock of purple martins, those swallow-like birds that take up Florida residence from early fall to late spring and then rush back North for the summer, were hovering, diving and skimming just above the surface where the hydrilla floated. They were eating breakfast out there a mile from the shoreline. That was not the normal place for purple martins that are notorious insect eaters on land in the low country where mosquitoes are abundant. They are so proficient at gulping down the pesky insects that harass people that numerous multi-family dwellings are erected for these birds by homeowners in many states. The sleek martins oblige by consuming literally thousands of mosquitoes and gnats daily, and perform a valuable service in insect eradication without the hazards of chemicals. For years, homeowners hung up an array of long-handled gourds that provided luxury hatcheries and nurseries for the martins. Some still do, but with a scarcity of gourds today, carpentry has replaced them with bird houses of two, three or more stories that are partitioned off into apartments with individual entrances. Anchored atop a 20 to 30 foot pole,

212

these modern martin houses attract whole flocks of energetic insect eaters. They destroy enough biting insects to allow lolling humans some outdoor peace at sundown.

There were, of course, no martin houses in the middle of Lochloosa, although there were some on the distant shoreline. But it was evident that there was an abundance of flying food available out here or the birds wouldn't be having such a heyday. I eased my boat close to the nearest floating hydrilla. A cork disappeared and the limber pole dipped and danced. I picked it up and gently set the hook while my heart pounded and I felt like minnows were flouncing in my veins. A 14-inch, pound-and-a-quarter speckled perch soon went in the live-box. For the next hour, I was like a one-armed paper hanger with the seven year itch, jumping from bow to stern after strikes on one hook or another. Each moment Xeroxed the past one. It was great, and I soon had a legal limit of 50 while dodging the islands of hydrilla and dragging my baited lures past the cover where the martins had led me.

I'll never forget the lesson. The high humidity and dense fog forced billions of gnats and mosquitoes to take refuge on the floating islands. They couldn't make landfall with their wings heavy from the moisture. They fought each other for landing space, some toppling into the water. This panic among the insects attracted the martins. The birds had a picnic. But those insects that fluttered on the water attracted millions of minnows. Obviously when this reunion of minnows flitted about the hydrilla patches, the larger predators were not far behind. Speckled perch schools were gorging themselves with gambusia, bluegills were sucking in the mosquitoes not caught in midair by the martins, and even largemouth bass, bowfins and chain pickerel had entered the fray. It was a bonanza not only for the fish, but the fishermen, and before the fog lifted in mid-morning, dozens of boats were milling around the floating, smelly aquatic material, and bent poles and light rods, along with the noise of flouncing fish on the water were proof enough that success was being enjoyed by all.

The tattler martins were responsible. Had they not flocked to where the insects had gathered, few fishermen would have taken the time to weave in and out of the hydrilla island patches. It usually resulted in losing lures, minnows and time when hydrilla fouled around the lines and the trolling motor prop. Most fishermen shunned these areas like the black plague, but it proved profitable then, and has since when I have found the

213

martins feeding and swooping gracefully along the water.

Birds have long been tattle-tales for striped bass fishermen as well as for saltwater anglers for blues, mackerel and other vicious predators of forage fish. Some striper fishermen in large lakes never go without binoculars and high-powered, fast boats. They cruise out into an area where stripers often school, stop, then begin looking for diving gulls. Gulls congregate above these schooling stripers for the tidbits of shad and herring left by striking stripers, often scooping up whole fish that have been crippled by the gluttonous "rocks." Once these active gulls are observed diving after surface morsels, these anglers rush to the scene and begin casting artificial shad look-alikes or jigs into the chaos. Stripers in their haste to fill their stomachs make mistakes and the live-box has another prisoner betrayed by the scavenging sea gulls, just as the martins tattled on the specks of Lochloosa that foggy morning.

Knowing the enthusiasm of striper fishermen for locating flocks of diving gulls that pinpoint feeding schools of rockfish, has prompted the Drose brothers, Don, Frank and Joe, all second generation striper guides at Santee-Cooper in South Carolina and frequent Florida anglers in the winter, to carry a box of soda crackers with them each time they guide a party fishing in that huge reservoir. Santee-Cooper is a 171,000-acre wilderness of water with dead forests everywhere, and submerged logs and stumps a threat to every careless boater.

"It is not uncommon for a boat to hit one of these logs and split its bottom open, Joe Drose says. "When that happens in this big water, you have to get help pretty quick, particularly when it is cold and you find your boat half-under and you hanging on for dear life. That's why I carry the crackers. You can crumble a handful of these on the surface and the gulls will come in droves from everywhere. There are always those human watchers in the distance who see the gulls diving and they rush in to what they think is a school of rocks. That gets help to us when our hollering for help is useless."

No one is carrying any crackers aboard speck-fishing boats on Lochloosa today as insurance in case of accidental capsizing. But there are more and more people observing the tattle-tale activities of the martins. They know these wily creatures can spot a food supply even in the fog and where one of nature's creations feed, other species are likely to gather as the survival of the fittest continues to be a first rule of nature on the water and the land.

Carelessness, Thievery
Disrupt and Ruin Many Best Laid Plans
for Fishing Holidays

Attention to all the details and a bit of caution at places where thieves may be looking for prey often make the difference between fun and futility for boat-fishing outdoorsmen on their angling holidays. There are myriad weird incidents and accidents that happen and ruin the best laid plans of mice and fishermen. Carelessness or thieves are generally the culprits.

The late Ruey Hewett and a fishing companion drove out from his Eastern North Carolina home in the wee hours of a spring morning. He was pulling his boat on a trailer behind his

Veteran angler teaches kids safety and technique.

station wagon. It was a sturdy, homemade bateau of marine plywood. A 10 horsepower outboard was clamped on the transom. The fishing buddies chatted and recounted fishing experiences for two hours as they moved along over several blacktop roads on the way to the Cape Fear River and a Wildlife Commission launching ramp where crappie and bream were biting.

Hewett made the turn at the ramp, got his car in position and looked through the rear window so he could back the trailer in the water. His mouth dropped open! His eyes flashed with disbelief! He had no trailer. Somewhere on the road it had quietly unhooked itself, and without disturbing the fishermen intent upon another day on the water, it was gone. Ruey spent the rest of that day looking for that unbuttoned trailer, boat and motor. He didn't find them. Somewhere there was a man who believed that finders are keepers, and he had a complete rig that was as cheap as stealing watermelons on a dark night from a neighbor's private patch.

George Tate and his crappie and striper fishing buddy were all set for a night fishing adventure at Lake Hartwell near Greenville, South Carolina on the Georgia border. They hooked their trailer to the sleek, almost new, bass boat and headed south. A dozen miles out of town the trailer began to bump. Dismayed with the unexpected problem, they stopped, got out of the car, and discovered a flat tire on the trailer. They had no spare. The night was still young. They would go back to Greenville, get another tire, return, make the switch and still get in several hours of fishing before the night was done.

They unhooked the trailer and rushed back to the tire store, bought the needed rubber and drove back to the trailer. A half hour later the flat was fixed. They joked about the inconvenience as they drove on to Hartwell and the launching ramp. George backed the trailer into the water. His friend parked the car, came back and sat down in the bow pedestal seat. George started the big 150 horsepower outboard, and looked upstream where he planned to go for the stripers. Alas! The boat wouldn't move even when George put the pedal to metal. He switched it off, thumbed the power tilt button, and the motor foot moved above the surface. He couldn't believe it! The propeller was gone. Some scoundrel had quickly removed the $400 stainless steel prop while the trailer was unattended on the roadside when they went for the tire. There was not a hook put in the water that night.

Arthur Prince was fishing in Orange Lake in Central Florida for panfish in his 14-foot Carolina boat with a 25-horsepower outboard. He was fishing alone, but friends were nearby in other boats, all pulling in shellcrackers from the spatterdock lilies in mid-summer.

"I believe I'll go in. I have enough fish, and it will soon be dark," he said as he put another fish in the live-well, and laid his rod and reel on the seat. He cranked his motor and was soon out of sight around the Cow Hammock Peninsula. He headed for the creek mouth. As usual, he was running flat out, as most boaters do, and steering the boat as he always had with the handle attached to the motor. His rod slipped off the seat. He turned loose of the steering handle, and grabbed for the rod, a reflex action. It was a near fatal mistake. As many boats will, his made a 180-degree turn. At full speed, Prince could not stay in his seat; he felt himself being catapulted into space. He grabbed the boat handle from midair, all in fractional seconds. The handle tore off from the motor. Arthur found himself treading water a half mile from the shoreline. He dropped the useless boat handle and tried to untie his shoes. He couldn't get them off. The boat motor stopped when the handle was wrenched off, and it floated a few yards away.

"I'll get back in the boat," Arthur muttered to himself as he used his best dog-paddling stroke. But fate was not on his side at the moment. A soft wind moved the empty boat away just a little faster than he could swim. After five minutes of futility and nearing exhaustion, he turned away from the boat and considered his other options. The first good luck was only yards away. A flotation cushion had fallen out of the boat when he did. For the moment, it was a partial lifesaver. He pushed it under his chest, and looked around. About 300 yards away was a grass bed. Perhaps it was shallow enough to wade. He had tragically discovered the cushion alone would not hold him up. He still had to kick and paddle, but not as vigorously as before when he had no cushion, and was scared and shocked.

Using all the stamina he had left, he reached the grass bed. But he could not touch the bottom. Completely exhausted now, he reached out and gathered as much of the tall, strong grass as he could, put the cushion on it, and let all of his body submerge except his face. He was slightly relieved to find he could breathe and stay afloat without working too hard. Maybe he would survive.

A half hour later, his friends whom he had left with the shellcrackers, rounded Cow Hammock and raced toward the creek. Providence played a hand. One of the fishermen spotted the empty boat on the horizon despite the dusk of early evening.

"That looks like Arthur's boat. What is he doing in the middle of the lake?" the fishing friend wondered. "We'd better go see," and he headed for the boat. Chagrin swept over the faces of the two fishermen when they saw the boat. It was empty, and everything inside was askew. It spelled tragedy.

"He must have fallen out," the driver sadly lamented as he

cut the engine so the boat could be towed in. That was the second lucky break for Prince. Boaters can hear almost nothing from any distance when their own outboard is running. With it quiet, sound travels well for long distances.

"I'm over here in the first grass bed," came a desperate but much welcomed yell in the near darkness.

Moments later, Prince was pulled over the gunnels, shaking from shock and exposure, but ever so thankful to be alive. He was saved by the bell, and the dislodged, wayward seat cushion that almost miraculously blew out of the boat.

Not nearly as dangerous, but yet disastrous enough to ruin a fishing day, was the unfortunate incident of the late Harry Bell in Lake Okeechobee in Florida. He was fishing in a bream bed a little further than he could conveniently reach with a 12-foot Lew Childres and Sons Breambuster fiberglass pole. He didn't want to move the boat any closer to the bed for fear of spooking the spawning panfish. They were biting his crickets as fast as he could get one to the bottom in the hat-size hole in the lilies. In desperation, he stepped up on the gunnels of the bow. That gave him a half foot, and he could reach the bream bed. Another boat raced by 100 feet away. Before Bell could brace himself, the wake churned through the lilies. The boat rocked and he fell flat on his face in the lake. The bream spooked, the spot was fish-less, and Harry came up spitting water and muttering. "The only thing I could think of was alligators." He hadn't forgotten the big 'gators he had watched a few yards away when the boat eased through the pads to the bream bed.

A little different trouble, but yet with shades of the same carelessness, happened to John Love, a veteran Tavares, Florida, angler. The water was high in Hanes Creek. Love had watched schooling bass playing in the creek all morning, but he couldn't reach them from shore. He climbed in his plywood boat, picked up a short, one-handed paddle, and was soon out in the creek's current headed for Lake Griffin. He would fish the edge of the creek for a mile or so, he decided, and he kept his boat near the middle of the stream as he adroitly maneuvered the ten foot boat. He put a couple of yearling bass in the live-box, but most of the jumpers were not hungry. Then, as he rounded a bend, he saw a 12-foot alligator looking at him from a mud bank on the shore. She had a nest there, but Love didn't know that. He did know that American 'gators do not normally attack people. It's unusual. They most often slide into the stream like a snake, and move away from the intruder. This was the rare exception.

John cast once, twice and a third time in the shadows of an overhanging sweetgum bush a yard from the big reptile. It was too much for the big mama. She roared her displeasure and splashed into the creek. Seconds later she surfaced alongside Love, slammed her powerful tail across the midsection of his boat, and split it cleanly in two. Had John been in the middle instead of in the bow, the flailing tail might have killed him. Instead, he found himself swimming with his fishing rod in his hand. He dropped it and headed for the shore 75 feet away.

"I swam so fast I reached the bank and I was only wet on one side," Love said jokingly when he walked out of the jungle to safety an hour later.

Alligators are big and tough, and while almost harmless generally, their very presence can cause disaster. A Louisiana angler in an old rented boat rushed up a bayou at full speed. An old giant 'gator was gliding unseen a few inches below the surface. The outboard foot hit the reptile, breaking the transom off the boat. It sank instantly and the angler drowned.

Jimmy Dicus had a double dose of bad luck one cold fall morning when he went after flounder in the Intracoastal Waterway in South Carolina. He had a 40 horsepower outboard secured to his 18-foot boat and a small 5 horsepower safety engine was alongside that would get him back to the dock if the big motor conked out.

He launched the boat and raced away. Two miles downstream, he looked back. The small motor was gone. He had not tightened the clamps, and it had bounced off. With two miles of 35-foot water behind him, he didn't bother to make a search.

Dicus fished out the day, drove the boat on the trailer and headed for home. Alas again! He forgot to raise and secure his long shaft motor. An hour later he stopped in his yard. The motor had dragged over some 35 miles of concrete and asphalt. Four inches of the foot were ground off. It was a costly oversight.

J. M. Strickland parked his boat trailer in the lot half a stone's throw from the wildlife access launching ramp on the Waccamaw River in Columbus County, North Carolina. He climbed into his boat, fished downriver a mile or two, and returned with his stringer of panfish.

Surprise is the word. His pickup was still there but the trailer had been purloined. He never found the thief or the trailer.

Twice, Alex Gore returned to his car and trailer at the Orange Springs, Florida, launching ramp to discover thieves had unlocked his car doors and stolen items from the glove compartment, vandalizing what they didn't want. Now he always opens the glove compartment and leaves it ajar so thieves can see there's nothing to steal. No more thefts! No more break-ins!

Some carelessness borders on the humorous. Frank McGougan is a North Carolina attorney who rarely fishes. But he accepted an invitation to go after the bream in a swamp pond near his home that was almost covered with standing trees. He was flipping crickets under the limbs and around the cypress trunks when he hung his line overhead. While his partner attempted to hold the boat, McGougan stood up and began retrieving his tangled monofilament line. Over-balanced and shaky, he grabbed for the limb, the boat shot backward. He found himself neck deep in the water still hanging on to the limber cypress limb. He was fortunate that he was not alone. But wet and miserable, his day was ruined.

A fisherman-hunter combined the squirrel season with casting for bass on Lake Lochloosa in Central Florida. He put his shotgun in the boat along with his fishing tackle and soon was working a lure along the grassline of Burnt Island. The bass did not cooperate. He put his rod down, pulled his boat up on the bank a little, picked up his gun and walked into the hardwood forest in search of the barking squirrels. He shot several and two hours later returned to his boat. A coiled diamondback rattlesnake stared him in the face from amidships. Frustrated at the intruder, the fisherman-hunter dropped his squirrels, leveled his gun at the rattler, and poured a load of No. 6 shot into the reptile. The snake splattered. A four-inch hole in the bottom of his boat allowed the water to rush in. The boat quickly filled with water

Two bass-fishing doctors were striking it rich in a lily-covered corner of Blue Cypress Lake near Vero Beach, Florida. Casting heavy Sputterfuss lures into the spatterdock growth and then retrieving the noisily splashing spinner with its weedless hook over the surface, they had four lunker bass in the boat before 9:00 in the morning. Trolling slowly around the fringes of the pads, both these normally astute anglers were excited with the action. Perhaps with too much enthusiasm, one of the MD's whipped his rod up and cast. The lure didn't leave the boat. The big steel hook buried to the eye in the hairy scalp of his partner. Seconds later, the blood streamed down the neck and face of the wounded fisherman.

"Just cut the line. Leave the lure in my head. We don't

want to lose these fish," the doctor said, with more outdoorsman attitude than common sense. He cut the line and they continued casting. A half hour later the blood was still flowing. The doctor felt dizzy and sick. He sat down. The fishing was over. They motored back to the dock and with the fishing excitement dampened, the doctor who made the careless cast removed the hook. The wound still hurt. They checked in at the hospital emergency room. The victim was OK, but he had lost a lot of blood. He agreed to a lockjaw shot.

Minor acts of carelessness sometimes ruin a fishing day. Fishing the Kings Bar shallows off the northern shoreline of Okeechobee in Florida is like finding a speckled perch paradise for many minnow and cane pole anglers from fall to spring. Many of these fishermen leave from the Taylor's Creek dock and putt-putt several miles to the bar with five and ten horsepower motors on small boats. Early one February morning, Sam Ward and his brother Jake left the marina and nearly an hour later found their honey hole on the west side of the bar in the cattails. They eased out the anchor, picked up their poles and were ready for action. It was not to be. They had bought their five dozen minnows and then left the bait and bucket sitting on the dock. By the time they returned to Taylor's Creek the wind was up. They didn't try it back to their favorite speck hole.

Somewhat similar to this carelessness is the story of the same Harry Bell who fell out of the boat while trying to reach a bream bed. He had chugged ten miles from a fish camp at Leesburg, Florida, through Lake Griffin to the Oklawaha River. The weather was warm and he was afraid his minnows might die. He picked up the bucket and tilted it to drain the water prior to refilling it from the lake. It slipped! He dropped the whole thing over the side. He retrieved the styrofoam minnow bucket, but didn't save a single bait. With a 5 horsepower motor, he didn't have time to return to the camp and then get back to this beautiful speckled perch hole! The day was done.

Fred Moore had a nice bass boat, and he and his wife ran for miles down the St. John's River in Florida to find a deep hole where the bluegills were hanging out. His wife questioned him about such a long run.

"You sure we've got enough gas?" she asked, when she looked around at the desolate swampland along both banks.

"Oh, yeah, I got another full tank," he said pointing to a spare six gallon tank.

Minutes later the motor sputtered, then stopped. Fred recognized the gas shortage, and plugged the line into the other tank. The motor wouldn't fire. He squeezed the bulb a few times. It made no difference. Confused now, he lifted the tank. It was light and empty. While he had filled it the previous evening, some envious thief had drained his extra tank. It was a long wait before he got a tow back to the camp. Fishing that day was over.

There is catastrophe in some carelessness by boat fishermen that does much more than ruin a fishing trip. Three natives were in a wooden boat on the Suwannee River and moving with the current while casting along a wooded shoreline. The boat moved under an overhanging willow and a five-foot snake dropped off a limb and landed in the bow of the boat. With reckless abandon, all three fishermen scrambled to the stern. It was too much for a boat with just six inches of freeboard. The stern went under. The boat sank. The best swimmer made it ashore. Two drowned. Life preservers could have saved their lives.

A striped bass tournament was scheduled for Cumberland Lake in Kentucky in May of 1987. The best striper fishermen in the country were there to vie for big prizes. In the wee hours of the morning before the event was to start at safe light, two brothers raced up the lake to a cove where they caught a supply of wild native shad that they planned to use in the Striperama event. They were experienced and long successful fishermen in the Carolinas.

With their supply of bait in the tank, they cranked the big 150 horsepower motor and headed across the huge impoundment for the dock. There had been a lot of rain. A big log had floated out into the lake. Wide open at 4:00 in the dark morning, the bass boat crashed into the log. The boat flipped, making a full 360 degree circle in the air. Both brothers were thrown in the water. Neither had life preservers. There was no kill-switch. One young man couldn't swim. He drowned in the 120-foot water and his body never surfaced. The other struggled to the distant shore and survived, but so grieved that he may never be the same.

The incident was tragic enough to prompt action by the Striper organization to require all future contenders to wear life jackets in every event. But it was too late for that young fisherman. Carelessness and thieves rob many outdoorsmen of the normal joy of fishing.

Zebco's Revolutionary New Bullet Reels Cast Long Distances with Ease

The Zebco .38 Bullet, a streamlined, jet black reel with " 90's styling " features a new line release system and low-profile thumb bar that make it cast with ease.

      Casting comfort and distance. Those are the attributes fishermen told Zebco they wanted in a spincast reel. And for three years, Zebco engineers worked to create such a reel. It is now reality and great for crappie fishermen.

      The result is the Zebco Bullet, a reel that casts easily and is comfortable to fish with.

      "The name reflects the reel's level of performance," says Zebco spincast product manager Rich Feehan. "Imagine your lure heading toward its target like a speeding bullet. Now, you have an idea how smooth this reel is."

The Bullet, which will come in two models designated the .38 Bullet and the .357 Silver Bullet, is the latest in a series of landmark reels developed by Zebco since 1949. "We expect that other companies will try to imitate the Bullet, too," says Feehan. "The shape may be similar, but the performance will not be able to match the Bullet. You can't duplicate overnight what it took us three years to develop."

There is more to the Bullet than its trend-setting, look-of-the-90's styling. A new line release system actually reduces friction to generate longer casts. An innovative low-profile thumb bar release puts the angler's thumb in a more comfortable position for casting accuracy. A quick-change spool enables anglers to change line quickly and easily for all fishing conditions.

But equally important are its fish-fighting features. Both new Bullets are equipped with Zebco's Magnum Gears (including a cut brass pinion gear for power, smoothness and durability). The .357 Silver Bullet features a ball-bearing drive system for smoothness and long life.

Both the .38 Bullet and .357 Silver Bullet come with Zebco's revolutionary 360-degree Magnum Drag System.

"The 360-degree design makes the Bullet's drag system ultra-precise," Feehan says. "The drag setting goes from full off to lockdown in just one revolution of the drag-setting wheel. That means you never have to guess what your drag setting is. When you find a setting that's right for a certain type of fishing, you can always return to it."

In addition, Zebco's Magnum Drag System gives the Bullet a smoother drag than any other spincast reel—and smoother than most spinning and baitcasting reels, too.

Both the .38 Bullet and .357 Silver Bullet come spooled with Zebco high-performance line. The .357 also comes with a free extra spool filled with 8-pound test line.

NEW Rebel CAT'R CRAWLER ™

S75 CAT'R CRAWLER™
1 3/4" 1/8 oz.

205 Woolly Bear Caterpillar

206 Catalpa Worm

207 Grubworm

208 Earthworm

209 Zebra Caterpillar

NEW

The latest in Rebel's Ultra-light "Look-alikes"!
S75 CAT'R CRAWLER™, 1 3/4", 1/8 oz.,

In some areas they're called Catalpa Worms, in others they're called Caterpillars. . .whatever they're called, they will soon be known as Rebel's hottest little fish catcher. The latest in Rebel's series of ultra light look-alikes is the Fuzzy CAT'R CRAWLER. This highbred Caterpillar/Night-crawler is available in 5 natural colors. . .three of them even have a fuzzy, life-like finish. When cast near shallow, visible structure, and allowed to sink for a few seconds. . .any nearby fish is sure to strike with the CAT'R CRAWLER's first move.

Early fishing reports confirm that Rebel's new Fuzzy CAT'R CRAWLER will be bringing fishing fun to ultra-light anglers everywhere.

Bass pro Ken Cook catches a crappie.

Jig for Crappies at Santee-Cooper

Jigs in a variety of colors and sizes had been tied on my line for more than two hours and retrieved and trolled all along the deep water of the shoreline of Santee's south side just a few miles from the I-95 bridge. I then moved in closer to the rocky cover in order to challenge the elusive crappies I knew must be hiding there. But fishing continued to be slow, to put it mildly, and only a couple of hand-sized, blackish males had been boated by mid-day.

"I have tried about every color and shape jig in my tackle box and they just won't take any of them. We're going to have to make some changes if there's going to be any fish to brag about when we get back to the landing," I told my partner. As any fisherman with savvy knows, showing off the catch can be a cherished part of the joy of any angling. The thrill of reeling in the catch and then the gourmet meal of tasty crappies completes the circle. "Let's try some minnows attached to some of these artificials and see if the fish can turn down such a combination of delicacies," I suggested.

A little re-rigging followed when we strung a small cork, one split shot and a tiny red lead-headed jig with a white plastic skirt on a light monofilament line. The unique combination looked like a baby squid had used its tentacles to envelop the 2/0 gold hook securely knotted on the line. On that small but strong hook I impaled an inch and a half long Missouri minnow through the eyes. Even out of water when the little fish wriggled and squirmed, there was assurance that no self-respecting predator of forage fish could resist such a temptation as this when flaunted right before the eyes and open mouth of a hungry creature.

I cast it with my ultra-light spinning tackle into a pothole in the grass line, allowing it to trickle down to within a foot or so of the bottom. The minnow kept twitching a moment and then the line tightened as that little cork disappeared. I set back on the rod and felt a pulsating struggling on the other end of the line. Soon a pound-and-a-half female crappie scrambled noisily over the

North Carolinian Bobby Nobles admires a nice shellcracker.

surface toward the boat as I lifted it over the side to safety in the live box.

Moving slowly along the high cliffs that afternoon, we easily caught near limits with those little jigs adorned with the real thing—small minnows similar to the natural food supply of these panfish that are so popular among veteran anglers in almost every state. We experimented with numerous colors and sizes of jigs from black to purple, chartreuse, white, and natural. They all caught fish when sweetened with a live forage minnow, but the clear and the white were by far the most productive.

We soon learned that while there is an added thrill and challenge to successful crappie fishing with spinning tackle that requires some accuracy in casting, hook setting, and bringing in the flouncing creatures over the cover, you could do just as well with much simpler equipment. An ordinary limber cane pole or telescopic fiberglass 12- or 14-foot rod (my favorite is the Super Bream Buster) rigged with an 8- or 10- pound test monofilament line and the same cork, sinker, tiny jig, and minnow was easier. It was faster too, and the crappies didn't spook when we moved in close enough to drop the bait straight down into the bedding fish. When the cork went down, you could fight the critter in the cover, then lift out even the two pounders right over the gunnels while the pole bent like an archer's bow the instant before an arrow is released.

And if you are really a fishing addict, is there anything more beautiful than seeing a cork go down? Maybe a largemouth hitting a topwater plug or a bluegill striking a popping bug on a flyline is comparable, but I never cease to feel the excitement in my veins when a cork suddenly eases beneath the surface and heads toward the bottom. You get this pleasure fishing for crappies at Santee with minnows and jigs combined in the spawning areas.

I think it is important not to have much lead on the line. The jig itself had a weighted head and often this is enough to carry the minnow down. Then sometimes another tiny shot eight or ten inches up the line helps get the bait to the bottom. Too much such weight ties the minnow and the jig so that there is not much action and crappies are notorious for preferring baits that move. Likewise, a monofilament line that is too heavy in pound test class, often is the difference between getting bites and just watching the cork float. Its stiffness takes away much of the minnow's liveliness and repulses your prey. No line should be used heavier than 10-pound, and I most often use 6- or 8- pound test. It's amazing how much fight and weight even this line test will take and it allows your minnow freedom to frolic.

Various other artificials are more productive when tasty natural morsels are added to the best man-made lures science can devise. The noted Beetle Spin will catch crappies frequently when trolled or cast into open water or near cover where the fish are congregated. But in test after crucial test with plain Beetle Spins on one line and the same color on another, a little minnow or grass shrimp attached just attracts more hungry crappies. And, of course, such spinning lures will cause a few largemouth bass in the yearling size to strike, too.

A relatively recent Rebel lure has gone on the market specifically designed for crappies and smaller bass, but it also definitely catches trout, walleyes, and catfish in some areas. This lure is the Super Teeny-R designed for ultra-light equipment on 6-pound test line in natural color patterns like bream, frog, rainbow trout, among others. It's only an inch and three quarters long from tail to plastic lip and runs about four feet deep when retrieved at moderate speed or trolled slowly. The 1/8 ounce little lure has a tuned noisemaker and is critically balanced.

Make no mistake about it—this lure will catch crappies in Santee waters. But in an effort to test it in several lakes, I have tried it straight and then also dressed with tiny minnows fastened in the lips or through the eye sockets on one of the treble hooks in the tail. In EVERY valid testing, the neat little lure was more successful with the minnow attached. You can catch specks on this lure simply trolling it on a long cane pole with light monofilament but it does a little better on spinning tackle. You have to cast with some delicacy to keep the live bait from snapping off, but it can be done with a little finesse plus some careful attention.

Mister Twister plastic artificials have been teasing crappies into making fatal mistakes for a long time and many individual fish in the schools will attack these life-portraying worms when they mosey through their habitat. But like the other artificials, it is much more productive with a minnow flipping alongside the twisting plastic tail. Yellow and white twisters have been by far the best for the anglers involved in recent Santee experiments and even the wariest crappies will often rise to such an offering.

White grubs with red heads are enticing baits for crappies when minnows are added to the hook. The grubs that I have tested have another distinct advantage to economy-minded anglers—they will last and last and last. One especially tough plastic grub just over an inch long was trolled for more than a week and accounted for more than 30 specks. It was still in reasonably good condition when I stopped the testing while many of the softer artificials that had caught fish during the period had been torn to pieces and replaced numerous times.

Once during the test we ran out of minnows when the crappies were hitting the artificials with the small bait fish impaled. We cut the anal fin off some of the smaller crappies and fastened these on the hooks just as we had the live meat. While there seemed to be some letdown in the catch rate, there was no doubt that this, too, was a better fish attractor than the artificial alone.

The most conclusive result that I have ever seen documented on how many more fish you can catch with a live bait addition as contrasted with the lure alone happened to me along with the late Ruey Hewett, a North Carolinian vacationing at Goat Island Resort on Santee's north side.

We had been catching our share of crappies with spinners fancied up with pork rind trailers and trolled behind an old stumpbumper boat and a ten-horse motor that we had rented. Then, one morning when a northeast wind was whistling down the lake we couldn't catch a thing on those spinners. We had long believed the spinners were more effective on sunny days than overcast ones like that, but it shouldn't have been enough to inflict lockjaw on the whole populace. But something had.

As a last resort, I put a small minnow on the hook behind a double gold spinner, trailing each other by an inch on a short piece of beaded brass wire material. On that hook I put the old-fashioned live minnow and began letting that new gimmick follow along behind the boat pushed by a stiff wind from the northeast. It worked like magic. Time after time the rod dipped and another crappie succumbed to the double temptation. We didn't catch a fish on any other line out that morning, but landed a box full on that gold spinning rig with a minnow helper. It was a positive conclusion.

There are some fishermen with expertise who can catch (on some occasions) as many or more crappies with just artificials as the best veterans can with live bait or a combination of the condiments. I tallied such a test between two equally adept anglers in Lake Marion's open waters a few years ago when the crappies there were as plentiful as sheepshead under a Murrells Inlet pier.

My two friends challenged each other to a one hour contest. One was using a small minnow on a monofilament line, No. 4 gold hook, the smallest lead shot sinker and a natural colored little bobber no larger than a thimble. He had the option of using various jigs with his minnows, as he saw fit, while the other fisherman chose a simple No-Alibi jig, one yellow and one white. Both were using short cane poles and fishing from the same boat where Potato Creek enters the river on the north side. It was the full moon in May and every crappie seemed determined to spawn at that very moment.

The fishermen started that bout on a three count and immediately began pulling in the crappies. They worked feverishly and jovially, yet with complete seriousness over the outcome.

Now I would like to report that the angler using the minnows and the jig together or just the minnow alone won the contest, catching more than the veteran jig fisherman. But that was not the case. The jigger angler caught 20 in an hour off that bed while the minnow fisherman landed 16. The difference was in the time it took to catch the minnows out of the bucket, impale them on the hook and get the bait back in the water again. The man with the jig just shook his fish off with their tender mouths unable to stand the flipping, and let them drop in the boat. He was back in the water with his lure in a second or two. It took several times that many seconds to re-bait with the live minnows.

But the mixed condiment fishing for crappies still has its place for the average angler. It will get strikes and fish when the species just isn't as thick and not nearly as anxious to bite as they were in Santee that day. This same test tried at another place at another time might have made a believer out of the strictly artificial angler who often said, "I wouldn't even eat a fish that I have to catch on a live bait."

Possibly it does take a little more know-how and expertise to catch crappies with artificials than with live bait. Devout lure fishermen seem to develop a feel, a sensitive touch that just every angler doesn't have and some never find. But there are far more amateur crappie anglers than trained, practiced veterans who can outsmart these specks. And for those who just want to bring home a mess of fish for the family dinner table, and aren't choosy about what legal means they use to catch it, they will more often succeed with a little of the old and little of the new, a bit of artificial and a bit of live bait.

Many fishermen measure success by the "Oh's" and "Ah's" they hear when the stringer is lifted out of the boat. They could care less whether they caused the crappies to mistake a feather for a shrimp or a piece of plastic for a forage minnow.

Warren Crabtree—
He Will Guide For Any Fish
But Guarantees a Cooler Full of Crappies

If he always had his druthers, Warren Crabtree, 45-year-old bachelor who guides out of Angel's Landing at Santee, would just fish for largemouth bass. Because fishing for these lunkers gets kind of slow in midsummer, he guides for any other species his customers want and is unique in that he guarantees his clients a 30-quart cooler full of crappies every day he takes a party out for these gourmet panfish.

"Any time that my customers are willing to fish all day if necessary, I guarantee them the 30-quart cooler full of crappies. It doesn't usually take all day and I normally expect to catch the 30 fish limit and fill the cooler between 8:00 A.M. and 4:00 P.M. with about an hour break for lunch. This gives real avid fishermen a chance to fish

Warren Crabtree gets a double in Santee-Cooper open water.

for largemouth bass early and late and still carry home a fine mess of fish for the table, the crappies, whether they do any good with their bass casting or not," the likeable, friendly Crabtree says.

233

"Crappies at Santee vary in size from season to season, within the same season and from one of these big lakes to another. But in the summer, they will average 1 to 1 1/2-pounds with some of them up to 2 1/2-pounds. I have caught one black crappie that weighed 4-pounds, 4-ounces, not far off the world record.

"My customers and I use live minnows for the crappies 95 percent of the time, but a few people still will use jigs and catch fish. We fish these minnows on rods and reels, no cane poles, and usually we are dangling those minnows in 20 to 30 feet of water. We start catching those crappie limits about May 20," Crabtree notes.

But how does this native of Alabama (his grandfather ran a fish camp there) who was raised on the Santee at Summerville, have the confidence to guarantee limit catches of crappies? Other guides make no such offer to anglers ready to pay $75.00 a day plus gas, oil, bait and lost tackle.

Crabtree makes a business out of catching crappies. Despite the fact that thousands of logs, limbs, stumps and other cover are on the bottom of much of these two giant lakes, this hard-working guide spends many of his off hours constructing man-made fish-hides in both the upper and lower lakes. He cuts the sweet myrtle bushes, similar to a small cypress, and submerges them with weights at likely crappie hangouts all over the lakes. He averages putting down 30 or 40 of these brushpile fish-hides a year. They constantly deteriorate but he never has less than 90 to 100 such secret havens around which crappies congregate.

He triangles their location in his mind and eyes and the hides are not easily located by just any passerby, but he also uses his depth-finder to find the bushes he plants in the 20 to 30 feet of water

"Sometimes I can catch the limit close in on my brush piles, but I'll still move the customers along to others from time to time. It gets hot out there in the summer and a good cool ride to another concentration just as good as the one we left is a welcome reprieve. I also use some of the same myrtle bush hides for bass, too. Any of the big predators will hang out around them. They attract forage fish and when these little fish get together, all the bigger ones will seek them out for their meal.

"I use no cork when I am fishing the hides for crappies. I make up a two-hook rig with a one ounce bell sinker. I bait each of these hooks and then let the line down right into and around the transplanted cover on the bottom. It doesn't take but a minute for the crappies to pounce on that tied-out food supply and we often bring in two at a time." says this veteran of ten years of guiding whose infectious smile lets you know he enjoys it.

"The biggest fish from my brush come from Lake Moultrie in the summer. But I put some hides in Lake Marion, too, so I have some places to get out of the wind even though the fish in Marion are smaller. You can catch some big ones in Marion just 'stump jumping,' but those around the brush are often small.

"Whether the weather is sunny, bright or overcast doesn't have much to do with my fishing success. If it is extremely bright, like in July and August, I have found that the crappies tend to bunch up more than usual. The fluctuating water level doesn't make much difference, either. My fish-hides are deep and the fish are in no danger of being exposed with normal water level changes.

"There is a time in February and early March when I catch some nice crappies in the open water, but most of the 200 to 250 days a year that I'm out there fishing, I'm around my brush piles or the stumps. When I have an off day, I haul more brush for new hides or work on one of my five boats, engines or trolling motors. I have a crappie boat, bass boat, striper boat, a back-up bass boat and then a big aluminum bass boat for winter," he says.

Crabtree makes it clear that while he guarantees creel limits of crappies, he makes no such promise to the bass and striper clients he guides, but the fee is the same. Acknowledged as a real professional at catching these large species, he knows it is too uncertain to make guarantees.

Warren fished four American Bass Association tournaments in 1976, coming in 2nd in the Florida Invitational. His largest bass put in the boat was a 12-pound, 4-ounce wallmount from Lake Moultrie. It was landed on a plastic worm in 1972. He stopped tournament fishing then for full-time guiding.

When fishing for bass, Crabtree thinks spinner baits and then worms are the best artificials early in the spring. Later in the year he goes to crankbaits and says you must learn to adapt to the cover, weather, water temperature, water depth and a variety of other variables.

"Finding the fish is the big job. You play it by ear until you come up with just the lure the bass is looking for. We release some of the bass we catch, but no one releases the striped bass. It's hard to land a striper and keep it alive. The fight usually takes the life out of it.

235

"When I'm just fishing for my own entertainment, I like to fish a flyrod in the Cooper River for bream and bass. That's real sport to me," he says.

Crabtree has some Santee-Cooper experiences worth relating but he has never had a serious accident.

"I did have a customer once who got so drunk that he fell face down in his own open tackle box. He had lures hung all over his face, and I had to get him back to the landing before we got all the hooks out. I got a hook in my own hand from pulling a Creek Chub lure off a bush that cost me $52.00 to have removed, but I have never had a boat capsize or split one open on a stump to cause any real accidents," he notes.

"You fish differently here for the various species. I like to cast or drift shiners for stripers in November and December in either lake and there are still some big ones out there. Last year I started with the shiners for the stripers before Thanksgiving and we caught a lot of 8- to 12-pounders, averaging 10-pounds. We had many 14- and 15-pounders and one 41-pound beauty.

"Earlier in the fall when I'm fishing for stripers, I look for the birds and watch my depthfinder. I drift six shiners at a time on rods set at the depth I can observe the suspended rockfish. Doing this kind of fishing, I use 10- or 12-pound Stren line at that time, but by Thanksgiving I go to 17- or 20-pound line because the fish get bigger. Stripers roam in the fall and then concentrate around ridges and hilltops. Shad start moving and come to the top in the afternoon. Stripers surface to eat them and you can have a heyday catching them then. You can easily tell the difference between the stripers and the shad when they are on your depthfinder and when the stripers are below the shad, it's hard to make them strike. When they move up into the shad, action breaks loose. Often these stripers are feeding deep and you never see them from the surface.

"But while I like to fish for stripers and prefer bass fishing to everything else, I spend more time guiding for crappies. There is a demand for crappie guiding services in the summer when things are slow for other species. I just put my Monarch bass boat that's rigged up for crappies over my brush piles and we catch fish.

"One of my customers fishing for crappies with 20-pound Stren over my brush couldn't reel in last year, and I thought he was hung on a limb. Finally, I told him to let me have the rod and I would get it un-hung. But when I took hold I could feel

236

something heavy and alive on the line. I gave it back to him and told him he had a fish. After awhile he started struggling and bringing a fish toward the top. I saw a flash of a big fish belly and I gaffed. That fellow had brought in a 50-pound blue catfish on that 20-pound line. It was freakish, too. We were fishing for crappies with the usual two hooks, but one of his hooks had the point broken off. That was the hook that he had the big catfish on. Even without a point, that hook was hung behind the gill plate of the monster catfish, wedged so tightly that it held, and there was no hook stuck in him at all.

"I usually use the 2/0 gold hooks for crappies and the 20-pound Stren in the brush because we get hung on that cover occasionally. But you can catch some fine crappies with ultralight line, and rod and reel fishing a Mini Jig or No Alibi," says Crabtree.

This unusual Santee guide who fishes for all game fish, had another freakish incident happen a few years ago. He was casting a homemade diving crank bait around one of his planted fish-hides when two bass, both weighing an even 5-pounds, jumped on the lure. He managed to land them both. Ironically, that same day, his party put an 11-pound, 2-ounce lunker in the boat, too. The giants were hungry that morning.

"Parties I have carried out have caught doubles on lures while fishing for bass many times, but that was the only day I ever saw two five pounders come in on the same artificial bait at the same time," says this smiling ten-year veteran of Santee-Cooper guiding.

Does Crabtree guide for the big catfish now making a name in Santee? No! He considers them easy to catch and no guide expertise is needed. "Anyone can just wait for them to bite and catch one," he says.

"But if you want to have some fun catching crappies on my fish-hides, drop in any time. There's a lot of time after we quit at 4:00 in the afternoon. Plenty of time to go back out and catch a mess of fish," he says.

Sounds good to me. I want to try those honey holes.

Winter or summer you can catch South Carolina low
country crappie.

Orange-Lochloosa—
Central Florida's Crappie Haven;
Lake Monroe—St. Johns Headwaters,
Full of Slabs

Author Carter gets a middle-size crappie in the
Lochloosa grass.

Contrasting in shoreline cover and inviting bottom structure, the twin lakes of Orange and Lochloosa in Central Florida
traditionally rank among the finest black crappie waters in the
country. Veteran anglers catch these speckled perch, as they are

locally named in the Sunshine State, the year 'round, and techniques vary from dropping minnows in holes in the spatterdock lilies during winter spawning months to trolling jigs and natural baits in the open water the rest of the year.

Cane poles are still among the most conventional tackle used for bed fishing the species in the heavy cover of grass, hydrilla and lilies, but in recent years a variety of rods and reels for crappie anglers has sophisticated the fishing. Super Jigs, Hal-Flies, Betts and Stanley jigs fished vertically around cover were popular in the 1980's and many of these devout speck anglers were using 10- and 12-foot B 'n' M fiberglass poles and 8-pound line with astounding success.

One of the most successful of these jig anglers is Ron Gilyen, who lives on the eastern shore of Lochloosa near Fin-Way Fish Camp on Highway 301. Ron uses two lengths of fiberglass poles and he cradles one under each elbow so he can fish two lines at a time in different holes. He ties on jigs, a tiny cork, uses no lead and moves slowly from hole to hole in the hydrilla. His cork floats flat and when it moves the slightest bit, he sets the hook and flops giant crappie over the gunnels in the boat. He is one of the few astute crappie fishermen who fishes two poles at once. He says he learned his technique from the late Catfish Ludwig and wouldn't trade his system with anyone, anywhere. Most of his strikes come on the falling jig.

After March or April when the specks have reduced their spawning, most crappie enthusiasts today go to the open water where they troll a dozen lines or more from a boat with a combination of jigs and live minnows on the hooks. Sturdy holders secure enough Johnson Crappie Spin rods, Cabelas, Zebco and Silstars to make the boat look like it is sprouting. Many still use cane and fiberglass poles in the holders. Enough lead shots to keep the jig-minnow enticers near the bottom are clamped eight inches apart up the line from the hook and a small, oblong cork on the surface is normally used.

Trolling must be at a speed sufficient to pull the cork to the surface (the lead sinks it when you are not moving). It is not unusual to have two and three specks hooked at once when you find schools in the open water of Lochloosa and Orange. Trolling with the wind on the stern is most productive. Anglers often mark spots with floats where they catch several fish so they can circle the area and stay with the school as long as they continue to strike.

Orange Lake, when full, (the water level was down several feet in '89-90 from the drought) covers 13,160 acres. Lochloosa to the east is connected by a short mile-long creek that then passes under the Highway 325 bridge at Cross Creek. It is 8,600 acres. The creek and other tributaries provide roughly 23,000 acres of fine crappie water and 2-pounders are not unusual. An occasional 3-pounder makes the scales.

Lochloosa, located along 301, is encircled with cypress trees along the banks, some growing well out into the lake. A good stand of grass laces the shoreline, and hydrilla is generally spread almost all over the lake. Big specks are caught around these cypress tree knees and in the grass patches. The hydrilla in the deeper water also provides refuge for feeding crappies. Lochloosa's deepest holes are only 14 feet deep, and they are in the northern end of the spring-fed lake. Crappies suspend in these holes during the hottest weather. Most spawning is in the cow lilies and grass beds, but generally if you can catch specks spawning in the shallows, they'll also bite trolled baits in the deeper water. Some anglers, adroit with casting in tiny hydrilla holes, catch big crappies with spinning tackle around the hydrilla islands that are plentiful all over Lochloosa.

Hydrilla is not as thick in Orange Lake. Again the Johnson Crappie Spin tackle, Silstar and Cabelas equipment is the most popular. Some wise old veterans make their own jigs with 2/0 gold TruTurn hooks, a half-inch piece of red plastic worm pushed up past the bend, and a minnow impaled through the eyes. At times it catches specks when all else fails.

Orange is a mucky-bottom natural lake with a low level dam on Highway 301 holding in the water that is fed into the impoundment from Prairie Creek at River Styx in the northern end of the lake. Most of Orange is no more than eight feet deep, and specks bed in the thousands of acres of lilies on the west shore next to Highway 441 and in the southernmost portion around the drainage creek

There are also good spawning areas off Sampson Point on the west bank. Good public access ramps, tackle shops, fish camps, camping areas, boat rentals, guides and snacks are available along Highway 441 on the west side and at the south end of the lake. At Cross Creek, where Highway 325 crosses the short stream joining the twin lakes, there are three good fish camps with cabins, tackle, boats, guides, campgrounds, etc.

There is also a famous restaurant, The Yearling, that

serves meals six days a week. It is closed on Mondays. The area was made famous by the late Marjorie Kinnan Rawlings who lived here and won the Pulitzer Prize for her novel, *The Yearling*, since made into a movie.

On the east side of the twin lakes is Highway 301, where there are excellent fish camps, bait and tackle shops, campgrounds, gas and guide services. (Unfortunately, extreme drought in 1990 closed many of the fish camps, but natives have seen low water several times in the past, and expect great fishing for crappies when the drought ends.) Anglers looking for more sophisticated lodging can find dozens of motels and restaurants at Ocala to the south and Gainesville to the west, both within 30 minutes of the twin lake complex of Orange-Lochloosa.

LAKE MONROE AT SANFORD

Near Sanford, Florida, the giant north-flowing St. Johns River has its headwaters in a series of connecting lakes with Monroe the best known. Other lakes in the complex are Jessup, Harney, and Puzzle, all connected to the St. Johns and easily accessible from Lake Monroe, where most tournaments are launched at excellent public ramps.

Monroe is a shallow lake of 9,406 acres with most of the shoreline covered with trees or marshland. The water is dark, tannic-colored from the abundance of cypress trees along the bank. The other three lakes bring the total water available for crappie fishing to 30,000 acres. Monroe has long been famous for its population of speckled perch and bream and in recent years has become a popular site for bass tournaments also.

The abundance of grass and lilies along the shore makes Monroe ideal for bedding panfish, and most veteran anglers here go after the spawners in the two to five foot water with minnows or small jigs. Experienced jig anglers tie on Super, Betts or Stanley jigs so they hang at right angles to the line and twitch them viciously in the cover. While some specks can be caught within rock-throwing distance of the ramps on the east side of Monroe where there is the most development, experienced slab catchers usually cross the narrow lake to fish the more desolate western shoreline or run to one of the other popular lakes in the chain where there is greater privacy.

Much of the Monroe water has a current flowing north into the St. Johns, and good speck catches are often made where the water eddies around obstacles, islands, stumps and aquatic tussocks. Quiet coves hold bedding crappies.

There are seven fish camps located around this series of St. Johns headwater lakes, five with campgrounds. All sell licenses, three have guides and restaurants, and two have lodging facilities. There are numerous modern motels at Sanford on the east bank of Monroe, and there are plenty of excellent restaurants nearby. Holiday Inn is located right on the water, and is a convenient facility for fishing and other club conferences. Monroe is on I-4 and only a few miles west of I-95. The region is in close proximity to Orlando, Disney World, Epcot, Sea World and MGM, and often anglers combine a fishing adventure on these St. Johns lakes with a family vacation at these famous resort attractions.

Monroe, like Orange and Lochloosa, is a renowned crappie fishing haven where slab-sized fish are the norm and often 50-fish limits are brought in at tournament weigh-ins. There are few disappointed crappie catchers with expertise who fish Orange-Lochloosa and the Monroe complex. They have a reputation for producing good catches, sometimes real trophy fish.

FISH CAMPS ON ORANGE AND MONROE

The Orange-Lochloosa twin lake area has the following fish camps located on the water: Southshore Fish Camp, 904-595-4251; Citra Fish Camp 904-595-3061; Orange Lake Fish Camp 904-591-1870; McIntosh Fish Camp 904-591-1302; Sportsman Cove 904-591-1435; Mike's Fish Camp 904-591-1135; Cross Creek Fish Camp 904-466-3424; Twin Lakes Fish Camp 904-466-3194; Palmeter's Cross Creek Lodge 904-466-3228; and Finway Fish Camp 904-481-2114. Lake Monroe area fish camps are Lindsay Fish Camp 305-349-5121; Lemon Bluff Fish Camp 305-322-6843; Marina Isle 305-322-4786; Black Hammock Fish Camp 305-365-9443; Osteen Bridge Fish Camp 305-322-3825; Monroe Harbor Marina 305-322-2910; and Hiley's Fish Camp 305-365- 3831.

Old and young in Central Florida thrill to crappie catch.

While it is often irritating to the fisherman, hydrilla attracts
Florida panfish.

Florida Specks Love Hydrilla But You Can
Get Them Out

Rapid infestation of the exotic hydrilla weed in 20 states
in the last decade is forcing crappie fishermen all over the
country to adapt to new techniques and systems if they expect to
continue carrying home limits of these gourmet flatfish once
caught in brushpiles, grass and lily pads where they spewed out
their eggs during spawning. They may still be in those spots, but
hydrilla that often grows as thick as 500 stems to a square foot
and in Florida in some lakes averages 120 to the square foot, can
make getting a hook in the old familiar places difficult if not
impossible.

Because it is not usually a topwater striker like its sister sunfish the largemouth bass, you generally have to put the bait or artificial near the bottom to attract crappie bites. But once you flaunt the proper enticement in his face, he'll bite and others from the same family may make a single hat-size hole a bonanza of several dozens. Where the hydrilla is thick and established for several years in a lake, some giants have lolled in the cover feeding on the forage fish long enough to reach maturity. That may mean real trophies from 2- to 3-pounds or more.

In the era before hydrilla was dumped into Florida streams and began its spread all over the nation, one of the best year-round ways of catching specks, as they are monikered in the Sunshine State, was to troll slowly for them with Mini-Jigs or Hal-Flies and a live minnow a foot off the bottom in open water of lakes and streams. It eliminated the notion that crappies could be caught only during the spring spawn. These fish fed year-round in the deep water and astute anglers came in with limits every month of the year. The system worked well in Florida where a trolled bait didn't hang up on submerged cover. You simply had to find deep holes and put the meat and jig where the fish were. When hydrilla was accidentally introduced and there were just little islands of the nuisance weed here and there, you could troll around it and catch fish. Indeed, it was a real honey hole— a haven for feeding crappies that helped the angler trolling the open water.

But the bonanza could not be permanent. Hydrilla wants a monopoly on all the water from shoreline to shoreline and bottom to the surface and every twig that was cut from a stalk took root and itself became a health plant instantly. Each new stem could and did grow an inch a day in Florida lakes with nutrient-filled water and bottom muck as rich as fertilizer. Nothing could stop it. It grows in South Dakota where the lakes freeze over four feet and more in the winter. It has grown from the bottom of lakes 45 feet deep to the surface when it got as little two candlepower of light. Its tubers in the muck can be exposed to the elements for years and still become virile and grow again when water covers them only a few weeks. It's almost indestructible with a few chemicals that will kill the live stems, but none that will eliminate its coming back. It's an uncontrollable plague once it gets the foothold that it now has almost everywhere.

Yet, with a little patience and if the hydrilla hasn't grown so dense that you can't power your outboard through it, there are

246

fine specks taking refuge in the cover and you can catch them with humble equipment. You will also renew a nearly lost thrill that once was the highlight of every angler's experience on the water—you can watch the cork go down. Watching a bobber shake, tremble, move off and then plunge toward the bottom gives the angler after crappie somewhat the same double thrill that a bass angler gets when he catches a lunker on a topwater lure. You couple sound and sight observations simultaneously with that unknown quantity — what and how big is the creature after your bait—and no outdoorsman can deny the experience that makes him feel like minnows are flouncing in his veins.

To catch specks in the hydrilla you revert back somewhat to the old fashioned way. A cane pole or Lew Childres' fiberglass Breambuster is as good or better than a rod and reel. If hydrilla is thick and you know every hooked fish is going to wrap around the stalks of a dozen plants before you get it to the surface, you'd better tie on a monofilament line in the ten- to 12-pound test size. You'll get more bites with six- or eight-pound test, but it might not stand the tussle when the fish fouls your line around the hydrilla. A 2/0 gold hook is a preferred size in most hydrilla-cursed lakes and the Tru Turn style seems to hold on better than some other brands.

The fewer lead shot you can use on the line the better. The crappie would like for your bait to look free and unencumbered. Heavy weights makes the minnow look tired out. A single middle-size shot eight inches above the hook is sufficient if the hydrilla has some openings large enough that you do not have to slither the bait down the stalk. If the holes in the cover are tiny, you may have to use two or three shots, but the more weight the less efficient the fishing.

You want a bobber that will hold that lead and bait a foot off the bottom. A big bobber is always a determent to catching crappie. It has too much resistance when the fish gulps the minnow and starts to move off. Often the fish will turn it loose when he feels the cork pull back. Thus, when you can get your bait near the bottom with a single shot, do it and use a tiny oblong cork that is barely large enough to support the weight on the line. It will disappear quickly when a crappie clamps down on the morsel on the hook. Set the hook by gently yanking on the pole, not a gusto hook setting like you would use on a bass tap-tapping on a plastic worm. The paper thin mouth of a crappie will tear with much jerking action and the fish will unbutton and be gone.

When you hook on your minnow for crappie fishing the hydrilla holes, you'll get the most action out of your live bait by impaling him just under the dorsal fin, but not deep enough to hit the hollow. A 2 1/2-inch Missouri minnow hooked properly and with a little weight will play and run for half an hour or more, enticing every gamefish in the neighborhood. It's a lazy man's way of fishing the minnows in the hydrilla. You can simply watch the cork dance and know there is enough action to attract attention. Crappie are reluctant to hit a still bait, although they occasionally will. They like the fluttering movement of a live bait struggling in their faces. If you haven't had a strike during the lifetime of that bait on the hook, don't let it hang there when it turns white. Put on a new bait. Life in the minnow is imperative if you are looking for a good stringer of these gourmet fish.

Don't get complacent and after trying a hydrilla island for a spell with no luck, assume they are not there, not biting, or you have the wrong approach. Move about from island to island, dropping that bait in every opening big enough to get your bait down. There's not much reason for ever letting your bait stay in one place more than four or five minutes if you have seen no evidence of a bite. Most times the crappie will bite within seconds after the bait gets near them. If they don't, they aren't there or your bait doesn't move enough to entice them.

If you are energetic and really don't mind working for your crappie strikes, then impale your minnow through the eyes or the lips, not the back. When it is hooked in this manner, you'll be able to jiggle the end of your pole or long rod constantly, giving the bait an up-and-down motion as if it were jumping, injured and yet alive. It takes a steady twitching but no self-respecting crappie will let that morsel get away with such temptation long. He'll rush in and run off with the bait. You'll feel the tug and the line running off. That's the time to lift the fish over the gunnel.

If you have tried a dozen hydrilla holes and still have had no strikes, maybe some noise will help. Many natives who fish lakes of the South purposely make a racket to attract fish to their baits. You can slap the end of your pole in the opening you are fishing for a few seconds, sending out rivulets on the surface and a noise that breaks the silence. Then let the bait drop back right where you created the Pandemonium. There will be times when the cork won't even stop. The fish will have heard the noise, apparently thought some cousins were feeding, and rush in to get their share. It works very well.

When you hang a fish, you can't always get the big 'uns

to the boat without some problem. With some line to play with, the crappie will circle and entangle in hydrilla. There is a tendency to pull hard to get the fish out quickly, but that isn't always the best method. Keep the line reasonably tight for a short time, hoping the fish will circle back and untangle himself. If he doesn't and you are beginning to suspect you will lose the fish anyway, give him a little slack after he rests in the cover for a few seconds. Often the fish will think he is loose and surge again, coming back into the opening in the hydrilla and to you.

Keep in mind that hydrilla often uproots easily from the bottom. It is not tough like maidencane or sawgrass. Sometimes you can move your boat a few feet, take hold of the clump of hydrilla that has you hung up, and pull the weeds and the fish to the surface in one simple movement. The fish will be draped in the stuff and almost hidden, but if he has been hooked through the tough upper mouth, he will often stay fastened until you get him.

Now there are purists everywhere who frown on catching any fish with live bait. One recently told me, "I wouldn't even eat a fish that I had to catch with a live bait." But then such renowned professionals as Ray Scott, founder of the Bass Anglers Sportsman Society, openly and unashamedly announces at a public meeting, "I'm one of those fishermen who still likes to see the cork go down." He means it, too. He likes to fish with a pole for bluegills and crappie with a live bait and a cork that trembles and disappears.

Purists can fish the hydrilla with some artificials and catch fish, occasionally even better than with live minnows. Sometimes you must have a combination of meat, metal and plastic; but with some experience in handling the right kind of jigs, the purists can do well even in the thickest cover of hydrilla infestation.

The best jig for dense cover crappie fishing that I've ever seen is the Lit'l Hustler by Southern Pro Lures in Jonesboro, Ark. It is made in weights from 1/16 ounce to 1/2 ounce in 36 different shapes and colors. Some are fluorescent and glow in the sunlight. It catches Southern crappie best when you use the 2/0 gold hook, 1/8 ounce red head and a white or yellow skirt. The little skirts have slits in the open end that will wiggle and move like tentacles on a tiny octopus if there is any current in the water. It is not weedless, but the skirt draped over the point of the hook helps keep it free of encumbrances.

and finger the line while it does its thing in the cover. Crappie obviously mistake the slight movement for forage fish suspended and nearly still. They'll hit it and hang themselves. Oddly, there are times when it is even more productive than the real thing—a live minnow on a hook.

There are other times when you can slide this Mini-Jig down the hydrilla after impaling a small minnow on the hook. That combination gives it more action and you can catch fish simply by watching and feeling the line until it moves off from vertical or you feel the strike of something alive. The combination of plastic jig, metal hook and live meat is a good way to fish the heavy cover for specks either during bedding season or when they are foraging for food the other months of the year. They will strike it the year-round.

The rod and reel fisherman gets his chance to show off and sometimes challenge the unsophisticated cane poler with these Mini-Jigs by attaching them to a 4- or 6-pound monofilament line with ultralight spinning tackle. Where there are holes in the hydrilla or other heavy cover as large as your living room or bigger, you can cast these enticing morsels into those holes and retrieve slowly, sometimes so slowly that it is almost still, and hook a lot of fish. It must sink a few feet below the surface and be light enough to plummet to the bottom when you retrieve it ever so slowly. It should not be twitched when fished in this manner. The crappie are looking for something easy to gulp down, not wanting to exert much effort. They swim up to it, mouth it for a moment and run off with your line. If you gently set the hook before the fish gets to the cover, you can bring in plenty of gourmet crappie even where the cover looks like a meadow, but with those few open holes where apparently this fish stalks the food that strays away from the hydrilla. When the holes in the cover are small, you can vertically fish with less chance of hang-ups.

These Lit'l Hustlers, Hal-Flies, No-Alibi's and other small lures have been effective in Florida waters for years. There are times at Okeechobee, Florida's giant natural lake in the tropical section, when specks will strike these jigs retrieved slowly near the cover better than they will live minnows.

Bait, Bobber, Line and Weight Critical in Crappie Fishing in High Wind and Big Waves

Often, when quizzed as to whether I can catch limits of speckled perch (crappie) in Florida lakes the year around, I hedge just a bit by saying I can catch them every day that the wind doesn't blow harder than ten miles an hour, and if it isn't too cold to troll the open water. While I never try to catch a 50-fish limit any more because I don't need that many specks, it's usually easy to catch about all that you need. But it takes some experience and know-how to put a stringer of fish in the boat in a high wind when the waves are a couple of feet high and you aren't prepared to adjust and cope with it.

When I refer to open water trolling for speckled perch, I am talking about dragging a combination lure and attached minnow near the bottom on either poles or lightweight rod and reel.

I think it is the surest way to put specks in the boat, and you don't have to wait half a year for them to spawn. They'll bite a Super Jig-minnow combination if it is presented properly. And properly means at the right depth, speed and motion so that even the most discerning crappie can't separate a morsel of food from a phony man-made trap. There are three "B's" to remember:

Control of the boat, the first "B," in a wind that raises white-caps on the lake and tosses your boat around is the first problem. Go with the wind with your trolling motor, and make sure your outboard engine on the stern is straight, or at least turned so that the wind that strikes it will not make your boat difficult to manage. Straight is the way when there is calm water, but you may have to turn it slightly in a wind to maintain a course.

Whether it is a windy or calm day, you will be looking for the deepest holes in the lake, hopefully where there is some aquatic bottom growth or other cover that holds specks winter and summer. Thus, it is imperative that you control the boat. You will also find your work easier if you'll keep the lowest possible profile. Standing in the boat is like holding up a sail, and makes steering more difficult.

251

The next "B" that is important in a wind is the bobber. Many times I have seen speck trollers dragging snap-on plastic corks as big as a baseball. Obviously a float of such size will catch a lot of the wind and wave motion. A fast speck that's full of hunger pangs might chase a bait being tossed around by a sailing bobber, but you'll have a much better chance at catching some fish with a small float that does not react much to the wind. A two-inch long, half-inch diameter styrofoam float, when properly trolled, will be only half out of the water or less. The wind has little effect on such a bobber so low in the water, and that's important. You want that jig-minnow combination to look just as natural as possible. And no crappie ever saw a real morsel jumping up and down and from side to side like one does when tied to a hook on a line with an oversize bobber on the surface.

Bait is the next "B" to consider in a high-wind trolling situation. I use a lot of No. 2/0 TruTurn hooks with jigs and minnows when I am trolling. Nothing is better when the wind is calm, and there is no wave more than a few inches high.

It seems to help a little on a windy day to use a No. 2/0 gold hook with a lead head, and a spur that will hold the jig up close to where the eye of the hook is tied to the monofilament. No speck will hit a jig very often that slips down on the bend of the hook where the minnow is impaled. I have dragged them for hours on the bend without any success, and then got quick action on the same hook and jig as soon as I pushed it back to the eye of the hook. The jig hooks that I use have enough lead on the hook at the eye to help keep my bait down, and the jig will hold for several strikes. You do eventually have to replace the jig because the live-looking tentacles will be torn and damaged from the strikes of the fish and your work in removing the hook from the specks' mouths.

Weight on the line is ultra-important when fishing lakes by trolling in wind . In calm water, I always try to press on three No. 2 lead shot, eight inches apart, above the hook and bait. I like the clothespin-type sinkers by Water Gremlin because they can be removed quickly or added without much effort. Conventional shot can be removed and added too, but it takes more work with a pair of pliers. Just press the shot and it will open. Logically, pliers is the way to clamp the shot on the line, but more lead has been pressed on line with teeth than any other way. Dentists must love fishermen who use their teeth to clamp the shot on the line.

On a cold day, you bundle up and still catch
speckled perch.

You can't catch crappie trolling in a high wind with just
three of the medium-size shot on the line. A little speck may hit
now and then, but the chances are that the bait is only a couple
of feet under the water if the boat is moving along rapidly and the
line doesn't have additional lead. I sometimes use as much as five
and six shot, always about six or eight inches apart up the line.
I do not believe bigger, heavier shot will work as well as additional
smaller shot. The heavier weight seems to detract from the life-
likeness of the trolled minnow and jig.
        Obviously speed of the boat that is dragging your lines
is paramount. You cannot just say "Set the troll motor on a
certain speed" and know that is what to recommend. Usually in
calm waters I run my Motor-Guide on No. 2 speed, sometimes No.
1. It will move directly in proportion to the load on the boat, and
the amount of energy stored in the batteries. The wind is a greater
factor, much more pronounced than either weight in the boat or
battery capability. The force of the gale teaches you where to run
your trolling motor after a few experiences. Often, all you need to
do is head with the wind, and occasionally touch your trolling
motor to keep the boat straight. The wind may be moving you at

the proper pace without any propulsion from your motor.

How then can a novice determine what speed is best for catching these fish? There is a proven way insofar as I am concerned. Put enough weight on the line and travel at such a speed that the angle from the rod or pole tip, to the cork on the surface is about 60 degrees. If it is 45 degrees, you are too fast, and probably have too little lead. If it goes straight down, you may be too slow or the line is weighted too much. The 60-degree angle is a fine rule of thumb that works. If you have so much wind that you can't move slowly and have the angle of 60 degrees, it's time to get off the lake. A storm is on and you are in danger in a small boat.

Other bits of advice will help you catch specks trolling in the wind or in calm water. Try to troll your jig as close to the bottom as possible, hopefully about one foot off the floor, and in Florida where most lakes are only 15 feet deep or less, it is not hard to drag a jig and minnow right in front of the fish when they feed on the bottom.

Speckled perch will rise from deep-water havens to strike a bait, but most authorities say the fish will almost never go down to take a bait. Douglas Hannon, the Bass Professor of Odessa, Florida, has observed largemouths and other species for over 20 years, and he has never seen any indication that a fish will dive down for a trolled bait. They will burst up for one when it appeals to them.

While these suggestions on how to catch specks in a high wind have been arrived at after a lifetime of fishing all over the South, let me point out that there is nothing quite as definite as death and taxes. The exceptions to all the fishing rules are legendary. One in particular is a classic with me. I was fishing in Lake Woodruff just south of Astor Park on the St. Johns River. It was around the middle of March, and the wind was huffing and puffing. Woodruff is a small lake , surrounded by woods, and it seemed to be the logical place to get out of some of the storm and still keep a hook in the water. I couldn't keep the boat headed with the wind as it swirled and tossed me around dangerously. In desperation, I decided to take in my poles and quit. I was then broadside to the wind, and the very small bass boat was tossing and dipping water on the sides. I put one pole across the boat with the line dangling in the water while I was attempting to wind up another line and leave for home. That hook in the water had no minnow and no jig, just a 2/0 gold hook that was naked after I

One of the thrills of fishing is showing off the catch.

had hung it on the bottom and lost my bait just before I placed it in the boat. I heard that rod rattling on the gunnels, and it started to topple over the side. I reached for the handle, and held it precariously as the wind had me all out of balance. There was a fish on that line that had defied all the rules. I struggled and eventually pulled in a 2-pound, 3-ounce speckled perch, the largest one I ever caught in the St. Johns lakes.

Sometimes the specks pay little attention to the rules. They just do their thing and it makes all the advice and expertise garnered over a lifetime seem useless. There are no absolutes.

Over the years of speck fishing I have repeatedly admonished fellow anglers in the boat for putting on a large minnow with a jig. "You just won't catch anything when you have such a jig and minnow. It's too big to interest most of the speckled perch," I often advised. "Don't ever put on a minnow longer than two and a half inches." And that is my recommendation. But the exception comes to light and makes me look foolish.

My nine-year-old grandson had become tired, and was ready to go home before I was ready to quit. He decided to play with the bait in the minnow bucket, and finding a real giant minnow about four inches long, he hooked it through the eyes in front of his pink Super-Jig, and tossed it out the stern of the boat. The line tightened, and the cork plunged under almost like something had been there waiting for his offering. He squealed and yelled, and hauled in the biggest speck we had caught all day. I knew I was in for an "I told you so."

"You see, Granddaddy? I told you we would do better if we had some big baits," he said, and I had no answer for that. His success had debunked my advice. Sometimes it just isn't my day.

The best laid plans of fishermen often go awry. Perhaps it is that uncertainty that makes the sport so intriguing. It keeps us guessing.

Arthur Prince catches a wintertime speck in
Orange Lake.

Rx—Fish a Day and a Half a Week

The widely-respected Duke Hospital, Durham, North Carolina, had a 40-year-old patient teetering on the brink of a nervous and general physical breakdown from long hours of overwork in the fall of 1939. He was Melvin B. Andrews, Sr., a farm boy, who for 16 years was an educator and then became a super-active insurance salesman in Goldsboro, North Carolina. He had tackled his new insurance profession with such dedication, setting himself a quota of 15 interviews a day, that he found himself on the go from daylight until 10:00 P.M. and beyond, six days in every week. With almost no time left for his wife and five children, he became ill, weak, anemic, virtually disabled after only a year as a salesman.

A graduate of Trinity College, later Duke University, Andrews called the hospital in Durham and asked to go through the famous clinic for a check-up to determine what was killing him. Accepted by the administrator, he reported to the internists and spent five days of intricate physical examination with nine doctors searching for every physical flaw in the patient. They could find nothing.

At the end of the physical exam, the doctors called Andrews to a conference room and revealed their findings.

"Melvin," they began. "You have no disease, no real physical illness. You have worked yourself almost to death, and indeed you may do just that soon. You must find something to do as recreation. Can you play golf, tennis, organize a softball league, or anything that will occupy some of your time and take you away from your work?" they asked.

"No, I can't do any of those things. I would like to fish, if I had time," he told them.

"Then that's the answer. We are writing a prescription for you today. You cannot fill it at the pharmacy. You are to take no treatment, swallow no medicine. The prescription is simply that you go home and from this day forth, you are to fish one and a half days every week. Do you understand that?" the senior

J. A. Herlocker, retired from the Charlotte, N.C., *Observer,* fishes two poles at a time for crappie in the grass.

physician asked. "You can continue working, but you must stop to fish."

"Yes, I understand it, but I don't know whether I can make a living and fish a day and a half every week." the sick salesman said.

"Well, it's either that or your family soon will not have a husband and father. The decision is up to you," they said.

M.B. Andrews returned home that September afternoon half a century ago and relayed the prescription to his family. Starting that week, he began fishing, often more than just a day and a half a week. He adhered to the advice strictly for 53 years and on September 6, 1980 he celebrated his 91st birthday by going fishing and driving his own car to get his license renewed for another four years. He fished alone generally, did not use a cane, and his doctor told him the week after that memorable birthday that he "was fit as a fiddle and strong as a horse."

Andrews continued to operate his successful insurance business until he was 82, and then retired to be free to fish every day he wanted to. "I have become a terrible crank about fishing. People just want to talk to me about fishing all the time," he said when he turned 91.

Until he was 75, Andrews continued fishing alone in his tiny boat and was adept at catching all the Eastern North Carolina species, especially, bass, bluegills and what he called "crappie perch." But when the water skiers became too rambunctious on the Wayne County Wildlife Lake, 11 miles from his home, he began fishing off the piers that are built out back of many of the homes that are on the 100-acre lake.

Fishing from the piers after giving up his boat, he still managed to catch limits of panfish and an occasional bass, all of which he gave to "the widow ladies of the community."

In 1946 N.C. State College, Raleigh, North Carolina, began sponsorship of a fishing school, or tournament, each year, and at that time it was held in fresh water. It has since become a saltwater event. That year the program was scheduled for the beautiful Fontana Lake in the mountains outside Bryson City, North Carolina. The entry fee was $175.00 and included everything—boats, motors, lodging, meals, guides, and bait. Andrews landed 16 different species, during the three-day event and was named "North Carolina's Champion Fisherman," a title he cherished.

"I have fished every hole, pond, lake and stream in Wayne County and many at other places all the way to Florida. I have saltwater fished off every pier on the Atlantic Ocean between Virginia and Murrells Inlet in South Carolina. Of all of those piers I believe Barnacle Bill's at Surf City, North Carolina, is the most productive," said this veteran of many thousands of days fishing.

The biggest fish Andrews ever caught in fresh water just might have been close to the world champion crappie. It was landed from a sand hole off the Neuse River and, oddly, he wasn't really there when it was caught, but he considered it his catch. He had set a line with a live minnow on it, tied it to a tree and walked away to eat lunch. The fish hit while he was gone, made a lot of noise with its splashing and another angler pulled it in. The fish weighed 4 1/2 pounds. The world record black crappie until recently was only five pounds.

The biggest saltwater fish he ever caught he didn't really land either. It was a six foot or longer sailfish and again it was in a tournament being sponsored by North Carolina State University. This time it was in the Atlantic. Andrews hooked a giant sail and fought it a long time. Finally the captain of the charter boat asked to handle the rod awhile. He quickly lost the fish, although it jumped and dived and was seen and admired by all on board numerous times. In that the captain lost the fish, not Andrews, the Goldsboro fishing champion was given honorable mention in the contest, even though the fish was never brought to the gaff.

"The largest fish I ever actually landed was an 18 1/2-pound black sea bass that I caught in the Gulf Stream off Morehead City. I'll never forget it. We set out that morning with a hundred or more people on the boat. They got up this pot of money by asking each fisherman to put in $1.00 with the catcher of the biggest fish getting the dough at the end of the day. They asked me to join in, but you see, I am an ordained, licensed Methodist minister and I preach, when asked, at churches of this area. I felt this was gambling and was wrong. I would have won the pot had I put in my $1.00 and they really ragged me about it when the boat docked. But I had to live up to my convictions and I wasn't sorry," Andrews said.

Oddly enough, while fishing was so good to him and left him in excellent health at the age of 91, it almost killed him too. In 1970, he was returning home from fishing with a friend driving the car. He was asleep at the time the driver crashed into the back of a truck. It was 45 days later when Andrews revived from a coma in the hospital having no recollection of the accident.

His wife passed away at the age of 76. She once fished with him regularly until he "scolded" her one day and she never went again. They were fishing off a crowded pier near Morehead City and catching spots and Virginia mullet. Rods and reels were not anti-backlash apparatus then as they are now, and Melvin would cast out for his wife in order to avoid the bird nests in the lines and possibly the accidental catching of someone's eye or ear with the hook, too. He walked away from her a few moments to fish the other side of the pier and when he returned, she was sitting down trying to untangle a terrible backlash.

"How did you do that?" Melvin asked his wife.

"I decided to cast a little further out and it tangled like this," she replied.

"But I told you not to cast, that I'd do it for you," Melvin reprimanded, with perhaps too much hostility in his voice for a wife he dearly loved.

"I'll never do it again," she promised. And she never did. The last 30 years of her life, she never again went fishing with her husband or anyone else.

As Andrews fished more and more in those years when his family of five was growing up and his wife had her hands full

260

taking care of them, she asked him one day if indeed doctors at Duke had really prescribed all that fishing, at least a day and half a week. He assured her that it was a legal, medical prescription, but try as he did, he could not find the prescription. Nearly two decades had elapsed since he had been told to fish and now his wife was questioning his putting so much time on the water. He wrote to Duke and explained the circumstances, asking if by some hook or crook they could verify the prescription issued so long ago. A few days later he opened his mail to find a Xerox copy of the exact prescription, taken from his efficiently filed folder in the hospital record room. His wife gave him no more argument on that subject.

Born a water-head child to a tenant farm family at Suttertown in the Coastal Plains of North Carolina, in 1889, he was abused by his father who whipped him and frequently told him he wished he had died when he was a baby. He was subsequently told by the same cruel father that he would beat him enough until he did die. Melvin Andrews survived because of the love of a compassionate mother who cherished and sheltered him the best she could in the face of unexplainable violence against him.

Believed to be mentally abnormal because of the oddly shaped head greatly out of proportion to his body, the child was not allowed to even go to school until he was 14 years old. Then, with normal learning ability, he managed to pass ten units of high school work by the time he was 18. Melvin wrote to Trinity College asking for admission and was refused because he did not have the 16 required high school credits.

He then penned a letter to the president of Trinity, who was to serve even after it was endowed by the Duke family and the name changed. He told them of his abnormal childhood, his abused body and lack of formal schooling but vowed he could make it if the school would admit him. The school asked him to come for an interview. He did, was given a job in the library and in 1913, graduated with a B.S.degree, cum laude. He taught school at Cary, North Carolina, one year and returned to get his Masters Degree in 1916. Before entering the insurance business 15 years later, he taught school at summer terms at the University of North Carolina at Greensboro, headed the public school system in Fayetteville and in Rockingham, North Carolina

That water-head baby grew to be perfectly normal and a brilliant, hard working American who resorted to fishing only when his life depended on it. For years he took a box of catalpa worms out of the refrigerator, drove to the Wildlife Club lake and caught a mess of panfish for his neighbors.

"Yesterday I caught 26 bream in an hour and a half off the same pier. Of course, I was here on the major period and you can just do better during those major solunar periods," Andrews said as he pulled a crumpled booklet from his hip pocket and quickly glances down the page to see if this was another good hour to catch his limit. Most devout fishermen believe in the solunar times that occur twice daily when the fish allegedly are more active.

"Some of my widowed lady friends really like to eat fish and I'll see if I can't make some of them happy again today," this great senior citizen who had a doctor's mandate to fish, would think out loud.

Author's note: *In 1983 this unusual outdoorsman died at his home in Goldsboro at the age of 94. He lived by a doctor's prescription to fish a day and a half a week for almost half a century and outlived almost all of his friends and many of his family.)*

Spawning season puts specks in the grass.

Tody Edisto Dukes. . .
Named After a South Carolina River, This Black Guide Is Institution

Edisto Dukes, known as Tody by thousands of fishermen, has the prescription for staying healthy, young and vital. He takes the medicine daily, and at 80, this black man who stands 6' 4" and weighs 225 muscular pounds, gladly takes his own medicine. He fishes the waters of the Santee-Cooper reservoir in South Carolina's low country every day the weather is fitting the year around. That's his medicine.

"They ain't nobody goin' have low blood pressure, high blood pressure, or any of them other things if he'll fish enough. They ain't no heart attacks for people who fishes. Out here you ain't goin' worry. That's what gives folks all these disease you hear about," says the senior citizen who has professionally guided anglers at Santee for the past 36 years. "I guides folks ever day they wants me, but effin I don't have a customer, I just goes by myself and fishes." His health and stamina at an age way past retirement for most, speaks for the success of his therapy, and the bass, stripers, bream and crappie he unloads verify his expertise as a knowledgeable guide, perhaps unequalled in the Palmetto State.

Named "Edisto" after a fast-running, gin-clear river in the South Carolina low country, someone nicknamed him "Tody" more than half a century ago. The name still sticks and customers from many states call the Goat Island Resort complex at Summerton, South Carolina, to ask for this congenial old native to guide them to successful fishing adventures. "We want Tody," they say, and everyone knows that's Edisto.

Tody was born right in those acres that surround Santee-Cooper, but then it was farms and forests with just the Santee and Cooper rivers running wild through the swamplands.

"They was 18 of us young'uns in my family, ten girls and eight boys, and we grew up fishing and hunting around here. Then in 1928, I worked on the railroad that came in to haul the

Dr. Rowell Burleson admires a Tody Dukes crappie
caught in Santee-Cooper open water.

logs away when the people decided to build a big dam here, and block up de water to make electricity. Then in the '30's, I helped 'em cut the trees and clear the land where de water was goin' be backed up. We cut a lot of 'em, but some just had to be left standing. They didn't even haul out all de logs, just tied 'em together and fastened 'em to the bottom. All that water out there just about has logs jammed down on the bottom. That makes it a real good place for de fish to hide," Tody says. And when the water covered the forests and farms early in the 1940's, Tody began guiding fishermen and quail hunters, and he hasn't done anything else for more than four decades.

That profession, which he dearly loves, helped him raise nine children of his own, and he is mighty proud of them, as he is of his 21 grandchildren and four great-grandchildren. Some of his offspring and brothers and sisters live in Philadelphia and other metropolitan areas. "I'll never die in one of dem big cities unless I do when I'm a vis'tin'. I ain't ever goin' live up there," he says, and you know he is married to the Santee and a fishing pole. Several of his children are avid anglers, including his 27-year-old youngest daughter who still lives at home just up the road at Davis Station. "She comes down here, and she fishes wid' me sometimes and sure enough she beats me," he says and grins like he was glad to be outdone.

"Things has been mighty tough for me plenty of times. I remember in the house we was raised in, that you could look through the cracks and count the stars when you went to bed at night. When it was real cold weather, we had to work hard to keep from freezin'. We didn't have nothin' but a chimney fire to heat the house, and some of us would chop wood while the others warmed up and then we would swap places. Someone had to be cutting wood all de time while the others warmed at the fire. Times was so hard the river only flowed two days a week. Then I got on the WPA durin' the Big Depression, and worked a whole week—hard— for $2.70, and furnished a wagon and two mules, too. But I sho' was glad to get dat $2.70, and it went a long way. I found out then you don't have to be a mill'onaire to be happy. Money ain't what makes folks happy. It's doin' what you like, like I does out here on the water," the old black man philosophizes. "I'd take my $2.70 to town on Saturday night and get ever'thing I needed. It would buy more than $100.00 now."

"Folks come down here to go bass fishing, and they want me to take 'em. I'm glad to do it. Sometimes they want to know effin' I'll guarantee 'em to catch a big fish. Sho'nuff, I'm not guaranteeing nothing like that. My life is all I can guarantee. How'm I going to know whether the fish is goin' to bite or not? I tells you, you don't never know when you'll catch a big bass. I don't care whether it's a young moon, old moon, full moon or no moon night. Them fish ain't goin' bite until he's hongrie," Tody says. "Some say they won't bite on no east wind. But sometime I catches limits on a east wind, and get skunked when it's not from the east."

Customers of Tody often want to know about how big his largest bass was. He is all truth and no bull when he answers the questions. "You only counts them you puts in the boat. I have had some big 'uns tear up my lines, my rods, reels and ever'thing. I know they was really big, but the biggest one I landed was 10-pounds. I carried it home, and we ate him. But I caught a 28-pound rockfish and a crappie that weighed 3-pounds and 12-ounces.

"Just yesterday I was fishin' the mouth of the creek at Cow Pasture (some shallow water near Caw Taw Creek and Goat Island), and I hooked an old bass that done stripped all the gears out of my reel. I had to borrow this 'un to fish wid today," he says.

Tody's fishing has no semblance of modernity. He has an old 12-foot aluminum boat with three metal seats built across it. On the front and middle ones, he has wired football stadium seats with folding backs. He sits in an old homemade wooden chair that has been his day-in and day-out perch for the past 16 years. It's sun bleached and without paint, but from that position he cranks and steers his 20-horse Mercury, the biggest most powerful outboard he has ever owned. He wants nothing bigger or better. With these meager facilities, he continues to successfully guide customers almost every day of the week and in 36 years of such work, he has never had anyone fall overboard, never been stranded on the lake, and has not even been towed to the landing but one time. His propeller fell off. "I've been pretty lucky," he says in an understatement.

"A long time ago, didn't nobody fish for bass 'cept rich people. Now all kinds of folks fishes for 'em. And back then didn't no lady folks fish either, 'cept some right here on the river to get a mess to eat. But I'se carried many ladies fishin' lately. Let me tell you somethin' too. Some of them women is better then men at catching fish. They'se got more patience. Some of 'em are real good.

"Some of the best times I have ever had fishin' was with some young children. I remember not long ago this crippled boy and his Ma came from Sumter and wanted me to take 'em crappie fishing. We was stump jumpin' with cane poles and minnows. That boy and his ma caught 72 crappies and one catfish that day. He was de happiest boy I ever saw. He kept kiddin' me. Wanted to know why I couldn't catch one. I really would've liked to catch some, but I was happy. I didn't get but three on my hook all day. That boy had a real ball," Tody remembers.

Tody uses a paddle in the stern to move his customers looking for bass in and out of the cypress-studded creeks and flatwaters. He has never had any use for a trolling motor. He'll go with you guiding for bass with your fancy bass boat, but he will cast from the stern and let you run the trolling devices. He'll put you where the fish are, but he only does the engineering of the boat when you ride with him.

"That log yonder is where I lost that big booger bass yesterday," he points out. "It's been lying dere a long time, and I've caught a many a fish beside that old log."

Tody is a believer in the old school when plastic worm fishing. That is, when he feels the bump he waits and waits and waits before he sets the hook. It seems like an eternity as compared with a fast one, two, three count practiced by most of today's bassers. But he still catches fish.

"When this water was first backed up over the logs and bushes, we didn't have no rods and reels. But when we got hold of one of them lures, we'd tie it on a line and a long cane pole and jiggle it along the edge of the water. We caught all kinds of bass on just that kinda' rig. But ain't no kind of fishin' good as it used to be. Old Bill Davis and me used to come out here at daylight an' catch all we wanted before eight o'clock. He would then go back and put in his day's work. Then many is de time when I come down here on the lake just before sundown and catch my family a mess of fish for supper that very night 'fore dark," he recalls.

"I carries some people out here fishin' and they keeps saying 'Wonder when they'se goin' bite?' They'se goin' to bite when they'se hongrie, and not before that. You gotta have patience to fish, and when I got them folks that's always aggrevatin' me, I'm glad to get rid of 'em. I put 'em in the best places, and if they'll put those wo'ms on dem plugs where I tell em, they'll catch some fish," he says with confidence.

"Then some folks come back to fish with me a year after we done had a good day and I carries 'em to a spot and tells 'em

Tody Dukes reels in a big Santee crappie.

to start here. They want to know why I don't go back to that same place we caught 'em at last year. Well, de fish ain't always at the same place they was a year ago, but you can't tell some folks that. They'se sure if they was fish there last year they'se there now.

"See dat old log right on that point? That's got a big old bass around it and, oh brudder, when he hits, he just wallows and cuts up and you can't git him out of dare.

"I likes a feller who likes to fish. He won't steal de stuff out of yo' boat, and you don't have to lock yo' doors at night against him. They'se lots of folks who come in yo' house to hurt you now, and you have to keep de doors locked, but they ain't fishermen. Christ had desciples that was fishermen, and he told 'em to cast de nets on the right side of the boat, and they caught so many they couldn't bring it up. De people believed what they saw, and they knew He was Christ, and He put de fish and de animals here on dis land fo' people to enjoy. They's lots of folks now who says it ain't right to hunt and fish. How can they be against huntin' and fishin'? God put 'em here for people," Tody again philosphizes, and you detect some of the Methodist religion in him.

"If you is one of dem people that's always sad, you just ain't no good. You got to be happy to be any good. Them sad people can't do nothin'" he opines.

Tody knows all the nuts and bolts of crappie fishing at Santee. He knows the where-to and the how-to, but in a day of fast food and fast boats, he is inclined to be a nonchalant, easy-going guide who still considers it a sport to fish, not a business and a struggle. He thinks all kinds of fishing is fun, and the meat delicious, even the bowfin. He is a great believer in wasting no fish, and is bitterly opposed to filleting any fish.

"De best meat on a fish is that around the backbone and on de ribs. Some folks come down here and just cut a little ole strip off both sides of the back and throws the rest in the garbage cans. We just takes that backbone they throws away and cooks it. That's de very best meat on de fish. I saw dis one fellow cutting little strips off the back of some lil' ole crappies. He wasn't getting a piece biggern' a lead pencil on each side. I told him iffen I'd knowed he wasn't going hurt that fish any more'n dat, I'd brought some band-aids wid me. I believe dem cuts would heal."

Crappie fishing at Santee is good any time of year, but it is best in the spring. Tody carries his customers into the shallows of the many creeks and tributaries where 'gator grass, cypress and sparkleberry bushes, briers and overhanging weeping

269

willows shade the spawning areas. Thousands of acres of such nesting ground is available on both sides of this vast expanse of reservoir and there's plenty of room for privacy for fishermen regardless of the number of anglers.

He urges his customers to put their baits right up close to the trunks of the trees and grass. A bait two feet away often doesn't entice a strike, but one right on the button prompts the fish to hit. Likewise, a carelessly flipped bait that doesn't slither down just inches away from the 'gator grass is likely to attract little attention, but one that rubs hard against the cover is irresistible to fish in those waters that are from two to five feet deep in the spring and early summer.

There's one particular acreage of the backwater, just minutes up Caw Taw Creek from Goat Island where Tody launches his boat, that is known as Caw Taw Hatchery. It gets its name because the really big fish find this two-mile long dark water ideal for spawning and raising young. While Tody hasn't hooked the famed "Aunt Samantha" lunker bass that lurks in a slough off Caw Taw, many others have. A Columbia, South Carolina angler says he has had the fish strike nine times and each time she got away. Most times the giant of the species just breaks the line and goes on her way, but the last time, she rose, shook her head in defiance, and threw the plug halfway back to the boat. The wall mount of Caw Taw hatchery still swims free.

This Caw Taw area is loaded with big bass. The water has a darkish tint in the hatchery area, but as it crosses under the black-top road that leads to Goat Island, the water is about the color of three-day-old apple cider. At least it looks like that because of the red and orange clay terrain. The veterans of bassing in the Santee say Caw Taw is one of the best big lunker areas in the entire chain. Striper fishermen trolling big lures here often land trophy bass instead. But Lake Marion has many other significant bass havens like the Red Banks, Potato Creek, Pine Islands, among many others.

Tody fishes dozens of these shallows where bass bed, using black, blue and purple plastic worms, often a Ding-A-Ling with a redtail, but Rebels and Creek Chubs on top, Charlie O, Mini-Max, and the Rebel R series crank baits are likewise proven Santee bass catchers.

As the weather gets hotter in July and August most crappie fishermen move out into the big lake. Often where the creeks enter the main reservoir there are sudden drops in depths from five or ten feet to more than 35 feet. Here is where most of the fish are caught in what the devout call "drop fishing." They simply anchor the boat at the shallow level, then cast weighted baits into the depths, flipping and winding slowly as these baits walk over the logs on the bottom and up the steep ledges. The crappie must call these havens heaven, and they school those areas in vast numbers.

A 25-year veteran of Santee fishing, and close friend of Tody, is Rusty Watson of Summerton. He says he has caught fish on the drops until he was completely given out, often catching one on every cast for an hour or more. Rusty releases most of his bass and keeps the crappie, but he vows the drops are the best way to land fish at Santee. The bass on these drops often weigh from five to eight or nine pounds, and the crappies are 2 to 3-pounds.

One of these most productive drops is at the mouth of Wyboo Creek, a few minutes run toward the dam from Goat island. The water here drops from six or seven feet to more than 30 feet in not much more distance than a couple of boat lengths. The fish accumulate here in vast numbers, and on weekends and holidays the area is often dotted with boats dribbling baits up the ledges. The upper reaches of this Wyboo Creek, in sight of the drops, is where Paul Flannigan caught the 16-pound, 2-ounce lunker 40 years ago that still stands as the Palmetto State bass record.

You lose a lot of lines on these drops because the bottom is latticed with sunken cypress from the forest that once grew here. Tody uses 30-pound monofilament line, as do most bass fishermen. When the hang-ups become too annoying, they will use a float worm, that is a worm attached to the line with a swivel several inches above the weight. Often you can drag this weight over the logs with the worm and hook just off the obstructions and get those live bumps you are waiting for.

The fish migrate up and down these creeks, often with the current or in pursuit of the schools of shad, their staple diet here. If the current is moving toward the dam, and the shad are present, the drops will be loaded. If the current is moving away from the dam, then most fishermen believe you are wasting your time on the drops.

Tody never goes up the river as far as Rimini, but Watson and others who fish those dismal, swampy waters, believe many of the really big bass are in that area. It has a lot of floating grass and some hydrilla. Also, some of the landings at Rimini are at such desolate end-of-the-sawmill-road locations that you can only get to them with good four-wheel-drive vehicles. A place in the Rimini area known as "Sparkleberry," named for the bushes that cover much of the flatwater there, is loaded with large lunkers. Watson fishes the area and has had some fabulous successes. He particularly likes to fish worm baits under the umbrella cypress bushes that make some of the lake there a dark, ominous wilderness. It's easy to get lost here if you are not an outdoorsman with experience.

While bassers almost always seem to prefer early and late hours for fishing, Watson believes that from mid-morning until mid-afternoon are the best hours for fishing the day of the full moon. Tody doesn't prefer any moon phase or any particular hours. His statement still stands that the fish will bite then they are "hongrie."

You'll probably catch fish, especially crappie, if you fish Santee with Tody Dukes. But more than that, you'll be absorbed with a feeling of peacefulness, contentment. You get caught up in his philosophy of not worrying about anything, and living longer by keeping a bait in the water. Dedicated to having his customers go home with a mess of fish for the table is a prime objective. Tody is quick to suggest his clients fish for something else if bassing "just ain't right" that day. He is the greatest crappie fisherman on Lake Marion, and takes pride in being called "King of the Santee Crappie Guides." He'll help you stump jump and catch a stringer of these crappies if you are not so determined on bassing that any other angling is degrading. If he can't find the crappies in the deep water that covers thousands of stumps, an unlikely eventuality, he just might spot the gulls diving and put you right in the midst of the giant stripers that have made Santee famous. He knows how to catch those, too.

One way or the other, no time is wasted when you are fishing with Tody Dukes. Indeed, no time is wasted that makes two people friends, and you'll make a friend when you fish at Santee with Edisto for a day or two.

Bamberg, S.C. Native Wayne Eller
Fishing Book Author Has South Carolina Roots

by Larry Cribb
Editor, *Living in South Carolina*

Having been an avid fisherman for about as long as I can remember, when I can't be on the water, my second favorite activity is reading books and magazines about fishing or watching outdoor shows on TV.

Several months ago as I was looking through the latest issue of *Crappie World* magazine, an ad for a new book on crappie fishing caught my eye. The book was titled: *Crappie Fishing—Secrets and Tips of a Game Warden.*

The ad read: "The author, Wayne Eller, serves as a Game Warden with the state of Minnesota. Originally from South Carolina, home of the world record black crappie, he brings the best ideas from both South and North to this book."

This was intriguing—a book that would give you a game warden's secrets and tips, and the author was a native of South Carolina too! I fired off a letter to the address in the ad and told the author if he would like, we would consider reviewing it in *LIVING IN SOUTH CAROLINA.*

It was only a few days later when the book arrived, and with it was a letter from the author telling me, among other things, that he was a native of Bamberg who still had relatives in the area (he mentioned two uncles specifically—Carl Cook and Rev. Charles Jeffcoat) and that he loved to come "home" to visit every chance he got.

I told some folks around our office about my discovery, and one staff member in particular was especially interested. It turns out that Bobby Blume, Job Training and Safety Supervisor for The Electric Cooperatives of South Carolina, had been a school classmate of the Minnesota author. Blume had quite a few boyhood stories to relate involving himself and Eller.

The next logical step, after reading and enjoying the book, seemed to be to call Minnesota and interview the author about fishing and his South Carolina roots.

A Gentle Man

Wayne Eller says one of the things he misses most about South Carolina is the gentleness of the people and "the etiquette that is even built into their common, every-day language."

One gets the feeling early in the conversation that Eller is himself a gentle man who loves the outdoors and the people he comes in contact with in his work. Indeed, the idea that initially spawned this book, came as a result of his feeling sorry for anglers, especially family groups, that couldn't seem to catch fish and from his desire to help them learn.

Born in Bamberg on what used to be called Reno Street, now known as Elm Street, Eller spent much of his early years moving back and forth between Georgia and South Carolina with his father. After finishing the 10th grade in Bamberg, he left to go to Minnesota to live with his mother and stepfather for a short time.

"I joined the service and spent two years in Alaska, so I had a quick initiation to weather much different than what I had known in South Carolina," he said.

After service, Eller returned to Minnesota, went to school and then married. "I worked as a house painter and a bus driver, among other things," he said, "but the desire to be a conservation officer became stronger and stronger and I eventually just had to take that exam."

He was accepted as a Conservation Officer (Game Warden) with the state of Minnesota, a post he has now held for 10 years.

He finds his association with fishermen and other outdoorsmen to be one of the greatest rewards of his job. "That and the fact that I feel I can really have an impact in protecting nature," he said.

Eller points out that the biggest difference in being a Conservation Officer in Minnesota as opposed to South Carolina is the weather. "It's definitely the biggest factor," he said, "although there is some difference in the wildlife and the methods employed here in hunting and fishing." (As we spoke on the

274

phone, he pointed out that the outside temperature was some 12 to 15 degrees below zero).

Among other things, he has learned to even enjoy ice fishing. "This time of year down there folks can go out in some of the shallow canals and catch crappie in a few feet of water, while up here now you'll probably find them anywhere from eight to 30 feet deep and you have to drill a hole through two feet of ice to get to them," he said.

In relating how he came to write the book, Eller said that being on the water all the time checking fishermen, he saw a lot of people who weren't catching fish who could be catching fish.

"I'd check one boat and a guy would have a real nice string of fish, then I come up on the next boat, maybe a family out fishing, and they wouldn't have anything. I'd really feel sorry for them and would spend some time with them trying to tell them something that might help them so they could get a few fish, but you know how hard it is to try to explain to someone in a situation like that in a short time what they needed to be doing.

"I got to thinking that there must be a way to get this information to them so they could really enjoy being on the water and catching fish, so I started trying to put together a little brochure that I was going to try to print up out of my own pocket and just hand it out to people who needed it," he continued.

"Well, the information just started growing and six years later I had this big manuscript. It turned into a full-fledged book with lots of drawings and color photographs, and a year ago it became a reality."

About the Book

When asked why someone in South Carolina would benefit from reading this book, Eller replied that crappie behave the same in South Carolina as they do in Minnesota. "In comparable weather and water conditions, they have the same habits regardless of which part of the country they live in," he said. "Up here we have much colder weather and for a longer period of time, but other than that there is really no difference in the behavior of the fish."

He also pointed out that he drew on his experience from much fishing in South Carolina, Minnesota and in Florida in researching and writing the book.

Written in the first person, Eller's book is down-to-earth, easy reading that covers just about anything an angler could want to know about crappie fishing, with tips included on fishing for other panfish and bass.

The drawings and illustrations are instructional as well as entertaining in this 140-page book which includes 47 full-color photographs and 38 illustrations and other features aimed at helping anglers catch crappie.

Topics in the book include: effect of weather conditions on successful crappie fishing; best crappie lures based on biological response and habitat; tying instructions for the most effective crappie catching jigs, how to fish for crappies in canals, bays, culverts, streams; how to find and catch crappie under floating cattail bogs, water hyacinths and other shaded structure; fishing flooded timber from small ponds to reservoirs; the crappie's favorite aquatic plants, post spawn and summer hideouts and much more.

Confirmed Jig Fisherman

A confirmed jig fisherman, Eller has a chapter on the secret of the marabou jig, and another chapter on how to make and use the jigs. He calls this lure the ultimate crappie lure and says in the book, "There is nothing more devastating to a fish population than a determined angler armed with an assortment of small minnow-imitating lead head jigs.

Eller tries to make it back to South Carolina at least every other year to visit relatives and do some crappie fishing. "I always drag my boat when I come home for a visit and I always head for Lake Marion while I'm there," he said. "I hop off of 301 right there near Jack's Creek and get me a nice mess of South Carolina crappie.

"I take great delight in coming home to fish at Santee-Cooper, then back in Minnesota going on the St. Croix River which is the boundary between Minnesota and Wisconsin—using the same lures and the same techniques at both places and coming home with fish from both places. Like I say, crappie act the same no matter what section of the country they live in and what works in Minnesota will work in South Carolina."

I'm sure Wayne would like to hear from some fellow South Carolina crappie fishermen. If you'd like to drop him a line or order a copy of the book, you can use this address:

Crappie Book
Box 85
Forest Lake, MN 55025

The Book—*Crappie Fishing, Secrets and Tips of a Game Warden*—is $9.95 and that includes tax, postage and handling.

For Greater Boating Safety
Remember to Stay in Touch

Many recreational boaters are finding out what captains of ships and larger boats have known for years: communication with the shore and other boats is essential for safe boating. Radios provide weather information, news and contact with other boats that even small boat owners need for their safety on the water.

With a VHF marine radio, boaters can keep in touch with their buddy fishing in the next cove, find out where the hot spots are located, and keep in touch with the shore in case of emergency. When a medical emergency occurs while out on the water, calling ahead can mean help is waiting upon arrival at shore, saving precious hours or minutes.

Today's marine radios range from small, portable, hand-held radios all the way up to the deluxe models with channel scanning and 25 watts of power. Power for VHF marine radios ranges from 1 watt to a maximum of 25 watts, with 1 watt providing close-range communication. The maximum distance most VHF radios will transmit or receive is about 20 miles, and VHF's are generally known as "line of sight" radios, transmitting only as far as the eye can see.

Because most recreational boaters are more familiar with car phones than VHF radios, it's important to know the rules and regulations that cover their use, as well as some radio etiquette.

Using a marine radio is not like using a telephone—you can't simply pick it up and call someone. The Federal Communications Commission regulates the use of marine radios and requires that all radios be licensed. There are 90 U.S. and international channels available for marine communication, with certain channels recommended and required for a specific use. Channel 16 is the safety and distress channel, with channel 6 reserved for intership safety communications. Channel 22 is primarily for communication with the U.S. Coast Guard. Knowing the correct channel on which to broadcast, as well as the proper radio etiquette for sending and receiving messages, not only helps get the message to the right people, but keeps from interfering with other radio communications.

With many types of VHF radios available, boaters can choose the unit that will fit their needs. For the small-boat owner who wants a radio for safety and essential communication, but doesn't want the risk of leaving his radio in the boat, a hand-held unit would be perfect. Impulse Technology makes a hand-held unit, the Impulse 600H, which features 82 channels, a rechargeable battery pack and instant channel 16 access. Small radios such as this one provide communication that can be taken with you at the end of the day.

Many boaters like the convenience and safety of having a radio installed in their boat, but don't need all the features offered on some of the larger, deluxe models, or don't have the space for large radios. Many companies make a compact VHF with all the features of the larger radio. These "mini VHFs", like the Impulse 6000, are perfect for the small runabout, especially if the boat is used as a shuttle boat for a houseboat or cruiser. When several friends get together to enjoy the water at the same time, VHF's are great for setting up a lunch or dinner rendezvous, or simply communicating between boats while at speed.

For anglers who fish on large bodies of water, even those lakes the size of middle Georgia's Lake Lanier, Lake of the Ozarks in central Missouri, or Lake Havasu on the Colorado River, a full-featured radio tops the "must have" list. Full-featured VHF's generally provide 90 channels and full scanning of all channels, and will handle the needs of recreational and commercial boaters alike. Most scan functions will pick up any pre-programmed channels with voice activity, so the boater can monitor several channels at one time. Impulse's top-of-the line 7500 VHF also has a dual scan function that allows scanning between channel 16 and another selected channel every second and a half. If a call is expected, the boater can still listen to the safety channel while waiting for the call to come in.

Boaters and anglers both have come to realize the safety and convenience features marine radios afford them. With today's FHF's, boaters can enjoy their time on the water, knowing that help is just a call away. For more information on VHF marine radios, contact: Impulse Technology, 329 Railroad Ave., Pittsburg, CA 94565.

Underwater Eyes—A Key To Taking Slabs

"Depth finders are one of the critical keys to successful crappie angling that s p o r t s m e n should utilize if they want to take large stringers of papermouths," Mike Howard, of Oxford, Alabama, explains. "My fishing partner, David Stancil, also from Oxford, and I have bought three depth finders for our boat to ensure we have the best possible chance of locating

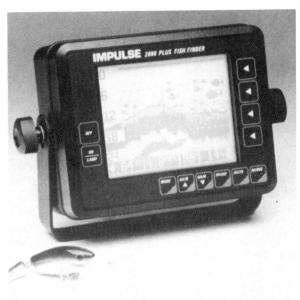

Use a depthfinder to locate Deep-water crappie.

and taking fish. And our investment is paying off."

Howard and Stancil are the reigning 1989 U.S. Crappie Association's Classic winners. Last year alone, the duo brought in over $24,000 practicing what they preach.

"We have learned that using multiple depth finders helps us locate prime crappie habitat easier and more efficiently than we do with just one depth finder," Stancil adds. "But pinpointing habitat is only one advantage that our electronics give us. We also can read the depth of the water, the temperature of the water and determine the speed of our troll besides seeing fish with our depth finders."

Although these two men know discovering suitable crappie habitat, such as a breakline on a point, brushpiles, ledges or drop-offs is crucial to productive days on the water, they also understand the role that water temperature and the speed of their troll play in their catching crappie once structure is located.

"The temperature of the water dictates to us the depth at which we need to keep our jigs to put them where the crappie

279

are," Howard reports. "When the water temperature is in the high 70's, we know we must run the jigs deeper than we do when the water is cooler."

"And the speed of our troll is the key factor in our ability to keep the jigs at the right depth," Stancil adds. "When we're trolling, we continually watch our electronics. And when the fish begin to hit we make a mental note of how fast we are trolling through the area. Then we maintain that speed to keep the jigs at that depth."

Stancil and Howard utilize three depth finders on their boat to guarantee themselves the best view possible of the bottom.

"The machine mounted on the console of the boat allows us to get a general idea of the underwater contours in a region we intend to fish," Howard says. "We also have two other units, one at the bow and one at the stern, to enable each of us, while we're fishing, to watch for structure and crappie the other person may not have seen. We've mounted one depth finder on the right side of the boat and the other on the left. When we troll across a site, we're able to watch twice as much area as we would with only one electronic device in use. And often David may spot fish or cover that I don't on my depth finder.

"Last year when we won the U.S. Crappie Association's Classic, that was exactly what happened. We located a shallow point that jutted out into deeper water. A roadbed with a few submerged, scattered trees on it that held some good-sized crappie paralleled a small portion of the point. Had we not had all our depth finders operating, we might have missed the roadbed, the trees, the fish and possibly the championship."

According to Stancil and Howard, getting involved in the U.S. Crappie Association is a way to learn more about crappie fishing and the secrets of the best papermouth anglers in the country.

"U.S. Crappie is a family-oriented organization," Stancil says. "And the tournaments are much more than mere fishing competitions. Each event gives area fishing enthusiasts a chance to meet other sportsmen, share ideas and tactics, make friends and get everyone in the family involved. U.S. Crappie even has parent/child and husband/wife categories in their tournaments."

Use a Depthfinder to Locate Deep-water Crappie

During the spring, almost anyone can catch crappie—just drop a line in the water and pull out one of those hard-fighting, fun-to-catch panfish. But many anglers stop fishing for crappies during the difficult summer months, when the sun begins to make sitting on the lake feel like being in a fry pan. Summer crappie fishing can be the slowest time of the year, but with the right equipment and some knowledge of crappie behavior, the challenge of warm-weather crappie can be conquered.

Although most crappie anglers are used to finding the papermouths close to banks, knowing that crappie hide in and around structure, many sportsmen fail to realize that crappie will also suspend and travel in schools in open water. Trolling has proven to be a very successful practice for taking these schooling crappie, and anglers have found that by using a depthfinder, they can locate these schools and the deep-water structure where crappies hold.

Finding schooling crappies and deep structure is the first key to success, say the experts from the Impulse Fishing Team, fishing pros from Impulse Technology. When the weather is hot, crappie move deep, often holding 10 to 20 feet below the surface and usually near submerged structure. Crappie can also be found on old creek and river channels, suspended above structure or in the mouths of creeks. Also, look for ledges where the bottom drops off, or shallow water close to deep. By checking a map of the lake before heading out, crappie anglers can chart out likely locations for crappies, using a depthfinder to locate possible crappie-holding structure. Then, anglers can try out several spots that look productive for crappie.

Depthfinders can also help the angler find schools of open-water crappie when trolling. To locate schooling crappie, cruise in a zig-zag pattern or troll slowly over spots with ledges or channels, where crappie like to hold. By using Impulse's 2800Plus fish finder, anglers can view the bottom contours on its

Brenda Carter catches a Lake George speck.

liquid crystal display screen, and have digital depth, speed and surface temperature displayed at the bottom of the screen. Once the angler finds the crappie, he lets out enough line so his jig will troll at the appropriate depth as he idles his boat forward.

To troll for crappies, most fishermen prefer a small, ultralight spinning rod and reel with 4- to 6-pound test line and jigs weighing between 1/8 and 1/64 of an ounce. Some anglers prefer to back-troll, thus keeping boat speed as low as possible.

Crappie are particular. On some days, they'll hit only one color. By trolling and changing the color of the jig the color that interests the crappie can be found, and the action starts.

If crappie are holding around cover, a ledge or a drop-off, the angler should try to stay over that spot with his trolling motor. Fish finder units, such as the Impulse 2800Plus, help the angler locate and stay on the structure by presenting a clear picture of what's below the boat. Dropping an anchor will scare the already skittish crappie, so anglers may want to anchor just upwind of their spot and drift back over it.

Although locating summer crappie can sometimes be difficult, the search is usually worth the effort. By using a depthfinder to look for schooling crappie, and to find the submerged structure, drop-offs and creek beds where crappie usually hold, anglers can improve their summertime crappie fishing to have one successful outing after another.

Florida's Speckled Perch—
The Panfish for Natives and Tourists

Florida's speckled perch, known more widely and scientifically as the black crappie, is the panfish for all seasons in the Sunshine State. It is sought by both natives and tourists from the panhandle to the Keys with lures and natural baits and it feeds more families than any other freshwater fish.

Mistakenly believed to bite only during spawning season from December until March by many, the specks of Florida will feed the year around, and can be caught once the angler understands their life-styles, and puts a bait within sight, sound or smelling distance. True, you can catch a limit without moving the boat when you find them bedding on the full moons from Christmas through March.

You have to work a little harder the rest of the year to catch a cooler full. But it can be done in summer as well as in winter when you put the bait where the fish are, often in the deepest water of the lake, and it doesn't matter whether it's morning or evening, sunny or cloudy, day or night. Speckled perch are always ready to eat.

Contrasting memorable catches come to mind. Both incidents occurred in Central Florida. The first fantastic experience was on a Sunday morning when my wife and I found some lilies and grass shaking in five feet of water in a Lake Lochloosa cove. Fish were obviously bumping the stalks of the clump of half a dozen lilies that floated peacefully on the surface. It was mid-February, and the spawning season. We anchored the boat, picked up a cane pole apiece, impaled a two inch minnow through the eyes on a 2/0 gold colored hook, threaded a small oblong cork three feet above the single lead shot weight, and dropped it near the bumping, shaking aquatic growth. The cork hardly stopped on the surface. It plunged out of sight, and I came in with a 12-ounce speck. My wife was fighting an even larger one on the port side of the boat. We re-baited, dropped the minnows back, and it was the same story over and over from dawn until we ran out of minnows.

Crappie like to forage for food in the lilypads.

We cranked up, motored back to the Twin Lakes Fish Camp, and loaded our perch in a cooler. We carried them to the dressing table and began work. We had caught 91 specks without moving the boat, some weighing 2-pounds. We had them caught, dressed, washed and in freezer bags in time to take a bath, dress and get to the worship service at the Cross Creek

Baptist Church before 11:00 A.M. We might still have smelled like specks, but we made it.

That adventure was at the time of year when most speck fishermen acknowledge that the species is easiest to catch—the nesting season. But it is no better than June or July if you unlock the open water speckled perch system secrets that have been learned, and now widely practiced throughout Florida over the last decade.

I like to think that I was the first to refine this system. Some fishermen have drifted in the open water with minnows and jigs for years and with some degree of success. But one hot June day when I was without wind and still trying to entice a speck to bite in the 14-foot water of Lochloosa, I decided to try two innovations. I would lower my trolling motor, and move at the speed I desired, and I would combine a Super Jig and minnow on the same hook and troll the deepest portions of the 8,200 acre lake.

I immediately began catching fish that morning, and I have caught them regularly ever since. I have continued to refine the system. Now I know that the trolling should be such that my lines will trail out the sides and stern of the boat from heavy-duty, fixed pole holders at about 60 degrees to the surface. I must clamp on three to four medium size lead shot eight inches apart up the line from the hook, and the cork must be about 2 1/2 inches long and easily sunk. The lead will pull it to the bottom immediately if you put it overboard with the boat stopped. But when you troll at the right speed, it will rise to the surface. Any strike will pop it under, and the pole will shake and bend.

Best speck results for me come when the poles are in the holders, and at 90-degree angles to the boat, parallel to the water. I prefer these to be 12-foot cane or B 'n'M fiberglass, but you can use long rods if you prefer. A pole directly out the bow of the boat will catch fish, and sometimes one will work well in the stern, but mostly the fish bite the hooks on the sides of the boat. My boat looks like it is sprouting, and when two people are fishing, I ordinarily have nine or ten set poles. I have seen the time when four or five had fish on at the same time.

I can always do better by trolling with the wind on the stern regardless of its severity. The hooks ride smoother than when you move sideways to the wind. And wind above 12 miles an hour in most lakes makes it difficult to put enough lead on the line to keep the hook near the bottom. I like for the hook to ease along about a foot off the bottom, and this is easy when the wind is not a real factor. It becomes more difficult when it has velocity above 12 m.p.h., and often reduces catch success.

I use Super Jigs in a variety of colors and Hal-Flies too. White, green and red all work well. I stick the minnow on the jig hook through both eyes, and he follows along like he is after the little jig. It does not kill the minnow. Crappies come after it every month of the year. And that brings me to the second of my most memorable speck adventures.

It was the last week in June. A friend and his wife from Germany were visiting. Neither had ever fished before, and the weather was warm. I wanted to catch fish for them badly, but had some qualms. My open-water system was new. The Germans had never fished before. Could I catch specks during what is normally the height of the bream season in Florida with my novice friends?

We left the Twin Lakes Camp at 7:00 in the morning and motored out near the center of Lochloosa. There was no wind. Fog slowly boiled up from the surface and the purple martins and other birds were diving over acres of the open water. On close observation, I could see literally millions of blind mosquitoes floating on the surface, some dead and others wriggling. Under this bonanza of insects, gambusia minnows and tiny shad were gorging themselves, keeping a steady turmoil over dozens of acres. When you are aware that where the bait fish are, there the predators will be also, you have learned how to go after speckled perch.

Each of us put out three poles with different colored Super Jigs and trailing minnows. The fish started hitting immediately. To shorten the story, we ran out of minnows three times before 3:00. Each time we went to the dock, cleaned our fish, bought additional minnows and returned to approximately the same spot in the lake where the insects were still everywhere. We marked the honey hole with an anchored Clorox jug that was easy to see from a long distance.

When we used our last minnow in the middle of the afternoon, we had boated 142 nice specks. Some were 1/2-pounders, but many were 2-pounders, with the average about 1-pound. It was a memorable day of fishing, and particularly gratifying to me. The Germans couldn't speak English. I couldn't speak German. We just hollered and waved to each other when one had an unobserved strike. The friends were so impressed with the crappie fishing that when they left they handed me a ten-mark German note, about $5.00 American dollars then, I pinned it to the wall over my typewriter, and it remains there today. It's a real conversation piece.

In this trolling-for-specks system, small minnows, about two inches long, will catch more fish than the larger ones. Do not horse them over the side. They have tender mouths and may tear out. Most people use a net, but I do not. I figure it is easier to catch another one than get untangled from the net.

Specks are unique fish. I have seen natives fish for them around floating islands or tussocks in Lake County in lakes Griffin and Harris, and in Okeechobee with cane poles, and when they were not getting bites as rapidly as they thought they should, they would beat the end of the pole in the water near the cover, then drop a minnow right in the splashes. Many then came up with nice specks immediately. They reasoned that the specks believed a cousin had found forage fish there, had attacked and made a lot of noise. I know the splashing helps bring the specks running sometimes.

Many times I have seen a single speck break the surface along the shoreline in the open, turned my boat to where he jumped, and then caught a fish pronto. Often, I was reasonably sure it was the same fish. He gave himself away.

Specks can be smelled on the spawning beds and the odor is different from that of nesting bluegills and shellcrackers. I can tell the difference. Beds of specks smell much more like fresh fish than the bream beds that have a musty-cellar odor. By learning how to discriminate between these odors, often you can be led by your nose right to a spot where speckled perch are congregated in great schools. When they are found bedding, it takes no expertise to catch dozens from the same hole in the cover.

It means that sight, sound and smell play a part in successful speck fishing. The angler who is serious about catching specks needs to use all his senses, and once he is intense and observant about this matter, he'll be a better angler than his buddies because he will have discovered how to locate the fish.

There are a few people who do not like the taste of speckled perch. Some few say it has meat that is too soft for them and they prefer the toughness of the bream. But most speck fishermen think it is the most gourmet freshwater fish in the Sunshine State whether you fry it, broil it, bake or smoke it. I prefer my specks fried a golden brown in hot corn oil with the bones, skin and fins left in. I do not believe in filleting specks. I think the skin is tasty, and I know there's more flavor to the meat when it is cooked with the bones in. I have no trouble "filleting" the speck in my plate with my fingers after it is cooked and smoking hot.

If we are expecting children or senior citizens for a meal and we are dressing specks, often we will fillet one side only. We leave the skin on that side, but cut it so that the fillet has no bones. Then the rest of the fish is left intact, and none of the resource is lost. If we do fillet both sides for the children, we still fry the backbone center portion for ourselves. We call that the "Harmonica," and it is the tastiest meat the fish produces. Regardless of how close you fillet a speck, you'll lose about 20 to 30 percent of the meat if you throw away the ribs, the skin, the backbone and the meat attached to it. Maybe that is fanatical conservation, but it's the way I think, and it's how to prepare specks for the dinner table.

Speckled perch get little attention from game and fish agencies, except in Tennessee, which promotes the species' propagation. Most assume that they are everywhere, and that there will always be a huge population for the novices to catch. But there is great pressure on these panfish today. Many times you can count well over 100 boats in the open water of a productive Florida lake, all going after this species with the revolutionary jig and minnow combination system in the deep water with few obstacles to hamper the catch. They are there seven days a week and almost 52 weeks a year when the weather permits. Millions of specks are pulled from many large lakes every year. Can they survive the pressure without some agency assistance?

They have mysteriously disappeared in a few lakes recently for no apparent reason. Lake Weir is a deep, clear water lake that has had no specks caught in it since 1984. The Florida Game and Freshwater Fish Commission is studying that problem now. The water quality is fine. It once was filled with specks. It would be a tragedy for some disease to destroy this species that is ideal for novices, even children fishing from the banks and bridges.

Speckled perch are the species for the common man, the hard hat American out for fun and food. Hopefully, he will always have lakes heavily populated with this humble species that is usually anxious to get on a hook.

High Water Can Hurt Crappie Fingerlings

The Tennessee Wildlife Resources Agency efforts to raise crappie fingerlings in Doakes Pond have been hampered by heavy spring rainfall. It has inundated the 18-acre nursery pond when it overflowed.

When the pond overflows it allows other species to migrate through the spillway out of the Norris impoundment into the pond. The spillway is 150 feet wide and it overflowed with about six inches of water all the way across.

Half of the black-nosed crappie, a color mutant of black crappie that has a stripe down the middle of its head, are kept in hatchery ponds, and those broods have not been damaged by the high water. These offspring have been stocked in the Cove Creek embayment of Norris.

"We didn't have all of our eggs in one basket," says Mike Smith manager of the Eagle Bend Hatchery, after the 1989 flooding.

The objective of the Doakes Pond experiment and crappie release is to determine if natural populations can be significantly influenced by stocking hatchery-spawned fingerlings.

Crappie Stocked in Center Hill in Tennessee

The Tennessee Wildlife Resources Agency stocked 220,000 black crappie fingerlings in Center Hill Reservoir in 1990.

The crappie were reared at TWRA's Eagle Bend hatchery near Clinton. This particular strain of crappie is known as "blacknosed" crappie because of a peculiar black spot which appears on the fish. According to Fisheries Biologist Anders Myhr, "These fish are in no way superior to our native crappie, but because of their peculiar color marking they are valuable in conducting research." Their "blacknosed" trait is a dominant characteristic and will usually appear for three generations among other black crappie. The parent fish came from Arkansas and were successfully spawned by TWRA hatchery personnel at Eagle Bend.

Tennessee Tech researchers have been evaluating the success of the crappie stocking in Center Hill along with TWRA fisheries biologists. Trapnetting and electrofishing techniques will be used to collect crappie for determining the status of the current population as well as the recent introduction.

TWRA chose to stock crappie in Center Hill because the present population in that reservoir is extremely low. "Hopefully, we can establish a year class of crappie, but it will take about three years for these fish to reach a catchable size of ten inches," said Myhr. The TWRA will most likely stock Center Hill with blacknosed crappie again next summer.

The TWRA first stocked 117,000 blacknosed crappie in Watts Bar Reservoir in 1988. The follow-up research showed that the experimental stocking was very successful in that reservoir.

Many states have long frowned on crappie stocking, and this Tennessee experiment could lead to hatchery release of species in many other lakes and streams.

Trolling a host of poles in the open is sure-fire for speckled perch.

Bill Lewis Lures Introduces Tiny Trap

One of the finest crappie baits introduced on the market in recent years is the midget size Rat-L-Trap properly named "TINY TRAP" by Bill Lewis Lures of Alexandria, LA.

Made in ten top-producing colors, the Tiny Trap in 1/8th ounce size and a little more than an inch long, is an effective crappie catcher when cast on ultralight spinning gear and retrieved, or jigged vertically on drop-offs and ledges. It will catch crappies right off the bottom.

With all the characteristics of its bigger, older relative, the Rat-L-Trap, it can be counted down. You can control the depth by the speed of your retrieve. It runs, rattles and vibrates exactly like the original Rat-L-Trap.

While spinning tackle is preferred by Tiny Trap users, it can be cast with bass tackle effectively.

Early field testers of the Tiny Trap have glowing reports of its success when cast and retrieved as well as when it is slowly trolled in open water near cover.

Bill Dance uses Overcast 15 for sun protection.

Bream and Other Panfish

Hack Curran shows off nice stringer of bream.

This warmouth perch weighed 1-pound, 15-ounces.

Natural Baits for Bream

Thrills often bring goose pimples to an angler when the sights and sounds of a game fish striking a topwater lure race through his mind at that memorable moment. But for me and millions of bluegill fishermen around the country, nothing makes the pulse pound out of control like seeing a tiny cork going under the water. It's an instant of ecstasy that many of the most avid anglers cherish from childhood, when they pulled their first punkinseed from a pothole, strung it on a forked limb from a creekside gallberry bush and rushed home to show it to Mama.

Fortunately, there are still many areas of the country where youngsters and adults can thrill to that experience in the out-of-doors where the population explosion hasn't gobbled up the branches, creeks, swamps and covered the tiny pools of the low country savannas with housing developments and industrial complexes. But enjoying the tug of a bream trapped on a No. 4 hook tied to a limber cane pole is not the exclusive domain of the youngsters. Old and young, both sexes and every nationality can still bring home creel limits of these gourmet panfish—and with simple, inexpensive tackle and free baits available with minimum effort if you know what you are looking for and where it abounds.

Live grass shrimp are the best bream bait you can use in many Southern states.

Only a few decades ago, the primary bait for bluegill, shellcrackers, warmouth perch, among other flatfish species that inhabited the country, was the lowly earthworm, and oldsters will remember when these squirming critters were threaded on the hook. You couldn't allow the point of the hook to show. That was a no-no and the fish would shy away. But that technique of impaling wigglers dug from around the drain pipe from the kitchen sink disappeared about the time of the Lucky 13 lure that doctors and lawyers bought in their quest for largemouth bass. At least that method of putting a worm on a hook went out about the same decade.

Those bisexual earthworms, and there are numerous species and all sizes, some that tunnel as much as eight feet into the ground ingesting the soil and straining for the nutrients for survival, are still fine bluegill baits, but every knowledgeable panfish enthusiast knows you push the hook through his middle and let him dangle loosely. He is a live, captive bait that is usually more successful if fished on the bottom or just a few inches above. There are times when two or three worms, a wad if you will, entice the copperheads from hiding in the brush tops and around the stumps better than a single worm. But you better be careful with a wad of worms on the hook. Any old lunker bass might come along and take a liking to it. That usually means a lost line, hook, cork and sinker, because most real bream fishermen use eight or ten pound monofilament line in this modern era. The line is more flexible, floats to the bottom better and catches more fish. And the tiniest cork and smallest split shot sinker is a must.

With a myriad of natural baits replacing the lowly earthworm, as well as a host of artificials, there are few baits of any kind today that will catch more shellcrackers than a worm dangled in a nest of spawners. But when it comes to bluegills there are numerous better naturals today.

In the same era that earthworms were the number one bluegill bait, the brown cricket, a domesticated species, began gracing the tackle shops. This offspring of the wild, black variety that fishermen found in the grass and weeds of the early morning for bream baits, could be dropped around the cover and allowed to slowly filter down toward the bottom. Few panfish can resist the temptation to strike what seems to be another insect dislodged from its perch. It can be most effective on a light line, small cork, single shot or no shot, No. 6 hook and a 12- to 14-foot cane or fiberglass pole. But for those more sophisticated anglers it can be

Author Carter picks grass shrimp out of hydrilla netted
along the shoreline.

cast on ultra-light spinning tackle or fly rods and prove deadly. Fishing thick, overhanging bushes on the shoreline, a cricket can be "slingshot" into the close places by firmly holding the hook in one hand and making a bow out of the limber pole. By aiming and releasing, a veteran of this type of angling with expertise can shoot that kicking cricket in a hole no larger than a pork and bean can. Often that's where the gripper-size bream are lying in wait for just such a morsel.

Another of the oldest bream baits is the saphead—an inch-long white grub-looking critter that eats on the pine wood of decaying slabs and logs. In the era when the sawmills went to the woods instead of the woods coming to the mill, fishermen often gathered their handful of these baits by snatching the loose bark off the slabs and raking off the sapheads into a cup or can. Today, avid bream seekers after these baits know where a felled pine is still housing these wood eaters or have a friend at the local sawmill who keeps on the lookout for logs with the tell-tale signs of worms. While crickets and earthworms are for sale at tackle shops around the country, few ever have sapheads available. But it is a fine bait, fished exactly as you would a cricket, one worm to the hook. Sapheads have many names and Georgians know it generally as a "sawyer." It's productive and is available winter and summer. Crickets and worms are not always easily found in the cold months.

Moving with the current down the Wyboo Creek at Santee Cooper in South Carolina, in a nine-foot, one man cypress boat, on an October morning, I was flipping crickets along the bank and picking up a bluegill now and then, but not as fast as I had hoped. In a little eddy, a dark hole under an overhanging gnarled oak, I noted an almost steady ripple in the otherwise calm water. Obviously something alive was moving and causing these circles of wavelets. Closer scrutiny proved the point. Caterpillars, those fuzzy, inch-long worms that build nests in the pecan trees and other flora of Santee, were feeling the first coolness of autumn and succumbing to the breeze, losing their grip and making the dive into the river. The bream had found a bonanza, like dinner on the ground at revival time at a country church. I flipped my brown crickets into the honey hole and I caught a few, but the difference in the offspring must have confused the bluegills. They were not nearly as hungry for my bait as for those loose morsels falling from the oak. I disturbed the area for a few minutes and picked a handful of the caterpillars off the tree, paddled off a few yards and let the serenity return.

The circles began forming again and you could often hear that mouth-sucking noise so familiar to every bream angler who instantly recognizes the feeding sound. I impaled a fuzzy worm and flipped it in the shadows. Bingo! Down went the tiny cork at a slow pace, and that's normal for the bigger bream. It's the smaller ones that race off with the bait like there is a predator after them. And there probably is. That makes them as nervous as a pregnant fox in a forest fire. In the following hour I loaded the live-box with hungry copperhead bream. Since that unforgettable morning, I watch for those early fall frosts, head for the black waters of the low country and then search for the falling "oakworms." That may not be their Latin name but for thousands of avid bream fishermen, that's what they are.

Like the oakworm experience, you have to perfectly time your fishing adventure if you are a mayfly believer. This is a short-lived aquatic nymph and these insects are plentiful in the South in early spring. Thus their moniker "mayfly." When these insects are covering the trees along the shoreline with a breeze lifting them aloft and depositing them on the water, bluegills have a mass meeting for feasting purposes. One or two of these impaled on a hook and dropped anywhere in the neighborhood will assure you of one strike after another.

Another coincidental observation one summer season in a narrow tributary draining into Santee-Cooper in the Jack Creek marina section, taught me a bream fishing lesson. I saw two or three red-winged blackbirds that hadn't wandered North yet, chirping and diving at a leafy bush just above the dark water. They were feeding on red wasps that had a nest as big as your cap attached to the bush. While they were catching a few, others were being swept off the nest and into the water by the diving predator birds. The bream seemed to be working in tandem with the birds. Each time a wasp was dislodged and didn't make the gizzard of the blackbird, it was gulped in by the waiting bluegills below. Obviously, this stinging critter was as desirable to the fish as to the blackbird. I was determined to get some on my bream hook.

Fortunately, it was a rainy, foggy morning and the wasps' wings would not propel them at bullet speed like they would on a dry day. I added troubles to the guardian wasps by splashing the nest with water with my paddle while wrapping my rubberized raincoat around everything but my eyes. That left any astute stinging guardsman a minimum of space to attack. It took only a minute or two to dislodge the last of the wet wasps. I quickly broke off the tiny twig that held the nest and rushed away from that area.

In each little chamber of the nest was a baby wasp in various stages of growth. But the bulk of them were whitish and roughly shaped like their adult parents. I put one on the hook and, as I was already positive, the bream all under those bushes were anxious to taste the larvae of the wasps.

The smallest of these larvae looks like a white worm or more precisely a maggot. And a maggot is that soft-bodied, legless grub that often feeds on the smelly, decaying carcasses of other animals. That bait doesn't appeal to the faint of heart and weak-stomached but it is a fine bluegill bait. And you don't have to hunt up a dead 'possum to get a supply. Many Carolinians raise their own by wetting corn meal and letting it spoil. The white grubs soon start gorging themselves on this gooey mess and are ready for the bream hooks. These are known as "mealworms" by many fisherman.

Catalpa worms have been among the most cherished bluegill attractors for a generation. These are huge black worms found only for a few short weeks on the huge leaves of the catalpa trees of the South. These trees are from the trumpet-creeper family and are the sole food supply of these worms. They are great for bream when picked fresh off the tree but that curtails your fishing to just the few days they are available. Enthusiasts of this bait pick them off the leaves in the summer and store them in jars in their deep freezers. You then have them the year 'round.

Catalpa worms are the most attractive to bream when turned wrong side out and cut into half-inch pieces. I usually turn them inside out by poking a country stick match against the head and then pulling the rest of the body over the match. On the inside, the catalpa is as white as cotton dipped in buttermilk. Bream can spot it for yards and will gulp it down.

For those using frozen catalpas, it is convenient to give them an hour or two to thaw before pushing the match through them, but one good Santee friend says his fishing buddy pops these frozen catalpas in his mouth and finds they thaw out in a matter of minutes. That's a matter for individual taste.

Another worm that is a proven bream catcher is found in all the Southern states where the giant lily pads are prevalent. This whitish worm bores right down into the stem of the lily. If you have ever fished the pads and watched the boat-tailed black grackle hop from one leaf to another pecking away at his breakfast, you can bet he was filling his crop with "bonnet worms." These resemble the same creatures you find in an ear of roasting corn, except these are a little tougher and make their homes in the lily leaves. You gather these baits by either splitting open the stems where you see a hole in the top or simply breaking off a dozen, tossing them in the bottom of the boat, and leaving them there until you need another one for your hook. You don't need the traditional bean can. They'll stay in the stems until you need them. No real conservationist would destroy a lily pad habitat of bream by taking such baits, but in many lakes it does no damage to gather these worms. They have generally sucked the life out of the aquatic growth by the time you find them anyway. The lily is dying.

Bonnet worms simply impaled through the middle and allowed to float to the bottom on your bream hook will draw attention from every bluegill in the community. Many times they will get strikes when all other worm forms are shunned.

But I have saved the best bream bait for last. And that bait is the fresh water shrimp, also known as "grass shrimp" or "hardback shrimp." These little transparent creatures are found in the coontail, hydrilla, and other aquatic mosses in at least nine Southern states. You can catch them easily in shallow water by scooping up the moss off the bottom with a fine mesh net on a handle no longer than your regular bass landing apparatus. It takes a little time to pick the flitting petite baits from the trash, but a handful of these will make you look like a professional when other veteran breamers are cussing about the fish having lockjaw and not biting that day.

They must be fished just right to bring the best results. And that means using a "nothing pole." This is a simple rig of a short, stubby six- or eight-foot cane or bamboo pole with a six-pound monofilament line not more than a foot longer than the depth of the water you are fishing. Use no cork and no lead. Just a tiny hook with one or more of the little shrimp on it. Let it down in the edge of the grass or in the holes in a brushpile or in the lilies where you know the panfish play. They will bite it by the time it hits the bottom more times than not. If it isn't attacked on the way down, flip it gently a time or two before moving it to another hole. When the bream or shellcracker strikes it, you won't need a cork to let you know you had a bite. It will be ingested—all the way down the fish's throat and you'll have the fight of your life to manhandle the bream over the gunnels of your boat. Ounce for ounce, there is no fresh or saltwater fish with the strength and determination of the bluegill and shellcracker.

You can catch bream with these shrimp and the conventional throw gear—that is a tiny cork, a single small shot, light line, a little hook fished along shorelines and grass lines. But you'll catch twice as many without the cork, lead, and usual longer line. Like a fine old black man who taught me the secrets of the nothing pole, said, "Lead is made for plumbers and corks are made to put in bottles." He knew what he was talking about.

Sophisticated fishing with artificials is considered more dignified, respectable by many Americans. One fine fisherman told me, "I wouldn't even eat a fish that I had to catch with a live bait." Those in that fishing fraternity are legion. But one man's trash is another man's treasure and for me, I'll take the thrill of catching bluegills on their natural foods and laugh all the way to the picnic table.

Even youngsters can catch fine bream.

Locating and Catching Big Bluegills

While many panfishermen actually prefer ordinary-size bluegills on the dinner table to slabs of the species, there's no doubt that all of us would rather fight the BIG grippers on the line. We like the bragging size that make the line sing, the rod bend and your heart speed up its pounding.

You can catch those big bream if you put your mind to it. You just decide you will land a lot of panfish lunkers by design rather than by accident. You can succeed as a big-bream catcher by studying their life-styles, and learning from the experiences of veterans who have become slab-catching experts.

Most panfishermen when trailblazing and experimenting with bream fishing, are not as analytical with what their exploration uncovers as they could be, reducing long-range success. When you locate a place, lure, time, natural bait, or system that is productive, your experience should be well recorded. It need not be on paper but at least in the recesses of your brain the factors that made that adventure different and worth repeating in your quest for giant bream, should be remembered. You learn from your successes and failures. Some wag has said you glow with your successes and grow with your failures. Remember success and failure can make you a better big bluegill fisherman.

You'll soon discover that there are more good places for giant bream than you at first believed. Then you begin to think. What makes this particular pond or stream more likely to have huge panfish than all the other places that I fish? What is different here?

You think about bottom cleanliness. Is this bream pond water with the sandy bottom the reason the fish are larger here? That's a logical conclusion, but it's not the real reason. There are plenty of mucky-bottomed ponds with many big bluegills. The hard bottom is not the difference.

It must be the abundance of food, you reason logically. It's not so. Many food-rich ponds and streams have just as many insects and other types of panfish forage food, yet you find that there are few big bluegills to be caught. Only baby bream get on the hook.

Carter lands a copperhead bream.

Last, you suggest that maybe this honey hole you have found that has so many big bream has more predators than most other waters. You have dredged up the answer. Ponds with a lot of big bass, pickerel, garfish, bowfin and other fish-eating species will have more of the huge panfish. Predators eat a lot of the young bream. Survivors then have less competition for the bugs, shrimp and minnows that make up their steady diet. By not competing with the smaller bluegills for the food supply, the bream devote all their time to eating. That means fast growth and huge fish.

It's axiomatic that the bigger the bream the bigger his appetite. That's what keeps big bream getting even bigger. They become gluttonous and reach giant size.

While certain ponds, like Merritt's Millpond in the Florida panhandle, is renowned as a big bluegill haven, that doesn't mean that only ponds have these slabs. Often you can find these trophy-size panfish in bays, sloughs, coves, reservoirs and even rivers where there is an imbalance of predators to bluegills.

Much of the bluegill fishing is done in waters where predators are not dominant. Baby bluegills plague the fishermen. There's too much competition between the big bream and the small fry. Little panfish gulp down the limited available food. All the panfish stay small and dwarfed. Eventually, even the old bluegills stagnate, stop growing and live the rest of their lives stunted with all the other three-finger-size midgets. The fisherman has to catch a stringer full to have a mess for his family.

There are times when you can pretty well determine the size of bluegills in a pond by the size of the scattered saucer-shapes on the bottom where they spawn. Often they are easily seen in the shallows, and some nests may be almost two feet across. Those usually indicate some huge fish rooted out the indentation. Males normally make these nests by pivoting around and around. Those that are almost a foot long make the largest nests. If there is nearby brush, weeds, logs, stumps or other cover, those giant spawners may not be far from the nests even though the eggs have hatched days ago. That cover makes the insect supply greater, and keeps the bream in the neighborhood.

To catch these slab bream, you must either appeal to their hunger or irritate them repeatedly with an offering right in their faces. A Beetle Spin, Super Jig, Hal-Fly, Mepps Spinner or other small artificial may bring the bream a runnin'. Sometimes any of these with a small sliver of white pork strip attached, will

Arthur Prince pulls in a big bream.

entice the reluctant bluegills to dart out of the shadows and gulp
down the attractor.

Even when there are no new or abandoned nests around
to mark bluegill presence, any submerged brush or other bottom
cover may hold bream. Around this submerged cover, there is no
better big-bream catcher than a popping bug on a fly rod or tied
on a light line attached to a cane pole and twitched in the shady
areas. Chartreuse, yellow and white are the colors normally the
most successful.

Sometimes a slight breeze helps locate these big bream.
If the wind is coming off a wooded shoreline, helpless mayflies,
moths, mosquitoes and other flying insects are often dislodged.
They topple into the water. Big bream suck them in, often giving
away their whereabouts by the noisy slurp that is a sure-fire
sound of feeding bream. No other species sucks in a surface
morsel with a sound comparable to the bream.

Once you have learned how to find slab-size bluegills, you

When you find a mass of white roots floating in the aquatic growth, you have found the mother lode—panfish are close by.

may have to hone your timing to the place and the season. Bream are not normally active feeders after dark, although occasionally on a moonlit night they will do some eating. But a good lantern light reflecting on the surface may attract such a flock of insects that the bluegills see an easy picnic. They rise to the surface and gulp down everything that squirms and floats. It can be a real bream bonanza.

Artificial bugs, spinners, crickets, grass shrimp, catalpa worms, maggots, sapheads and the old-fashioned night crawlers will catch blues. Spinning tackle lets the fisherman stay a safe distance away to keep from spooking the bream, but a long line on a 12-foot pole is a good way to catch these night-feeding panfish, too. Don't be surprised if crappies compete with the bream for the bait. They too, flock to a light that has drawn insects to the spot. They like the easy pickings.

Bream often bite better before sunup and after sunset because they can not shield their lidless eyes from the brightness of daylight. They have their fixed eyes wide open, and the dimness of the early and late parts of the day helps them see better, thus they can hunt and find food better. The light on the surface after dark does the same thing for them as the natural light of dawn and dusk.

307

You'll probably catch more big bluegills with large baits than the snack-size offerings when fishing the night light. The bream often gulp down fluttering meal-size moths on the surface as large as a half dollar. They get accustomed to large bites. Yet, occasionally the largest blue in the territory will hit even the smallest bait. There are no absolutes for big bream.

Big baits catch big fish was never brought home to me more vividly than one evening when I was in a hurry while fishing with catalpa worms that I usually turn wrong side out, cut into half-inch pieces and impale on my hook. Instead, I hooked the whole huge, black catalpa through the midsection and flipped the bait near my lantern light. The cork popped under. I came up with one of the few 2-pound bream I have ever caught. That fish wanted to get a stomach full with one gulp. The big bait paid off.

Hooks are important when going after any size bluegill. They have small mouths. If you fish a jig, select one with a No. 10 hook and a spherical head no larger than the head of a country match. A small piece of night crawler or mealy worm tipped on the hook will make it more productive. Don't thread it on the hook; let it dangle naturally a half inch or more.

Natural baits probably catch more bream than the artificials. When fishing these naturals, use hooks no larger than a No. 4. Most veteran panfishermen use No. 8 or 10 hooks. A tiny cork or no cork makes the bait look natural, as does the smallest lead shot eight inches up a six-pound test line.

Bluegills rely heavily on their sense of smell. They use it to scent food. It helps them, especially in muddy or tannic water. Live, natural bait usually smells better to the big blues than decaying ones, and it is a prime reason why you should keep your bait fresh. They will find it better.

Regardless of how many years you have hunted for big bream, you do not get too old to learn new tricks on how to find them and how to catch them. You become acutely aware of the presence of big bream when you hear one sucking in a mayfly on the surface, observe a bumping stalk of a spatterdock lily in the six-foot water, sense the tell-tale smell from a spawning nest, see tiny bubbles of oil bursting on the surface, and note a collection of tiny, hair-like white roots in an eddy near the grass and weeds that the spawners have nosed up. All these signs mean bream are marauding in the neighborhood. Using all your senses and learning what your observations teach will help you track down the big bruiser bluegills. It's the difference in the thrill of victory and the agony of defeat.

The One-Man Boat Bream Fishermen

One- and two-man homemade boats are bream fishermen's favorites in Eastern North Carolina.

I sat motionless in the bow of a tiny nine-foot one-man cypress boat and guided it in the slow current with a short homemade paddle, easily maneuvering the petite craft downstream no more than 35 feet from the dense wilderness shrubbery that draped the dark shoreline of the shallow waters of Lake Moultrie near St. Stephen. In my right hand I fondled my favorite bluegill fishing equipment, long proven successful when everything else failed in this productive area with its dark waters flowing just inches beneath the outstretched gallberry bushes, popash, willows and gnarled oaks that laced both banks of this spawning area for giant-sized bream.

309

Every foot of this scenic swampland is little changed from its natural wilderness beauty when Columbus landed in the New World, but the bream and largemouth bass are falling prey to modern technology. Technology is uniquely practiced here, artificial lures adroitly dropped in the dark shadows under the bushes near the mucky bank where roots, stumps, limbs and other cover shelter giant panfish in ideal habitat unpolluted and unspoiled by man.

Natives three decades ago learned that a popping bug on a light line cast into these honey holes was a greater temptation to the fat bream than the conventional earthworms, grasshoppers and crickets. The artificial popping bug floated life-like on the surface and few finny creatures could look up at this swimming insect and resist it. And the sportsmen who succeeded the meat hunters in these waters got a bonus thrill from catching these big bluegills on the topwater lures that gave them broad smiles from witnessing both sound and sight. It was like having minnows mingled in your marrow.

But along a river so narrow that regular flyrods and lines made it almost impossible to properly place the flies and bugs in just the best, most inviting havens for the panfish hiding there, native anglers came up with a country-style rig that proved much more practical than the usual sophisticated rod and reel tackle.

In the early stages of this innovation, before the time of monofilament lines, fishermen simply tied number eight black sewing thread to a 12- or 14-foot, limber cane pole, impaled a natural bait on a tiny hook and flipped it under the overhanging cover. But such line easily tangled, and often, when a big bass gulped down the bait, the line and tackle was no match for the fish.

Better cane poles came on the market and after that, the fine fiberglass Bream Busters with great strength and action. Eight- and ten-pound test monofilament line were on the shelves of every tackle shop and good flyline was available even in the tiny villages and crossroads where these river fishermen could examine it and experiment. In time, they came up with the rigging used widely today all along the rivers of the East Coast of Virginia, the Carolinas, Georgia and Florida, among other low country waters in other states. It's a regular system in Santee Cooper Country where several fishermen load three or four boats on a pickup truck and hustle off to the bream bed areas. No trailer is needed.

The fishing tackle I was holding that overcast morning at

Lake Moultrie was typical. It was a 14-foot fiberglass pole with a yellow conventional flyline tied to the end. Then I had tied on four feet of 8-pound, clear Stren monofilament leader. The line and leader combined was about four feet longer than the pole. And on this clumsy-looking apparatus I had tied a chartreuse popping minnow after clipping about a quarter inch off the rubbery legs that protruded. This color, and white, had long proven the best of the popping minnows, called "bugs" by most fishermen of the section, and I proceeded to flip it quietly into every nook and cranny along the shoreline.

Pop! And that familiar sucking sound recognized by anglers with topwater flies everywhere was the tell-tale noise that meant the swirl under the bushes was made by another bream inhaling what he thought was a tasty morsel that had lost its footing on the leaves above.

I set the tiny No. 6 hook and watched my line literally split the water as the giant bluegill raced from hiding and into the open water as the tension directed the fish away from cover and toward the little bateau. Moments later, I took hold of the line with my paddling hand and lifted a real "titty bream" into the boat. Titty bream are those grippers so large you have to hold them against your chest to get the hook out of their mouths.

Repeatedly I grinned as the bluegills tore up my popping bug time after time. Often when the nooks under the bushes were so tiny that I could not flip the fly right where I wanted it, I would use the old slingshot method—taking the little lure between the fingers of my left hand and pulling on the line so hard that the limber pole arched like an Indian bow. Then, aiming the lure for the desired spot, I turned it loose. A good river fly fisherman can set that bait right in the mouth of a quart Mason jar, and it is from such hiding places that the real giants of the bluegill species are often rousted and landed.

Other fine game fish succumbed to my offering too. Redbreast bream in the faster water often rose to these flies. Largemouth bass couldn't resist it, either, although I prefer a larger popping minnow for this species, with a bigger hook. I also like to move it more, jiggling it on the surface like it was swimming for its life. On the contrary, most bluegills in these bush-draped waters hit the bug moments after it settles on the surface and without any twitches or jerks on the line. Crappies like the popping minnow too, and they usually infest tree tops and brush piles in the more eddying places of the river or in some of the

The late Curt Layser of Pennsylvania was an expert panfisherman.

hundreds of little lakes that branch off from the stream to flood some tree-covered acres of swampland.

This unique fly fishing is widespread in the Santee area, but relatively few anglers have perfected the system. It is imperative that you stalk the fish and the smaller, lower profile the boat, the better your chances. Before sunrise or after sunset or on overcast days the success record is much greater. The fish simply can't see you as well. However, some of the dark holes under the cover will produce strikes and fish any time of day.

Such fishing is always more productive in the spring and summer months when real insects indeed do fall off the overhanging branches to feed the waiting bluegills below. While some success can be enjoyed even in the winter, most river fly fishermen find the months that mayflies, wasps, bees, mosquitoes, and the like, are active also prove the most productive for the anglers.

While the Santee Cooper traverses much of five counties, has adequate public launching ramps and is among the best waters for this fly fishing, other streams are also excellent sites in the low country of South Carolina.

In Southeastern South Carolina, there's the prolific Little Pee Dee River in Dillon and Horry counties, as well as the Big Pee Dee. Tributaries and backwaters of the Santee-Cooper complex of lakes and rivers at Summerton, and Moncks Corner, among other places, offer excellent fly fishing with either this unique and antique tackle used by the natives, or in some areas, the conventional flyrod and reel in the big water.

You can flip your fly only about 35 feet, but that's far enough where the stream is not much wider than that and there's little room for handling line on the back cast. Try it! You'll like it!

Buckets of Bream From
Bridges and Banks

When some of the biting cold of winter winds whistle, and you have the urge to go fishing but not the courage to face the weather out on your favorite stream in a boat that would be buffeted and battered while you kept your hands in your pockets, face protected and wrapped up, find a bridge or high shoreline bank and return to the basics. Go after a bucketful of bream from the bank or the bridges.

Often there are bridges across tiny creeks and swamplands in the South where giant cypress, gums, maples and oaks break the force of cold winds, and an angler with a little outdoorsmanship and adventure in his veins can wet a line a few hours in winter when he just can't wait for spring. He can salve the fishing urge that draws him away from the television and warmth of his den whether he brings home a mess of fish for the

Kids often learn to fish by catching bream from
the seawalls.

table or not. But if he knows something about bream fishing, and has the astuteness to pick the right spot, he just might make this event successful enough to talk about.

The best results on a winter day, even a windy one, often occur when there's a reasonably bright sun that stirs the bluegills and warmouths from near dormancy as they await a temperature change that will send them scurrying for spawning beds a few months hence. They may forage around for a few morsels if it doesn't take too much energy in the cold water. The angler who has pulled himself from the comforts of home to dream of pulling in fish, watching a cork go down or feeling the tug of something alive on the line, just might have that morsel in the face of the fish, and thus get his fishing thrill early. It's not a time of guaranteed success, but it is not uncommon.

There was the time a few years ago on a January day that would have been reasonably comfortable in a bass boat on a lake had it not been for a gale-force wind coming out of the north. Not wanting a small thing like that to stop the fun of fishing when the television offered nothing exciting on a Saturday afternoon, I picked up an old spinning rod and a cane pole and I drove off alone to Prairie Creek, a small stream that flows out of Lake Newnan and under Highway 20 east of Gainesville, Florida. It empties into Orange Lake after meandering through a jungle of growth a mile or so south of the highway.

There was an abandoned railroad trestle, a highway bridge across the creek, and fortunately there was plenty of water. A freshet had swallowed the little stream, and it was being pressured to hold the water within its banks. I have long found that in the winter you can catch more fish from such structure when there's a lot of water flowing. The fish seem to leave areas of the lakes to forage through the swamp, perhaps looking around for food.

I chose a seat on a crosstie of the railroad trestle, baited my hook with a long dangling Georgia jumper worm, and let my spinning reel unwind as the bait trickled down near the bottom, a few inches from a piling that supported the structure. With no bobber, I kept the line reasonably tight, and by fishing the lee side of the piling, the current didn't wash my bait away. Protected from the harsh wind by the giant trees along both shorelines, and with my coat buttoned tightly and cap down around my ears, I could make myself believe that this was really fun even if nothing picked up my bait and ran with it.

But the adventure was more rewarding than just being outside with the osprey, raccoons, crows and redwing blackbirds. I felt a tug on the line at the same instant I saw the angle of the monofilament change from vertical to 45 degrees. Something was running off with my bait. I reeled in with great excitement. A fine 12-ounce copperhead bream came to the surface, and soon into my hands and on a stringer.

It suddenly wasn't so cold any more. It is amazing how such a January experience from a railroad trestle can stop the wind from blowing and the cold from biting. A fish on the line makes every day a pretty one.

Dangling similar baits around a dozen pilings of this structure for the next hour, I pulled up eight hand-sized bluegills and a couple of warmouth perch, all I needed for a Saturday night dinner. I carried the stringer of fish home proudly. I had succeeded on a day when most of my fishing cronies in the South wouldn't have braved the elements.

On a subsequent trip to the same place in search of bream, I found the water too low, and the fish were not there. Piling after piling proved fruitless, and I soon realized that I would go home with the proverbial hungry gut unless I tried something different. I picked up the old cane pole I had carried with me on the first trip, but didn't use when the spinning reel and rod were all I needed from the crosstie perch ten feet above the surface. With my pork and bean can of worms dug from the swamp nearby, and the cane pole with a tiny bobber, a single lead shot and No. 4 Eagle Claw hook, I crossed a couple of wire fences, and ambled down the creek bank. I was no virgin here. Both shorelines had been worn slick in times past when other fishermen had deserted the bridges looking for greener pastures from the banks of this creek that flowed through a wilderness. At least it was too cold for snakes to be lolling in the path. I didn't have to worry about that in the winter weather.

A few hundred yards downstream, I walked up on an elbow in the creek, where the water turned abruptly to the east, and it had worn out a hole in the bottom near the clay bank. A few limbs from a decaying oak had tangled with exposed roots and were hanging half submerged in the oxbow. That looked like the ideal spot to drop my hook with the enticing worms. Bluegills must know that a spot like this will have some food washing in from the aquatic growth above, and they suspend, wait patiently and stalk whatever forage comes their way. Any smart bream should know this is the place where he should hole up. Some obviously did, because the very first time my hook went to the bottom, the cork disappeared by the time the line was tight. I fought a 1-pound bluegill through the brush and onto the bank. In the half hour that followed, I had a dozen instant replays in that one hole. It was no larger than the couch in my den that I had left to try my luck here. Then there were no more bites. I surmised that I had caught all the fish in that hole, and I probably had.

Moving from one bend and deep hole in the creek to another, oblivious to the swaying tree tops being pounded by a 30-mile-an-hour wind above and disregarding the near-freezing temperature on this winter day, I caught a stringer full of bream on that excursion. I never walked down the road to my car with a greater feeling of accomplishment than I did that day when most anglers, even avid ones, would have elected to pass, wait for another more acceptable weather period. You get the thought running through your mind on such a unique adventure that you are closer to nature than you have been before. You have discarded the sophisticated for the humble and what could be more humble than a $2.00 cane pole, hook, line and can of worms. Somehow you have a little pioneering spirit gushing through your mental processes. You have outwitted your prey at a time when neighbors in the South voted no.

The message of such an experience is that bluegills, speckled perch, warmouths, catfish and even largemouth bass often live around these bridges, and in holes of creeks that lace through swamplands. When you can't stand the wind and weather of open water where you have no natural protection, you can put the right bait at the right spot, and often come home with the dinner meal you usually can't catch until April or May. You get a head start on your neighborhood revivals, but you'll confess when tales are being told around a skillet of frying bluegills. The next weekend you'll have company along the bank, and sitting on the railroad trestle.

Most of the fishing from the bridges and the banks of Florida streams is done by natives. Few tourists show much interest in such unsophisticated fishing. But for those who get their kicks and some of their food from catching panfish, the system is not important. As long as it is legal and successful it's fun, and for many in the angling society, there is no thrill greater than seeing a cork go down.

316

Birds, Wasps and Worms Betray Bluegills

It was mid-morning on a beautiful spring day. All of nature's creatures were busy in the air, on the water or along the lush shoreline of the century-old millpond now converted for recreation and named Lake Tabor in Columbus County, North Carolina. Once this impoundment stored water that powered a clumsy waterwheel, turning the gristmill gears to grind corn for the local farmers.

Lake Tabor served an agrarian populace long before the advent of electricity in coastal North Carolina. Today, these 388 acres of tannin-colored water filled with standing cypress trees, stumps, half-submerged logs, limbs and weeping willow flora provide an excellent panfish haven for anglers who live along the North-South Carolina border less than a mile away.

Bill O'Quinn, a veteran panfisherman from nearby Loris, South Carolina, was stalking Lake Tabor bream, a catchall term for bluegills, shellcrackers, redbreast, warmouth perch, and other flatfish species that abound in the South. He eased his 10-foot homemade plywood boat around and over numerous obstacles that were great fish-hides for feeding and nesting bluegills that thrive in shallow swamp waters. He looked for the dark shade where bream ambush passing forage food.

Quietly, Bill flipped a live cricket impaled on a long-shank No. 6 TruTurn hook into the inviting nooks and crannies of the cover. Every flip tempted the nearby bream to gulp down the tasty morsel that looked so natural and unencumbered on a 4-pound test, clear monofilament with a tiny shot eight inches above the hook and a fingernail-size cork that kept the wriggling cricket a few inches off of the sandy bottom.

This cricket-flipping among the dense cover is a typical panfishing technique in the eastern Carolinas low country. O'Quinn, like many other veteran natives, fishes with a 12-foot limber cane pole or B 'n' M telescopic fiberglass rod. He whipped

317

Jeffrey Burleson gets a thrill from showing off this shellcracker.

his bait into the darkest shadows of overhanging bushes and along the shady side of stumps and logs. Sometimes he has to use a slingshot-like maneuver to shoot the cricket into the seemingly impenetrable shade under the willows. He accomplishes that easily by putting pressure on the line just above the hook until the limber pole bends like a Fred Bear hunting bow. Some of the more sophisticated panfish stalkers catch fish with flyrods in these waters, but there is so much overhead flora, and the holes where the fish hide are often so tiny, that O'Quinn has stuck to the humble tackle of his forefathers. He has perfected a technique of bait presentation that permits him to entice bream in spots where novice anglers would fear to tread. Even experienced flyrodders would have difficulty.

O'Quinn fishes the dense dark spots, always difficult to penetrate, but his expertise minimizes line hang-ups.

Despite the ideal water level and his favorite June moon phase (three days before the full), Bill was striking out even in the productive bream havens where he has often dragged in hand-size copperheads. Today he is getting no strikes as the panfish act like they are afflicted with lockjaw. Strange! This is the spawning season and normally he can pinpoint the feeding and nesting fish. He consistently takes home a mess for the family dinner table. It is usually a matter of locating the fish, and Bill has been unlocking that secret for decades, especially when the full moon nears in the spring. Why not today?

Suddenly, Mother Nature offers a little unexpected assistance, changing O'Quinn's luck on this day and enhancing the bream-fishing success of many others. That is especially true of those who observe and react to the revelations that unfold around them when fishing the lakes and streams of the Coastal Carolinas.

Silently musing about his ineptitude, Bill glanced up at a noisy but graceful mockingbird that was tiptoeing from twig to twig near the top of a tall, leafy maple. It leaned precariously over the water. Erosion had eaten away at its root system and it would soon give way and the tree would topple into the water.

The mama bird was moving toward a half-concealed nest in the uppermost fork of the tree and the squeaky chirps from several open-mouthed offspring that plainly announced the presence of hungry babies. They were begging for a bit of worm or maybe a colorful, tasty ladybug or grasshopper.

Trapeze artists could take lessons from that agile

319

mockingbird as she danced ever closer to the anxious and impatient baby birds. It almost seemed like she was teasing them to scream louder and louder. Then came disaster.

A haughty bluejay, a much-despised species among many songbird lovers because it kills the young of other birds in the nest, swooped down upon the noisy infant birds. The startled adult mockingbird forgot her feeding chores and turned to face the imminent danger. She quickly confronted the jay, squawking and screaming with every breath as she challenged the invading predator. In that weak moment, the mockingbird betrayed the panfish of Lake Tabor, as other wild birds have been betrayers for generations. As her mouth opened to scream at the jay, a wriggling red worm fell, descending through the limbs and leaves of the maple and plopping on the shady surface. It was doomsday for the worm, a revealing moment for the observant fisherman.

The familiar sucking sound that is a trademark of surface-feeding bluegills snapped O'Quinn to attention. That unintentional release of the worm from the mockingbird's beak pinpointed a honey hole for the intruding human. By the time the rings disappeared from the surface, he had flipped a cricket within inches of the spot. Obviously, this old bird had dropped food before, a fact apparent from the congregation of bream positioned beneath its nest. It was here that they often received this manna from heaven.

Bingo! Bill's cork popped under and he fought a "titty bream" (one so large that you have to clutch it against your breast to remove the hook) to the gunnels and over the side. Instant replay kept him busy for the next half hour as a dozen bluegills entered his livewell. He had only to flip the wriggling insect in the water to catch fish after fish. The bird's nest bonanza would continue for a week.

O'Quinn would also learn on subsequent trips to this spot that the bream would hit a small, white popping bug flipped in the area almost as often as a live cricket. By shortening the length of the bug's rubber legs, the topwater bait proved to be more productive. The fish seemed to gulp it down easier.

They also hit orange-and-white Beetle Spins. Anything that looked like an insect (whether dead or alive) enticed these bream to strike. Clear Super Jigs twitched so that the slender trailing tentacles fluttered near the surface brought other bream sucking sounds and more fish to the boat. It helped to tie the jig on the line so that it hung at a right angle to the line.

Max Clarke, formerly of Greensboro, N.C., watches the birds and finds spawning bream.

Spring gave way to summer. O'Quinn continued his bream fishing, moving from Lake Tabor to the Waccamaw and Lumber rivers—fast-moving low country streams that lace along the Carolinas border. Using his short one-handed paddle, O'Quinn sculled his little boat from the bow, as all veteran river anglers along the coastal region have learned to do. Still using the cane-pole tackle that scored under the mockingbird nest, Bill deftly flipped the cricket into strategic spots along the shoreline, a technique referred to by coastal natives as "throw-gearing."

A stray copperhead, the native male of the species, soon became the next victim. But fishing then became slow. With faint sounds of "Taps" playing through his head and the sun descending, O'Quinn was about to surrender when Lady Luck and an astute observation changed his plans.

A hat-size wasp nest hung on a mulberry bush just inches above the dark water of the Waccamaw. It was covered with busy, buzzing red wasps. They almost obscured the greyish tough paper that housed the larvae that were now adult wasps. They were leaving the incubator, stretching their wings for the first time. Many were shaky and weak. Some of the newborn lost their footing, toppling into the current and exciting the guardian parents. In an effort to save the young, some of the oldsters fluttered on the surface, where a stiff breeze moved them along. Bluegills stalked food along the shoreline and these ready-made dinners were like morsels from the supermarket. Every wasp that hit the water was quickly consumed within a few feet of the nest. Obviously, these bream had experienced falling food from these insect nests in the past. They suspended near the surface to fill their stomachs. The bream had found the mother lode on this day, and so had Bill.

Time after successful time he used slingshot-motions to propel the cricket under the wasp nest. He then saw, heard and felt the strike of the fat bream as they sucked in crickets. The bluegills dashed toward open water and he yanked them into the boat, fluttering and flouncing. O'Quinn filled his livewell before he left the spot as darkness settled.

The action slowed at times when the young wasps stopped falling into the water. Bill would then create more excitement by helping them fall. He simply splashed water on the nest with his boat paddle, after taking precautions to cover his bare arms and face with a poncho to avoid painful stings. Guardian wasps keep surveillance on the perimeter of their nests and attack molesters.

These wasps were so busy trying to save their drowning offspring that they paid little attention to the fisherman. As they buzzed around the nest, Bill continued to boat the feisty panfish below them. Fall soon followed the wasp nest incident and O'Quinn continued his pursuit of the Carolinas low country bream.

There was the nippy feeling of first frost in the October dawn as he slid his small boat into the Lumber River at the Fair Bluff bridge. He quickly moved down the clear river in the strong current, using a short paddle only to maneuver around any obstructions and maintain a course close to the shoreline. Despite floating about a half-mile of the river, O'Quinn had picked up only two redbreast off its shallow sand bar. Was this shaping up to be another tough day to catch fish?

As the sunshine burst over the treetops, he welcomed the warmth. Frost glistened like diamonds on the leaves of an old red oak tree on the bank that leaned precariously over the river. There was an eddy under the oak tree and O'Quinn paddled across the narrow stream to try a cricket or Georgia Wriggler in what appeared to be a choice bream spot. Bill's mouth dropped open and his eyes flashed. The frost was killing a population of oak worms that were living in a big web nest atop the tree and feeding off the green leaves. These caterpillars, known in the Carolinas only as "oak worms," could not stand the killing frost. They hung on the icy leaves until the sun began melting the frost. The worms quickly began losing their grip and toppling into the water underneath the oak. It was like ringing the dinner bell for every panfish in the territory. There was a bluegill reunion under the tree with dinner on the ground. Bill quickly took advantage of his discovery. First, he tried flipping crickets and earthworms where the bream were breaking. They struck a few times, but showed an obvious preference for the fuzzy oak worms. He eased his boat under the lowest limbs and snatched off a dozen worms, then backed away, looped a line on a snag to hold his boat, and adroitly flipped the impaled juicy worm into the shady eddy under the oak.

Pop! His little cork noisily disappeared. He set the hook and came in with a monstrous bluegill. Another quickly followed and the action continued until he had as many nice bream as his family could use. The frost and killing freeze on the parasitic worms had opened the door to bluegill success again for the wily old veteran panfisherman. This was a fall season discovery that he had heard about for years. Only this time he was the one who reaped the benefits.

Nesting songbirds, wasps and oak worms are not the only creatures of nature that help bream fishermen catch panfish throughout much of the country.

In the nine southern states that have alligator populations, many fine catches are made around 'gator beds in the grass and spatterdock lilies. These big reptiles cannot out-swim a bluegill, but they stalk them so quietly in bedding and feeding areas that many meals are snatched as fish pass too closely to avoid the ambush. A moving alligator is not a good omen. He is looking for fish just like a human angler does. But a still, quiet 'gator often has found a school of fish and is patiently filling his belly. The 'gator will always leave when the angler moves in, vacating a productive fishing hole.

Like the alligator, water snakes, especially cottonmouth moccasins, feed on small panfish. Their jaws come unhinged, allowing a snake no more than an inch in diameter to swallow a bluegill more than four inches wide. These snakes find bedding fish and take up residence. They are so still that bream are caught in the snake's teeth with the speed of lightning. When you spot a motionless snake in cover, the chances are good that a school of panfish is nearby. Again, a moving snake doesn't mean anything. It's when you see one or more in cover and perfectly motionless that you may have made a helpful discovery.

In areas where the great blue heron, white egret and

limpkin wade along the shallows, often stopping and looking like statues with their outstretched necks, you can be sure there is a bream food supply nearby. These water birds are generally stalking freshwater shrimp, minnows, bugs and worms in the ankle-deep water—the same food that the bluegills live on. If the birds find these creatures in abundance, the fish may not be far away.

Sea gulls are not good creatures to help bream fishermen find a bluegill bonanza. They are more helpful in attracting attention to bass, stripers and other large predator schooling fish in open water where residue from shad and other forage fish has been left floating. But there are times when the gulls will dive after shrimp and minnows along the fringe of grass beds and lily patches, revealing the presence of food that might mean panfish are there too. Osprey and bald eagles catch fish and give away secrets, too.

Part of the natural food base for bluegills in much of the country where the cow lilies grow, is the bonnet worm. This white worm bores down into the stalk of the lily from the top. Often they move up in the morning, particularly on warm days. They will wriggle on the top side of the leaf. Bream in the area will quickly swallow every worm that falls into the water. The red-winged blackbirds and grackles come to the aid of the angler in many such instances. These birds walk on the lilies, pecking in the holes and eating the bonnet worms. Where there are several birds on the lilies (often making a lot of noise) there are likely to be bream underneath. The very presence of a lot of lilies with holes in the tops made by the bonnet worms, often means the panfish have gathered here to await a worm in the water. Bonnet worms impaled through the middle on a small hook and dangled near the bottom in open spots in the lilies will catch every bream in the territory. Noisy birds often reveal this.

O'Quinn found his bream bonanza in three seasons by careful observation of nature's critters. These accidental discoveries made his excursions successful memories. There was some luck involved, but his alertness and understanding of the situation at hand paid off. He would not soon forget. Other bluegill anglers with expertise have capitalized on alligators, snakes, herons, wasps, worms and birds to find and catch fish.

Fishing help sometimes comes from the most unexpected sources. Insignificant wildlife creatures unknowingly play Judas roles that betray the panfish and help anglers put tasty meals on the table.

324

Panasoffkee's Bluegills and Shellcrackers

A hop and skip off U.S. Highway I-75 at Coleman and north of Wildwood, is the shallow, gin-clear Panasoffkee Lake that has experienced great shellcracker fishing in recent years. June is usually the hottest bream-fishing month as both shell-crackers and bluegills fight for bedding space. Interestingly, Panasoffkee, when there is normal rainfall, is so clear that you can drop your bait to the bottom and observe the shellcrackers picking it up. You can set the hook with confidence when you see the bait dangling in the fish's mouth.

Shellcrackers like to feed on the bottom, and that's one big reason why they are caught in limit numbers by cane pole anglers who impale worms and grass shrimp on a tiny hook with a single lead shot under a small cork. That morsel entices the shellcrackers to nose it up and gulp it down.

This father-son team with the family's best friend, look for Panasoffkee bluegills.

Handled adroitly, shellcrackers either bedding or feeding will also strike a Hal-Fly, SuperJig, Beetle Spin or other small jig flaunted in their faces. They hit with the violence of an unleashed coil spring, and ounce for ounce will put up as much fight as any species anywhere.

Shellcrackers particularly like Lake Panasoffkee where there is an abundance of insect food throughout much of the 4,460 acres of clear water with acre after productive acre of aquatic growth. There are miles of eelgrass, peppergrass, lilies, maidencane, sawgrass and water hyacinths in the Panasoffkee that averages only five feet in depth with the deepest holes only ten feet. Housing dots the western shoreline, but much of the east bank is undeveloped.

Panasoffkee Lake is connected to the Withlacoochee River by the two-mile-long Outlet River and Princess Lake. You can find June shellcrackers by using your nose, eyes, ears and other senses. The water is shallow enough that you can actually spot your quarry on calm days. If you are a natural bait fisherman, you'll do better by anchoring both ends of your boat and floating your bait to the bottom with little or no lead on the line. You'll get more fish with an 8- or 10-pound test monofilament line than with anything heavier. Your hook should have a long shank for easy removal from the mouth. Number 4 or 6 steel hooks are best. If you do not anchor, the swinging movement of the boat will drag your bait back and forth, and shellcrackers are not as likely to strike it. Some people use no bobber, but most natives put a cork on the line that floats free on the surface without any downward pull when the weight and hook are on the bottom.

A local tip for shellcrackers is chumming the area around your hook with handfuls of coarse sand. The sand filtering from the surface to the bottom seems to attract the fish that need some action to wake them up.

Purists who wish to catch their dinner table meal with artificial baits need to know how to jig a jig, either vertically or cast along cover lines and retrieved. Small spinners, crawfish crankbaits, tiny silver Rat-L-Traps and Rapalas will trigger strikes. Some of the Panasoffkee shellcrackers reach weights of 2-pounds and above, and have mouths large enough to attack some of the same lures that bass and crappies hit.

Bluegills are plentiful in Panasoffkee, and prior to the late '80's when an unusual rainfall made the water dingy with tannic acid, the bream were caught in greater numbers than the shellcrackers. The bluegills still are caught when the water is higher than normal, but shellcrackers seem to be more easily caught than the bluegills.

Bluegills bed in the same kind of habitat as the shell-crackers, but they have a tendency to nest every full moon from April through September. Shellcrackers may bed each month, but the species generally spawns early in the spring, skips a few hot months, and goes back on the nest again in September.

You can catch bluegills with shrimp, worms, crickets, mealy worms, wasp nest larvae, catalpa worms, sapheads and a variety of other naturals. These baits are fished under a cork, off the bottom, impaled on little hooks and light monofilament. They will hit a moving bait better than a shellcracker will, and they are not as likely to strike a bottom bait as one dangling a foot or two off the bottom. If you can handle a bait on a line without a cork, and with no weight on the line, you'll catch many more bluegills than you will with even a single lead shot and a cork. The bait fluttering down from the surface just looks more alive and wild than one cluttered with lead and a cork. A 6- or 8-pound monofilament line is best, and even with no weight except your grass shrimp, the best of the naturals, you can still feel the bottom when you fish with a limber B 'n' M fiberglass rod. This "nothin' pole" will also catch some shellcrackers, yearling bass, crappies, catfish, pickerel or anything else in the neighborhood. Twitch the bait near the bottom.

Some shellcracker purists catch bluegills on tiny spinners, especially Beetle Spins, little crankbaits and jigs. Topwater enthusiasts who can handle a popping bug on a flyrod can mop up in the shallow waters around the grass and lilies on dark days. Accuracy is important, and often the bream will not venture out more than a foot from the cover. But a twitched popping bug in his territory will frequently bring that sucking noise that means another copperhead has found your bait to his liking, and made a fatal mistake. Those end up in the skillet where many seafood lovers declare there is no better fish to eat than those panfish from the pure water of the Panasoffkee.

There are nine fish camps scattered around the shoreline of Panasoffkee Lake, and there are several good launching ramps. Among the best of the full service fish camps is Pana Vista Lodge, operated for two decades by Jim and Eloise Veal. They have boats, bait, guides, cabins, campsites, tackle and are aware

You seldom catch a bluegill this size, but this one hit a spinner.

of where and how the fish are biting. They freely share their knowledge of the lake, and are anxious to help visitors catch limits of bluegills and shellcrackers.

"Recently we have had some of our very best shellcracker seasons. We need high water that makes the fish easy to get to when they are spawning, and we see some fine catches of really big shellcrackers come from the Panasoffkee. The shellcrackers are giants some seasons. The bream will be biting good, too. We need good water levels," Jim Veal, a veteran angler said.

Fishermen interested in learning more about the Panasoffkee Lake panfish can contact the Pana Vista Lodge, Route 2, Box 100, Lake Panasoffkee, FL 33538, Telephone 904-793-2061.

Panfish enthusiasts have hundreds of fishing holes to choose from in Florida, but there are no better spots than Lake Panasoffkee for bluegills and shellcrackers.

Briery Creek Lake
Hottest Bream Hole in Virginia

These are called "titty bream" . . . so large you have to
hold them to your chest to unhook.

When David K. Whitehurst, chief of the Fisheries Division, Virginia Department of Game and Inland Fisheries, saw a stringer of 12 bluegills caught in Briery Creek Lake that was unbelievable, he estimated the catch at 20 pounds. While his eyes may have stretched the weight a mite, this 845 acres of wooded water is now rapidly growing many species of bream to bragging size. Impounded in 1986, by mid-year of 1989 big bluegill catches were the talk of the town around Farmville, Virginia.

Bill Kittrell, biologist with the fisheries division who has

Briery Creek Lake in his 12-county territory, says he has documented some bluegills at 1-pound, 4-ounces, not much below the average the 12 Whitehurst bream would have weighed if they indeed had tipped the scales collectively at 20 pounds. Maybe the 20-pound estimate was a bit off, but it was a stringer to remember, anyway. Whitehurst obviously does.

One thing is for certain, ever since the lake that is half-covered with standing trees, was opened to the public for fishing in 1989, larger than normal Virginia bluegills have been pulled from these tannic waters by hundreds of native anglers enjoying panfishing experiences that almost guarantee plenty of fun and food. Tourists anglers have got the message, too.

Why does this relatively new lake that was built exclusively for freshwater sport fishing appear to be a fast-growth honey hole for panfish that reach weights of a pound or more in four or five years?

Kittrell, who was a biologist in Ocala, Florida, before accepting his present post in Virginia, points out that Briery Creek at first was designed to grow lunker-size largemouth bass. With that in mind, the Virginia wildlife agency stocked the lake with a studied mix of the Florida strain of bass and the northern largemouths native to the area. It's too early to document the long range bass growth, but the transplanted predator bass seem to be constantly hungry. Feasting on the smaller bluegills, those that escape the onslaught have the food supply to themselves, and they are reaching a healthy obesity quickly. Their length and girth are larger than normal for most Virginia bream.

"The three-quarters to one-pound size is the most frequently caught bream in the lake as they congregate around the tree trunks and feed off the insects and tiny minnows. But we truly do have many of these panfish that have surpassed normal growth for Virginia waters. Tourists and natives are having a lot of fun catching them and showing them off, then enjoying them at the dinner table too," Kittrell says with some obvious pride in his domain.

With half the 845 acres covered with standing timber, Briery Creek Lake is unsuitable for speedboats and water skiers. That's in keeping with the plan by the Game and Inland Fisheries for this particular impoundment that was built to enhance freshwater angling opportunities for the Farmville area. Briery Creek is on U.S. Highway 15, just south of Farmville. It is easily accessible.

Plans call for a paved launching ramp and parking lot to be completed this year. But the aggressive nature of the bluegills to date has erased the slight inconvenience of the dirt ramp and parking area. Fishermen have been delighted with the robust bluegills that cherish crickets, night crawlers, grass shrimp and bits of catalpa worms impaled on No. 4 or 6 hooks and dangled under a cork a foot off the swampy bottom of this cypress-covered reservoir. Catching the legal limit of 50 fine panfish has become a common experience—and you can count on many of them being "titty bream" size.

Kittrell also notes that in addition to the bluegills, electro-shocking studies have turned up fine 8-inch punkinseed panfish and redears (shellcrackers) as large as those on the stringer the Chief Whitehurst recalled. All the panfish are obviously doing very well at Briery Creek.

Currently there is a two-a-day limit on largemouth bass at Briery Creek Lake, and they must be 18 inches long or better. Some are being caught, but the bassing seems to be a little slower than originally forecast. The impoundment still may be a lunker bass honey hole in this decade, but for the moment, the panfish are getting the headlines.

"The Briery Creek Lake project was designed to be a great fishery, and it well may be in a few more years. But today the bass fishing is kind of slow. An abundance of small bass are constantly chasing the bream all over the place. They have been gulping down enough of these small panfish to leave plenty of nutrition for those that escape the predation. That's the bright spot in this new impoundment, and panfishing is going like gangbusters," Biologist Kittrell happily recalls.

There's little doubt about it. Briery Creek Lake is the hottest panfish hole in Virginia, and you just might drag in a stringer of slabs with unsophisticated cane poles equipped with bream hooks and the traditional natural baits used by outdoorsmen since the era of Izaak Walton and before. It doesn't require a fancy boat and expensive tackle to catch a mess of panfish in this watery forest, but the purists succeed, too, with Beetle Spins, Super Jigs and Hal-Flies. When the really big bream are as plentiful as they are at Briery Creek, almost anything will catch fish.

The lady was fishing for crappies, but got a bream on
the hook.

Black Lake's Bream and Barfish Bite When Bass Go On Strike

Big bass enthusiasts pour into Louisiana's Black Lake complex from early spring until late fall, and stalk the species that often is so abundant around the standing forest of cypress trees that 25-30 lunkers a day is not uncommon. But when these largemouths are turned off, many tourists and local anglers still score—they go after the bream and barfish that abandon caution and know no season.

A narrow ribbon of tannic-colored water stretches about 65 miles from the Red River into north-central Louisiana near the village of Campti on Highway 9, and except for some winding channels through the woods, all of this watery swampland is literally a live-cypress forest draped with Spanish moss. A prettier place to fish would be hard to find. The fish obviously agree, as the habitat affords great food and cover for a myriad of freshwater species that seldom reject natural or man-made morsels twitched around the tree trunks, knees and drooping limbs in this wilderness of water.

Guides like Richard Childs recall spring days when the marauding bass were prowling, and astute anglers hauled in literally dozens of lunkers in the 5 to 7-pound range in an hour.

"They school on top around the trees, and will bite just about anything that you cast within eyeball distance. They chase thousands of small shad, and are in a feeding frenzy. They seem to be panicky, dashing to gulp down all the food before a hungry cousin beats them to it. Constant splashing around the trees often covers half an acre. It's unbelievable," Childs describes a Black Lake bass bonanza.

"But bass fishing is a bit unpredictable. They seem to turn off from changing weather conditions more often than the other species that are so plentiful here. So when the bass don't cooperate, we can still enjoy success and a memorable experience here. Bream, white perch and the challenging barfish will keep your lines singing and poles bent," this talented native from near Shreveport testifies.

333

White perch and barfish? Those are Cajun names. They call crappie white perch or sac-a-lait, and expect listeners to know what they are talking about. Shellcrackers are chinquapins. And barfish? That's their moniker for white bass, striper, and hybrids. They are marked with horizontal black bars from tail to gills, grow fat and chunky off the crawfish and other forage species that abound on the brush-covered bottom, and will bite everything from a tiny sinking jig to maggots, minnows, crickets and grass shrimp. A combination of jig and natural bait is deadly.

Bill and Jean Baker own Chandler's and Black Lake Lodge, a full-service fishing complex, the only one on this unique lake that looks like it might have been transplanted from the low country in Georgia, Florida or the Carolinas. Bill is a lawyer in Jonesboro, and his wife Jean has worked with him for decades. They live at Black Lake and fish from a 20-foot pontoon boat. While they are not professional guides, few people know the lake better or can catch more panfish than this husband-wife team. They are veterans with a lot of expertise who know these dark waters as well as anyone. Furthermore, they know virtually every fisherman they chance to meet in the cypress trees by name, profession and family history. If anyone is loading the boat with bream and barfish, the where-to and how-to information is courteously shared. It saves a bit of trial and error.

Bill maneuvered his sleek pontoon away from the dock at the Highway 9 bridge. He headed right into the cypress forest. Within rock-throwing distance of the bridge and only a minute or two from the launching ramp, he cut the motor. Jean tied the pontoon to a tree. We were ready to fish.

It's at this point that the how-to comes into use. "You can catch these barfish, crappie and bream a lot of ways, but Jean and I prefer to fish for them with the smallest jigs we can find. We add meat to the hook to make it a little more enticing. That's when we impale a maggot or grass shrimp or even an earthworm or cricket. Sometimes in four or five feet of water you can catch all the barfish and other species you want without adding the meat, but we think tipping the hook helps. We use light line, about 6-pound test, no cork, and we fish close to the bottom. We get a lot of strikes as the little tipped jig settles slowly. The line runs off, you set the hook, and enjoy a good tussle to the gunnels," Bill says.

"We like to find the four and five foot deep holes just off the channels that run through the trees. The fish seem to gather

334

in these holes, especially on pretty, fair days like this," Jean adds to the how-to, where-to.

Almost before the waves from the wake subsided, Bill grunted and groaned with a fish on the line. He was fishing a 1/32-ounce, clear crappie jig distributed by Armstrong Cricket Farm at nearby West Monroe, Louisiana. With a light line and a 10-foot B 'n' M telescopic pole, he was not equipped to fish for trophies. But he had the right tackle for the Black Lake panfish. It required no casting, no sophisticated technique—just let the little jig flutter toward the bottom in 5 to 10 feet of this dark water.

Bill landed his first strike, a fine slab-size crappie in the 1 1/2-pound range. Now it was Jean's time and quickly it became apparent she was the expert when it came to catching panfish here in her own backyard.

Impaling multicolored larvae, maggots to most fishermen, on her tiny jig, Jean immediately wrestled a fine shellcracker (redear) over the gunnels, and in a matter of minutes she put a half dozen other assorted bream in the bucket. None were giants, but all were gourmet seafood at the dinner table. They were fun to fight on the limber B 'n' M poles, too. The larvae were alive, and had been dyed red, green and yellow. One color seemed to be about as productive as another. Kept dry in a cup of sawdust, the wriggling, inch-long larvae can be preserved for days.

With the 5-gallon bucket with ice in the bottom covered with assorted species of so-called bream, Bill moved the pontoon a hundred yards to another spot that looked just like the one we had left. Again, Jean tied up the boat to a cypress. We were ready for more action.

"There's no better bait for the barfish (white bass, yearling stripers and hybrids) than the live grass shrimp that we catch here with a fine-mesh dip net around the aquatic growth. Try a couple of these little translucent critters on a No. 4 hook on or near the bottom. No cork, no lead, just the grass shrimp on a small hook or added to a jig. The barfish often go for them right here in this deep hole," Bill advised.

He was right. Jean came in with a 14-inch, fat hybrid striper, quickly followed with another, and then a white bass. Instant replay made the bluebird afternoon exciting for two hours as the big bucket was filled with a great mixed bag of bluegills, shellcrackers, white bass, hybrids and a few crappies. For early spring, mid-March actually, you could not have caught a finer mess of fish than those pulled from the cypress groves at

Black Lake anywhere in the country. It's truly a panfish paradise for both novices and experts. On a stringer, the mixture made a postcard picture.

Black Lake Lodge and Chandler's Camp have cabins, boats, bait, meals, licenses, guides and advice. They can be contacted at Route 2, Box 240, Chestnut, LA 71070. Phone 318-875-2244.

Young and old catch panfish.

Georgia's Two Pounder Is Not Really a World Record Warmouth Perch

My tiny bream cork disappeared like it was alive and the strike was obviously vicious. But then the line stopped. The bobber stayed down and you wondered if a real lunker hadn't carried the bait under the cover, disgorged it and left you hung but good on the bottom, where decaying brush made sheltered nesting havens for a variety of Santee panfish.

I yanked on the cane pole, expecting resistance of one kind or another. But the line came up straight out of the water with only the tiniest trickle of life and motion. Unbelievable! I had a two-finger sized warmouth perch not nearly as long as any of the gob of night crawlers used for bait, and yet that little critter had jumped on my hook and carried my cork to China almost like he had hands. Honestly, when I eased the little fellow off the hook he seemed to be grinning at me with an expression like, "Fooled you that time, didn't I?"

Such experiences with the warmouth perch, that ranges from Minnesota east through the Great Lakes and Pennsylvania and inhabits about every mudhole in the Carolinas, Georgia, Alabama and Florida, among other Southern states, are legendary. There's not a freshwater game fishing enthusiast in the country who hasn't had a myriad of momentary thrills from this gallant little species that will bite anything from a crayfish as big as he is to a Broken Back Rebel lure with three sets of treble hooks trolled along the bottom in search of stripers or largemouth bass.

These stumpknockers, as they are known by some anglers, are not afraid to attack anything dead or alive that is flaunted in their faces and if they get by without feeling the hook the first time, they will come right back and strike again and again, much like the chain pickerel. Even if you do land the critter, he may well come back to bite again within moments if he hasn't been hurt substantially and you keep on fishing where you caught and released him.

And most warmouths are released. They are generally caught by mistake because few anglers go out to catch a creel limit of warmouths except in some remote rural areas where the native fishermen have sought them for food for generations. Those select few know that whether this species is large or small, it is a fine gourmet meal if you catch them early before the water gets too warm and they get that strong or muddy taste. They are not appetizing then, but neither is a bluegill under the same circumstances.

337

Warmouth inhabit dense weed beds, soft muddy bottoms, around stumps and brush, rocks or logs, anything that offers cover and protection from the larger predators and any territory where minnows and other panfish fry are likely to provide an abundance of nutritious meals for a species with a healthy appetite. They are generally morning feeders and will gulp down any kind of larvae from the aquatic growth and any fish that swims that isn't too big to go down. All insects and crayfish, too, are among the favorite foods of this hungry species. They generally do not feed much in the afternoon and the really devout stumpknocker anglers go after them at safe light and either have their cooler filled or have struck out before noon.

Those warmouth fishermen who actively seek the species have perfected this system. Mostly they "lead line" for the warmouth with several big shot on a strong monofilament line, a stubby cane pole, No. 4 Eagle Claw hook, load it with a wad of worms and jiggle it on or near the bottom in the thickest brush piles and log jams in the still waters of lakes and streams. These fish are not very fond of fast moving water, preferring instead the still waters from a few inches deep to four or five feet. They have an amazing ability to live in muddy water, much like the bowfin and catfish, where most more actively hunted panfish wouldn't want to be found. They will hit that wad of worms being moved around them and you have a good momentary tussle with one of average size. And that means one in the 7- to 10-ounce class.

But they are not all just average. Those that live to be senior citizens in the fish family, seven years old or more, reach lengths of 8 1/2 inches or thereabouts and many have been caught in the one-pound class. The largest one on official rod and reel records was landed by Carlton Robbins, of Sylvania, Georgia, on May 4, 1974. It was officially weighed in and recorded at 2-pounds even. But don't let that fool you—South Carolina's Willie Singletary beat that recorded world champion.

There may be no best time of the year to catch a warmouth. But those who study their life-styles and fish for them with intensity, believe that they are bedding and therefore the easiest to catch in the Southland waters, like Santee, when the dogwood trees begin to bloom. By the time the petals fall, they have about ended the spawn but are still caught frequently right in the bluegill, shellcracker, bass and crappie beds. They recognize a good dining table when they see it and will make their home there as long as the eggs and fry are plentiful. It is during these months that anglers for other species most often put warmouths over the gunwales whether they are casting an artificial minnow into the grass, jigging a fly for bream, dropping crickets, shrimp or worms in the lilies, or even trolling live minnows in the open water nearby. Warmouths are not that persnickety about what they eat. If it moves, they'll come after it.

There are warmouth fishermen at Santee and in other Southern honey holes who use the old throw gear system and still catch good messes of this species. This is a light monofilament line on a limber cane pole, tiny cork, little hook with a cricket, worm, live grass shrimp, grasshopper or crayfish for bait. They flip this bait in the thick cover, under overhanging bushes and around the maidencane and cattails to hustle the warmouth out of the cover.

Many today use a small piece of Uncle Josh's white pork rind on the shank of the hook, above the live bait. It is an attractor that often brings the warmouth a-runnin'. Before the time of the more sophisticated attractors now commercially available, these avid fishermen cut tiny pieces of white fatback meat and threaded it on the hook above the bait. Either addition seems to be a little more enticing for the warmouth than the plain bait, but brave little fellows that they are, they will attack just about any offering.

The largest warmouth I ever put in the boat was caught on a lead line with a gob of Georgia wigglers on the hook. It weighed 14-ounces and the very next time I dropped the bait to the bottom, I pulled in another one exactly the same size. It was an instant replay situation. Both looked huge for warmouths, and I have never again caught one that big. Those two were caught in the Waccamaw River in North Carolina where they are called "Morgans" by many for some unknown reason. Other names by which they are known in the South and other parts of the country include "goggle-eye" and "goggle-eye perch." It is also often mistaken for a rock bass. The thick-bodied sunfish does resemble the rock bass but it can be distinguished by the three spines on the anal fin, teeth on the tongue and small spots on the anal and dorsal fins. It has a large mouth extending beyond its reddish eyes and it never is larger than 11 inches. It is olive or gray in color with mottled markings on its sides and back.

One of the great attributes of the warmouth perch is its lack of fear that makes it readily catchable for even the rankest amateur or first-time-out child. Regardless of the noise you make, splashing that ruffles the water, and ineptness in putting on the bait and presenting it to the fish, almost any angler can bring a warmouth out of the water. Fishing from the humblest bateau, jonboat or even from the bank, warmouth are usually catchable.

Never was this more dramatically exhibited than a few years ago when a Cub Scout was out fishing from the bank in the upper reaches of the Sparkleberry Swamp. One of the youngsters had never had the pleasure of doing any kind of fishing in his life, and when I handed him a cane pole with a worm bait on it and gently let it sink a couple of feet in the water near a cypress trunk, I casually remarked that he would have to watch it for a bite in that good-looking place.

"How will I know when I get a bite?" he asked, and I was astounded that an eight-year-old didn't know when a fish bit.

"Well, you'll know you have a bite when that cork on the surface goes under," I told him patiently.

Several minutes later when I had the other dozen youngsters anxiously expecting a bite and a big fish on the line, I came back to the little scout who didn't know how to recognize a bite. Amazingly, he was using the end of the pole to push the cork under.

"What are you doing that for?" I inquired.

Just as sincere as a deacon in church, the little fellow said, "Well you told me I would have a bite and could catch a fish when the cork went under."

At that same instant, the cork stayed down and the line was almost tight. Sensing something on the line, the cub jerked with all his might. A little warmouth went flying through the tree tops like he was shot from a cannon and came to a bouncing stop in the palmettos 40 feet from the river bank. Moments later a happy eight-year-old was clutching his catch in both hands and beaming a smile worthy of the most professional basser with a wall mount in his net. It was an incident that truly dramatized that the warmouth, minor species that he is, still has a place in America's waters and that he will bite regardless of the lack of expertise or knowledge of the angler.

And there should always be plenty of these little critters for the young and old to enjoy. A single female will lay up to 126,000 eggs in a season. They become sexually mature when they are three inches in length and will grow half that long the first year of life. In the scheme of nature, there is no such thing as an insignificant species. For a lot of anglers who take up a hook and line only once or twice a year, the little old warmouth is important.

But what about the 2-pounder listed by the International Game Fish Association as the world record? Well, it was caught with more sophisticated tackle, and met the guidelines for a world record—that is, it was caught with a rod and reel. But it certainly was not the largest warmouth legally landed, as far as we can learn. Willie Singletary has that documented record with a humble chinaberry limb for a pole. Here's what outdoor writer Bob Campbell had to say about Willie's real, documented record in 1979:

Willie Did It With A Limb

Some are lucky, some skillful. Some do it with very little investment, others spend a lot. But Willie Singletary of Lake City did it with a chinaberry limb late one hot summer afternoon deep in Douglas Swamp.

Singletary caught the world record warmouth perch sunfish.

His fish, caught in May of 1973, weighed 2-pounds, 3-ounces and while the story has been told, it bears telling again, because a man who catches a world record on a chinaberry limb is some kind of a special fisherman.

Singletary was not in pursuit of giants nor did he intend to catch a big fish. What he had wanted when he and friends set out on that hot summer afternoon was a change of pace from laying too many bricks in too short a time.

They were also looking for a change of pace at the supper table.

Sometime in the late afternoon after the men had entered Douglas Swamp near Olanta, Singletary landed his record fish on the makeshift equipment and a fat earthworm.

That equipment cost Singletary about 50 cents and the fish "a whole lot of mosquito bites," said the fisherman in an interview shortly after he made the catch.

He said the record fish didn't fight much, but "popped" about two feet off his limb-fashioned pole. What fight the fish didn't make on the line it made up for in the bucket.

Placed in a five gallon lard stand, the fish promptly "turned over the bucket," said Singletary with a smile exhibiting an ample set of teeth.

"We might have caught some more fish," the soft-spoken fisherman said, and his friends wanted to fish more, "but after I catch this one," he said, "then I leave."

The point of the story is you don't have to be a high-powered fisherman to catch a record fish. More than one state record has been landed with rather modest means.

State wildlife officials say Singletary's catch is one of the most memorable of the state record catches because it is near pure "man and fish story," something akin to Hemingway's *Old Man and the Sea.*

Exuding a certain unpretentious presence, Willie Singletary is a sturdy fellow with solid features. He looks you

341

squarely in the eye, but behind his eyes there is a discernible element of doubt.

His is altogether a presence that tells you he is here with a firm purpose in mind. He is ready to talk business...no kidding, and it is enough to make anyone a little uneasy, even those of us who are talented at avoiding such things as business (not to be confused with fishing.)

Willie wants to register a state record fish. He also wants to know how he is to benefit from being the holder of a state record. The slightest hint of doubt eases into his friendly eyes when I tell him there's no money to be made from a record. "Then why did I come all the way to Columbia?" he's asking himself... the question is clear in his dark eyes.

But his smile never wavers. Mine is beginning to weaken at the edges, however.

"No money?" he asks, mildly suggesting disbelief.

"No money," I reply.

"Then what do I get?" he asks pointedly through that invulnerable smile.

Were I playing poker, it would be a losing proposition.

"A certificate," I say, holding my breath.

"No money?" he asks again, as if just maybe he hadn't heard correctly the first time.

"No money," I reaffirm, not wanting him to remain in a state of uncertainty. "But holding a state record is a prestigious thing," I add hopefully, "You should be proud."

There is another poker pause from Singletary. But finally he looks me dead in the eyes and says, "You keep the pride, I'll take the certificate." After all, he says silently, a certificate is better than nothing, though neither it nor pride will help feed the children.

Willie was not in pursuit of giants nor did he intend to catch a state record fish. What he had wanted when he and a friend had set out on that hot summer afternoon was a change of pace. Welcomed too, would be a change of fare at the supper table.

But two fishermen with no tackle weren't going to catch many fish. They had no rod, no reel, no fully rigged bass boat with carpeted deck and a spiffy little seat up front, pushed by a 150-horsepower Merc outboard. So they improvised, and that is how Willie Singletary of Lake City, South Carolina, came to hold the world record for warmouth, caught with the limb of a chinaberry tree.

Carolina Sportsmen Get Change of Pace with Unique Yellow Perch in Winter

When deer hunters have harvested their season limit or weariness from sitting in a tree stand for too many days causes your spirit to rebel, you can continue an outdoor pursuit even when snow and ice blanket the Eastern Carolina low country swamplands.

The unique yellow perch that love to migrate in the coldest months of the year up the Waccamaw River, are hungry for live bait in the white water narrows and in the tailraces. The tasty species spices up the lives of those sportsmen who never find weather too cold for going fishing. There's no better place to bring home a stringer of these elongated perch, known in some areas as "raccoon perch," and by many Tar Heel anglers on Tobacco Road as "redfin trout," than behind the low-level weir in the south corner of Lake Waccamaw in Columbus County, North Carolina. This natural lake was formed by a giant meteor aeons ago, and measures five by seven miles, averaging only about eight feet in depth. The crystal-clear lake is the headwaters of the 50-mile long Waccamaw River that crosses the Carolinas state borders east of Longs, South Carolina, and flows around a myriad of oxbows, into the Intracoastal Waterway at Bucksport. Yellow perch can be caught in many of the upper reaches of this scenic, wilderness river, but by far the most popular spot in January and February is directly behind the dam in the whitewater of the tailrace. Many local anglers let their boats ride up against the dam, and then cast with light tackle into the fast current in the narrow river mouth a few yards downstream. A free-lined live minnow on a No. 4 TruTurn hook with a couple of lead shot eight or ten inches apart a foot up the line, will attract the marauding perch. Other veteran yellow perch anglers use roughly the same system, but with a snap-on cork two feet from the hook that dances and streaks in the fast water until a perch decides to gulp it down and run. Both free-lined and cork-supported baits are successful in the fast current in the coldest weather of winter.

Perch hold at the weir in the worst winter weather, eventually crossing into the lake when the water temperature moves up. Other perch stalkers show disdain for the ice and cold and wade the knee-deep water, casting small crankbaits, spinners or grub lures against the shoreline where eddies and swirls on the edge of the current hold the yellows.

Perch lounge in lazy water awaiting onrushing forage that is swept over the weir and into the river mouth. Always yellow perch in the tailrace are there in numbers, never just a stray. If you catch one, you'll likely catch a dozen or more in the same honey hole. They move up the river early in the year in schools to explore spawning areas in the lake prior to the reproductive nest-seeking antics of bluegills, shellcrackers, crappies and bass.

A yellow perch weighing more than a pound is a big one in the Waccamaw. Mostly they are 10- to 12-ounce fish, but occasionally a 2-pounder comes flopping in on a line. Regardless of the size, the Carolina yellow perch are great fighters on the line as well as excellent table fare.

Most native perch-jerkers feel that the yellows are too small to fillet. Instead, they scale, gut, de-head and wash their fish, and then fry them whole in deep fat after a salt, pepper and cornmeal-flour sprinkling. These succulent perch are delicious. There's not much problem in filleting out the bones with your fingers after the fish is fried brown and crisp. Like the well-publicized, fast-food chicken drive-ins, the yellow perch is finger-licking good. Scaling a yellow perch is not easy. The scales seem to be fastened with crazy glue. They almost have to be cut from the skin and this makes filleting desirable by a few perch dressers. But if you have the patience to scrape the Carolinas' scales loose from the skin, you'll have a much better tasting protein in the dinner plate. Leaving the skin on also expedites removing the bones from the rib cage.

This unusual species is caught more often in the dead of winter than later when they spawn in the grass beds and around the cow lilies in Lake Waccamaw. Occasionally, bream fishermen encounter the perch spawning in the cover early in the spring and make good catches with worms, crickets, mayflies and grass shrimp baits. But primarily, the Carolina yellow perch is a winter-time delight, offering outdoorsmen a chance to oil up their tackle early for a little fishing at a time when most sportsmen pick up guns and dogs for hunting the plentiful local whitetail deer.

Yellow perch fishing when the ice and snow cover the marshland is a change of pace anticipated and enjoyed by an elite society of Tar Heel anglers always a step ahead of other sportsmen. Traditional freshwater anglers in this largest natural lake between the Great Lakes and Florida schedule their adventures here from late March until December.

The heartier fishermen have unlocked the secrets of yellow perch shenanigans in the fast water. Then, rather than chase another deer or go to sleep in front of the fire, they challenge this tasty species with hook and line. Many come home wearing satisfied smiles. Like bream and crappie, it is another fine panfish for the dinner table that the unsophisticated anglers love.

Yellow Perch Despised in Ireland

Following an annual conference of the Outdoor Writers Association of America at Harrisburg, Pennsylvania, in 1987, a contingency of fishing communicators accepted an invitation from Northern Ireland's Tourist Bureau to fish a few days in that green and beautiful country. We went to fish for salmon and brown trout in the prolific waters near Kesh. Trout and salmon did not cooperate. But you could see natives dragging out tubfuls of yellow perch that they considered a trash species. They fed them to the gulls. With a little prodding, the guide agreed to let us fish for the perch. He bought some domesticated maggots for bait, and we immediately caught dozens of foot-long yellows. We carried them to our bed-and-breakfast facility where we borrowed knives to scale and dress the fish, a hard job without the proper tools. We sat on the ground with a pine board in front of us and worked diligently for an hour getting the fish ready for the skillet. A typical, pipe-smoking old Irishman walked by, stopped and gazed at us working on the yellow perch. He shook his head and muttered, "That's the first poor Americans I ever saw." He couldn't believe we were going to eat "trash" fish. The lady proprietor cooked the perch for our breakfast They were great. The cook agreed. Her husband-guide said no. He wouldn't stoop to eating perch. We discovered something else—cornmeal is unknown in Northern Ireland.

Way Down Upon the Suwannee River You Catch Fine Redbreast

Thousands of lakes and dozens of rivers provide Florida natives and tourists with a mecca of great sunfish waters, but none is more outstanding than the historic Suwannee River for redbreast and Lake Panasoffkee for bluegills and shellcrackers.

The scenic Suwannee was first recognized for its beauty and attraction by Stephen Foster's homely ditty "Way Down Upon the Suwannee River," but in recent years the freshwater anglers of the area have enhanced its image by setting the two, four, eight and 12-pound line class redbreast sunfish records with fish pulled from this winding stream. The biggest of these pretty panfish, also known as yellow bellies, longear sunfish, sun perch and redbreast bream, weighed 1-pound, 2-ounces and was caught by Alvin Buchanan May 2, 1984.

Redbreasts are river species, and they are usually found in association with smallmouth bass and rock bass as they range from Canada to Florida in all states east of the Allegheny Mountains. The Suwannee is not a smallmouth stream, but redbreasts abound in virtually all of the 265 miles of water that starts in the Okefenokee Swamp in South Georgia and empties into the Gulf of Mexico at the tiny town of Suwannee, 24 miles west of Old Town on Highway 19. The last 50 miles of the Suwannee is navigable by boats of great size, including 42-foot houseboats with tag-along fishing dories pulled off the stern. Anglers can fish from the comfortable deck of the houseboats along steep shorelines or board the dory and flip natural and artificial baits under the overhanging flora that decorates beautiful, uncluttered shorelines for mile after scenic mile.

Despite the Suwannee's fame as a wilderness river where you can visit historic springs, sanctuaries and old Indian stomping grounds, it remains one of the least used streams in the South. Designated as an "Outstanding Florida Waters," and now attracting attention for its redbreast records, this river that laces its way past cypress hammocks, palmetto stands and around 30-foot cliffs of rocks in some oxbows, it is a freshwater angler's paradise. While largemouth bass are plentiful and bluegills, shellcrackers, warmouth perch, catfish, pickerel, crappie and other species are at home in much of the Suwannee, it's the rambunctious, never-say-die fight of the redbreasts that is today's subject of many conversations at anglers' 19th holes.

Redbreasts like surface lures and professional bass fishermen like Shaw Grigsby, Jr., and his father forget the cast-for-cash business a day or two every week to have fun on the Suwannee. Some of the best waters of the Suwannee are only an hour or so from their Gainesville home, and when you are an artificial lure enthusiast as the Grigsbys are, you can fish and experience thrills without pressure on this river.

While redbreasts will rush after live crickets, earthworms, and grass shrimp when floated along sandy bottoms near deep holes on No. 4 hooks, lightweight monofilament line and a little cork bobbing in the current, the Grigsby father-son team prefer to catch their panfish with small spinners, little topwater plugs or the ever-popular popping bug. A chartreuse or white popping bug flipped in the eddies along shorelines early or late or on overcast days will attract as many hungry redbreasts as any artificial or natural bait.

Fly rodders who can keep their lines out of the trees that almost overlap the river at some of the narrows, have a field day with the popping bugs. The much less sophisticated rigging of a 16-foot monofilament line on a 14-foot cane pole with a popping bug attached can be slingshot under the bushes, and maneuvered around limbs and vines better than a fly line. A mature redbreast sucking in a surface lure, couples your sight, sound and feel, and devout river anglers recognize this experience as second to none in panfish excitement.

The redbreast fishermen who do not subscribe to the preference of the purists and go after the panfish with cane pole or rod and reel with natural baits, often fill a live-box when they anchor upstream from a sandbar, let their worms, crickets or shrimp trickle along the bottom in a fast current, and then check it when it drops off in a hole on the sandbar fringe. Few self-respecting redbreast can refuse the offering. It's in just such a spot that they stalk their food as it washes in from the swamp tributaries of the Suwannee. Food with a hook in it is not rejected by feeding red bellies.

Redbreasts can be caught at night better than most of their sunfish cousins. They tend to feed along grass or lily lines after dark and rush to attack surface lures or small Mepps spinners retrieved rapidly. Natural baits get strikes too.

Redbreasts spawn in the spring in the Suwannee when the water reaches 68 degrees F. The male noses out an indentation in the gravel or sand and the female deposits her thousands of eggs. Both parents guard the nest a few days after the hatch, and it is a good time to put redbreasts in the boat. They are always plentiful in June when they spawn, and the reproduction may continue well into summer.

The first year, a young redbreast may grow to only two inches, but will jump to as much as five inches the second year. By the fourth year he will reach six inches, and when full grown may measure almost a foot. A 1-pounder is considered a big redbreast, but in the Suwannee today they are nearing 2-pounds as the recognized records prove. Veteran redbreast enthusiasts will not be surprised to see a 2-pounder weighed in any season as more and more anglers are going after the gourmet species.

Redbreasts are easily identified by their long black gill flag that has no yellow or red trim. They are the brightest color of any medium-size sunfish with yellow sides and a crimson belly. They have small mouths and short, round pectoral fins. In many areas of the country they are called "sun perch" and thrive in clear, fast water that is free of pollution.

Fishermen interested in pursuing the Suwannee redbreasts, can launch their boats at Fanning Springs, Old Town, Rock Bluff, Branford and many other upstream villages on the river. But those who prefer to start at the river mouth will find excellent facilities at Miller's at Suwannee overlooking the Gulf. Houseboat rentals, camping sites, tackle, guides, bait, boats, motors, maps and friendly advice are available at this modern dock and marina. Their mailing address is P.O. Box 280, Suwannee, Florida 32692. The phone number is 904-542-7349.

Foster's song made this America's favorite river of music. It flows into your heart and when you become infatuated with the record size redbreasts available for the asking, you'll have an additional attraction for this swampland with its twisting, devastatingly beautiful, untamed river. In many ways, the Suwannee is Florida's best kept freshwater fishing secret. Just now it is being unlocked.

Catfishing—For Fun and Food

The line with a gob of worms squirming on a hook, sank slowly toward the muddy bottom of Lake Moultrie, a part of Santee-Cooper in South Carolina. Six inches below the surface it stopped. There was no movement and I wondered if a warmouth or even a crayfish hadn't decided to partake of my enticing bait that warm spring morning, when a rush of muddy water was pouring in from the swampy forest following a near cloudburst the night before. I flicked the end of the rod, only half expecting any resistance, but the tip bent, the line tightened and in that instant I knew there was no ghost taking my bait. I had a fish and he was running like the devil was chasing him.

It didn't last long. The fish stayed down, but he soon tired and I reeled a three-pound channel catfish alongside and dropped another tasty meal in the livewell.

Once called a trash fish, "cats" are a gourmet
meal for many now.

All over Santee-Cooper many species of catfish await the sport and commercial fishermen with everything from traps, rods and reels to cane poles and bows and arrows. These omnivorous feeders will eat anything, spoiled or unspoiled, dead or alive, and that gives sportsmen and meat hunters plenty of leeway when it comes to putting a mess of these whiskered critters on the dinner table. They do not have to be giants of the

349

species like the blue catfish and flatheads. Even the kittens, as some natives call the smaller catfish, make real gourmet eating. Indeed, those tiny critters the size of jumbo shrimp fried in deep fat are a dining delight, something special. You have only to know how to eat the meat right off the flexible backbone and ribs to know you have a protein that is truly finger-licking good.

Virtually unprotected by law at any level, catfish have been netted, trapped, gigged and trot-lined by commercial fishermen for decades and shipped to seafood markets of many states. Public waters have teemed with catfish of various kinds for generations and no particular body has had any monopoly with lakes, creeks, rivers and even the man-made ponds, readily acceptable habitat for South Carolina's several species. While some lakes have had enough commercial pressure to curtail the harvest for brief periods, the catfish always bounce back, and become plentiful again as a single big mama cat may produce as many as 50,000 fry in a single season. It's so prolific that it often infests lakes where it is not welcomed and hasn't been stocked by any agency. They just seem to miraculously appear and thrive.

Always caught on purpose by some sports fishermen, catfish often are pulled from the water on hook and lines by accident, frequently an unwanted variety that was loosed from the hook carefully to avoid the painful sting of the needle-sharp spines on either side of its slick head. It is equally disliked by many sports fishermen who frown on having to skin rather than scale the critter before putting him in the skillet, even if he is tasty.

But there is a growing fraternity of catfish sports fishermen at Santee who are discovering the simplicity of catching these cats in a myriad of manners, none of which is very costly or sophisticated relative to other freshwater angling. It's a way of providing protein that is tasty without damaging an already overspent family food budget. You can often catch them closer to home and save that high-priced gasoline, and the bait that attracts them is free—often those scraps that you toss in the garbage. It is fast becoming the practical fish to catch, even though unfashionable in the minds of many bass and other game fish anglers who show only disdain for followers of the lowly catfish.

Whether you are fishing a low country farm pond, lake or river you'll catch more cats immediately following a freshet when the water is rising rapidly. It even seems to help if the water is muddy from the rushing runoff that brings in worms and insects from the surrounding soil and vegetation. The food wash-in stimulates the catfish to feed, and it behooves the fisherman to get there as soon as the water starts rising or the foraging feeders will get their fill quickly and not be interested in your hooked bait. But as long as the water is rising and the channel cats haven't satisfied their appetites, you can keep right on catching them.

The ideal place to cast your bait in this freshet situation is where the onrushing fresh water slows down in the existing water. It's there that the drowning insects are deposited, sinking to the bottom, and the whiskered fish lie in wait. This type of catfish angling is particularly successful after a long drought when the insects have been scarce on the water.

Often when the water is rising, you can detect the movement of catfish in the grass and weeds along the shoreline. This is like shooting ducks in a barrel and the cats will eat anything you drop in front of them.

In fishing for these catfish in this situation, there is no better bait than grasshoppers, but if you have a really hot spot, you probably can't get enough of those insects to keep fishing long. Earthworms are the classic bait for these fish any time. But you will probably do better with some kind of blood bait. Skinned beef melt or spleen is a good blood bait, as is any type of animal meat or organs.

If you are fishing for channel catfish at a time other than the freshet, you'll do better with the liver, heart or kidneys of a wild rabbit or squirrel. Entrails from quail, doves, pheasants and ducks are also good blood baits for catfishing. The wildlife organs are better than domesticated species, generally, because the tame ones are bled out thoroughly and quickly, leaving almost no blood. Wild animals are almost always left longer with the blood in them and it settles in the internal organs.

You can freeze these wild animal parts in bait-sized pieces. Then when you are ready to cat fish, you thaw them out and dangle them in the honey hole where you believe the critters hang out. As the blood dissolves in the water, the catfish pick up the scent and they will rush to strike. These blood baits are great for fast-running water, particularly just above obstructions. Often catfish congregate in a brushpile near a rapid flow of a stream and you may catch a sack full when blood baits are allowed to drift toward them.

A nice catfish will feed the family.

All Is Calm, All Is Bright
It's Time For Good Will Toward Men

Winter sunshine peeked through the cypress trees on the shoreline as the first faint rays of dawn glistened on the peaceful surface of Little Lake Henderson in the Tsala Apopka chain in Central Florida. Mark Whitley glanced up from his pedestal-seat perch on the bow of his sleek fishing boat at the horizon, and then settled back to carefully watch his half dozen bobbers floating in the stillness. Any moment Mark expected a bobber to disappear. It was speck-biting time.

Nothing happened. But so what! Everything was beautiful, and he surely would catch a mess of crappies that Martha expected before the morning passed. She wanted enough fillets for the small grandchildren who would be arriving late in the afternoon. He fished on and other boats settled down around him, propping out enough poles on the gunnels to make the crafts look like giant spiders. Maybe they were sprouting. But then his boat looked like those of his neighbors.

Mark flipped the switch on his trolling motor, adjusted the speed so his hooks would pass a foot or two off the bottom, and set a course toward a distant water tank at Hernando. If a breeze sprang up, it would probably be from the northwest. That would put it on his stern where he wanted it.

Lady Luck was smiling. Corks disappeared on both sides of the boat. Mark carefully, steadily lifted one pole after the other from the holders, and three pound-size slabs soon flopped on the deck. He was off to a good start. In the hour that followed, he put ten more fine specks in the livewell. He was pleased.

"Hey, fellow, what you doing in that boat? I been watching you catch a stringer full of specks, and I ain't had a bite. You must know something I don't," a bearded stranger from a nearby boat hailed Mark. A tiny quiet figure in the back seat held a pole in

353

both hands, intently watching the corks. He stole a quick look at Mark, glanced at his dad, and his eyes returned to the lazy, luckless bobbers.

I'm fishing like I always do in the open water. I got several colors of Super Jigs on my lines with a small minnow hooked through the eyes. You see how I troll them slowly through the water with the oblong corks making tiny wakes on the surface," Mark relayed a bit of his technique.

"I just got minnows on my hooks. I ain't got no jigs," the unsuccessful fisherman muttered with a little chagrin.

Corks continued to pop under, and the tips of several of Mark's B 'n' M fiberglass poles splashed in the water as big specks struggled to get unbuttoned. He admired the big pop-gutted female crappies that were ready to spawn, but gulping down another meal before heading for the shallows. They splashed in the livewell.

The neighboring fisherman wore a tragic, disappointed countenance. He hadn't had a bite despite trying so patiently. Mark suddenly was obsessed with a feeling of guilt. Little voices seemed to be telling him something. He sat upright in his seat and looked around. He was letting his imagination play tricks on him. Or was he? The compelling urge to do something engulfed him. He got the message.

That neighboring angler could use some help. Why not live a little of the golden rule? Mark turned his trolling motor toward the other boat, put his port side poles on the deck, and moved a few yards to boatside of the fishing stranger with the wisp of a child huddled in the stern.

"Fellow, would it irritate you if I shared a few things? I know you haven't been catching any fish. I think I can help," Mark cautiously approached the unknown fisherman almost apologetically.

"I would appreciate any help. This youngster I have with me is fishing for the very first time. We will have a mighty disappointed child if we go home skunked."

Mark held on the side of the boat, and for the first time looked at the quiet child. Bright steel braces were fastened to the shoes on both feet. The face bore the semblance of a smile and long, blonde hair tucked under an old fishing cap testified that this was a little lady. Polio or meningitis had made her a cripple. Yet, she wanted to fish with her daddy and was trying ever so hard.

354

"I have plenty of these small Super Jigs that help me catch fish. Here, take this handful! Put one on every line you have. Make sure you have pink jigs on some of your hooks. The specks seem to go for pink this morning. Use your smallest minnows. Those four-inch minnows with a jig make the morsel entirely too big for most crappies to strike. Also, slow your trolling motor down a little. Put a couple of more lead shot on your line a foot above the jigs, and let's see if your luck changes," Mark shared his jigs and advice. He started to push away from the boat.

"That monofilament line looks mighty heavy. What test is it?" Mark asked as he saw the little girl's line flitting in the air.

"I think it's 25-pound. It's been lying around the house for a long time," the fisherman said. "I don't get much chance to fish."

"It's far too heavy," Mark said, and he pushed his boat back alongside. "Little lady, hand me your poles. I'll change your lines." Ten minutes later, Mark had put new 10-pound test line on the little girl's poles and helped her dad re-rig his with the new, lighter line.

"You're all set now. Let's get back to fishing," Mark said as he trolled away and watched his new acquaintances drop the jig-minnow baits in the water.

Almost like a miracle the child's yell signaled success. She struggled with a big speck that slammed against the boat, took a ride across to the other side, and finally, like a pendulum fluttered in the air above the deck. Smiling, her dad turned around, unhooked the fish and said, "Get the hook back in the water. That's a real beauty."

Instant replay kept the rest of the morning thrilling. The little cripple had the time of her life as she put eight or ten nice specks in the boat. Her dad concentrated on helping her, often forgetting his own strikes. And Mark didn't even bother to fish. His reward was the yells and smiles of the little lady.

It was time to head for home.

"Well, maybe I'll see you around again. And be sure to bring that youngster back fishing often. She's going to be a real pro," Mark chided as he cranked his outboard and roared toward the dock.

There was a unique warmth in Mark's chest he had seldom felt. It lingered even as he began dressing his fine catch. He had more fish than his grandkids would eat. The old widowed lady at the end of his street might like a few fillets. He put four in a plastic bag and dropped them off at her house on his way

355

home. The warmth increased.

Mark wiped the dirt off his wet shoes at his back doorstep and went in. Martha was putting lunch on the table. "What are you so happy about?" she asked, observing the glow on his face and the glint in his eyes.

"Oh, nothing at all, it's just the season," Mark smiled broadly.

It was Christmas Eve.

Convenient Order Form

I would like to have additional copies of this book,

Crappie Secrets

Please mail me _____ copies to the address below:

Name:_____

Address:_____

_____

Enclosed please find check or money order in the amount of $13.50 that includes postage and handling, for each book.

Please mail to:
W. Horace Carter
Atlantic Publishing Company
P.O. Box 67
Tabor City, NC 28463
Phone 919-653-3153

(Tear out & mail this sheet to publisher.)

Please ship me one copy of Atlantic Book checked below:

Hannon's Field Guide for Bass Fishing	$ 9.95
Creatures & Chronicles From Cross Creek	9.30
Land That I Love (Hard Bound)	14.50
Wild & Wonderful Santee-Cooper Country	8.30
Return to Cross Creek	9.30
Nature's Masterpiece at Homosassa	9.30
Catch Bass	8.30
Hannon's Big Bass Magic	13.50
A Man Called Raleigh	9.30
Damn the Allegators	10.95
Bird Hunters Handbook	11.50
Lures for Lunker Bass (Paperback)	12.95
Lures for Lunker Bass (Hardback)	16.95
Best Bass Pros	10.95
Deer & Fixings	9.95
Hunting Hogs, Boar & Javelina	10.95
Trophy Stripers	12.95
Forty Years in the Everglades	9.95

Convenient Order Form

I would like to have additional copies of this book,

Crappie Secrets

Please mail me _____ copies to the address below:

Name:_____

Address:_____

_____

Enclosed please find check or money order in the amount of $13.50 that includes postage and handling, for each book.

Please mail to:
W. Horace Carter
Atlantic Publishing Company
P.O. Box 67
Tabor City, NC 28463
Phone 919-653-3153

(Tear out & mail this sheet to publisher.)

Please ship me one copy of Atlantic Book checked below:

Hannon's Field Guide for Bass Fishing	$ 9.95
Creatures & Chronicles From Cross Creek	9.30
Land That I Love (Hard Bound)	14.50
Wild & Wonderful Santee-Cooper Country	8.30
Return to Cross Creek	9.30
Nature's Masterpiece at Homosassa	9.30
Catch Bass	8.30
Hannon's Big Bass Magic	13.50
A Man Called Raleigh	9.30
Damn the Allegators	10.95
Bird Hunters Handbook	11.50
Lures for Lunker Bass (Paperback)	12.95
Lures for Lunker Bass (Hardback)	16.95
Best Bass Pros	10.95
Deer & Fixings	9.95
Hunting Hogs, Boar & Javelina	10.95
Trophy Stripers	12.95
Forty Years in the Everglades	9.95